Collins HANDY WORLDATLAS

D0715842

Collins Handy World Atlas

Collins
An Imprint of HarperCollinsPublishers
77-85 Fulham Palace Road
London W6 8JB

First published 2004
This edition produced for W H Smith 2004

Copyright © HarperCollinsPublishers Ltd 2004
Maps © Collins Bartholomew Ltd 2004

Collins® is a registered trademark of HarperCollinsPublishers Ltd

Printed in Germany

ISBN 0 00 719523 0

RY11670 Imp 001

Everything **clicks** at
www.collins.co.uk

Collins HANDY
WORLDATLAS

contents

INTRODUCTION

The atlas is introduced by details of the world's states and territories and by maps and information on major geographical themes. The reference maps which follow this world section have been compiled to provide the best coverage for each part of the world through careful selection of scales and map projections. Maps are arranged on a continental basis, with each continent being introduced by maps and statistics on the continent's physical features and countries. Maps of Antarctica and the world's oceans complete the worldwide coverage.

Map symbolization

Maps show information by using symbols which are designed to reflect the features on the earth that they represent. Map symbols can be in the form of points – such as those used to show towns and airports; lines – used to represent roads and rivers; or areas – such as lakes. Variation in size, shape and colour of these types of symbol allow a great range of information to be shown. The symbols used in this atlas are explained here. Not all details can be shown at the small map scales used in this atlas, so information is generalized to allow easy interpretation. This generalization takes the form of selection – the inclusion of some features and the omission of others of less importance; and simplification – where lines are smoothed, areas combined, or symbols displaced slightly to add clarity. This is done in such a way that the overall character of the area mapped is retained. The degree of generalization varies, and is determined largely by the scale at which the map is drawn.

Scale

Scale is the relationship between the size of an area shown on the map and the actual size of the area on the ground. It determines the amount of detail shown on a map – larger scales show more, smaller scales show less – and can be used to measure the distance between two points, although the projection of the map must also be taken into account when measuring distances.

Geographical names

The spelling of place names on maps is a complex problem for the cartographer. There is no single standard way of converting them from one alphabet, or symbol set, to another. Changes in official languages also have to be taken into account when creating maps and policies need to be established for the spelling of names on individual atlases and maps. Such policies must take account of the local official position, international conventions or traditions, as well as the purpose of the atlas or map. The policy in this atlas is to use local name forms which are officially recognized by the governments of the countries concerned, but with English conventional name forms being used for the most well-known places. In these cases, the local form is often included in brackets on the map and also appears as a cross-reference in the index. All country names and those for international features appear in their English forms.

Boundaries

The status of nations and their boundaries are shown in this atlas as they are in reality at the time of going to press, as far as can be ascertained. Where international boundaries are the subject of disputes the aim is to take a strictly neutral viewpoint, based on advice from expert consultants.

MAP SYMBOLS

Settlements

Population	National Capital		Administrative Capital		City or Town	
over 5 million	⊡	**BEIJING**	⊙	**Tianjin**	⊙	**New York**
1 million – 5 million	☐	**MADRID**	○	**Sydney**	○	**Madurai**
500 000 – 1 million	☐	**BANGUI**	○	**Douala**	○	**Barranquilla**
100 000 – 500 000	☐	**WELLINGTON**	○	Mansa	○	Yong'an
50 000 – 100 000	☐	PORT OF SPAIN	○	Lubango	○	Puruliya
under 50 000	☐	MALABO	○	Chinhoyi	○	El Tigre

Styles of lettering

Country name	**FRANCE**	Island	*Gran Canaria*
Overseas territory / Dependency	**Guadaloupe**	Lake	*Lake Erie*
Administrative name	**SCOTLAND**	Mountain	*Mt Blanc*
Area name	PATAGONIA	River	*Thames*

Physical features

- Freshwater lake
- Seasonal freshwater lake
- Salt lake
- Seasonal salt lake
- Dry salt lake
- Ice cap
- River
- Mountain pass 2188
- Summit △ 6960

Other features

- ∴ Site of special interest
- ∿∿ Wall

Communications

══════	Motorway
──────	Main road
----------	Track
‒ ‒ ‒ ‒ ‒	Railway
✈	Main airport
┼┼┼┼┼┼	Canal

Boundaries

──────	International
----------	International disputed
‒‒‒‒‒‒	Administrative (selected countries only)
··············	Ceasefire line

introduction and map symbols

EUROPE COUNTRIES		area sq km	area sq miles	population	capital
ALBANIA		28 748	11 100	3 166 000	Tirana
ANDORRA		465	180	71 000	Andorra la Vella
AUSTRIA		83 855	32 377	8 116 000	Vienna
BELARUS		207 600	80 155	9 895 000	Minsk
BELGIUM		30 520	11 784	10 318 000	Brussels
BOSNIA-HERZEGOVINA		51 130	19 741	4 161 000	Sarajevo
BULGARIA		110 994	42 855	7 897 000	Sofia
CROATIA		56 538	21 829	4 428 000	Zagreb
CZECH REPUBLIC		78 864	30 450	10 236 000	Prague
DENMARK		43 075	16 631	5 364 000	Copenhagen
ESTONIA		45 200	17 452	1 323 000	Tallinn
FINLAND		338 145	130 559	5 207 000	Helsinki
FRANCE		543 965	210 026	60 144 000	Paris
GERMANY		357 022	137 849	82 476 000	Berlin
GREECE		131 957	50 949	10 976 000	Athens
HUNGARY		93 030	35 919	9 877 000	Budapest
ICELAND		102 820	39 699	290 000	Reykjavík
IRELAND, REPUBLIC OF		70 282	27 136	3 956 000	Dublin
ITALY		301 245	116 311	57 423 000	Rome
LATVIA		63 700	24 595	2 307 000	Rīga
LIECHTENSTEIN		160	62	34 000	Vaduz
LITHUANIA		65 200	25 174	3 444 000	Vilnius
LUXEMBOURG		2 586	998	453 000	Luxembourg
MACEDONIA (F.Y.R.O.M.)		25 713	9 928	2 056 000	Skopje
MALTA		316	122	394 000	Valletta
MOLDOVA		33 700	13 012	4 267 000	Chişinău
MONACO		2	1	34 000	Monaco-Ville
NETHERLANDS		41 526	16 033	16 149 000	Amsterdam/The Hague
NORWAY		323 878	125 050	4 533 000	Oslo
POLAND		312 683	120 728	38 587 000	Warsaw
PORTUGAL		88 940	34 340	10 062 000	Lisbon
ROMANIA		237 500	91 699	22 334 000	Bucharest
RUSSIAN FEDERATION		17 075 400	6 592 849	143 246 000	Moscow

languages	religions	currency
Albanian, Greek	Sunni Muslim, Albanian Orthodox, Roman Catholic	Lek
Spanish, Catalan, French	Roman Catholic	Euro
German, Croatian, Turkish	Roman Catholic, Protestant	Euro
Belorussian, Russian	Belorussian Orthodox, Roman Catholic	Belarus rouble
Dutch (Flemish), French (Walloon), German	Roman Catholic, Protestant	Euro
Bosnian, Serbian, Croatian	Sunni Muslim, Serbian Orthodox, Roman Catholic, Protestant	Marka
Bulgarian, Turkish, Romany, Macedonian	Bulgarian Orthodox, Sunni Muslim	Lev
Croatian, Serbian	Roman Catholic, Serbian Orthodox, Sunni Muslim	Kuna
Czech, Moravian, Slovak	Roman Catholic, Protestant	Czech koruna
Danish	Protestant	Danish krone
Estonian, Russian	Protestant, Estonian and Russian Orthodox	Kroon
Finnish, Swedish	Protestant, Greek Orthodox	Euro
French, Arabic	Roman Catholic, Protestant, Sunni Muslim	Euro
German, Turkish	Protestant, Roman Catholic	Euro
Greek	Greek Orthodox, Sunni Muslim	Euro
Hungarian	Roman Catholic, Protestant	Forint
Icelandic	Protestant	Icelandic króna
English, Irish	Roman Catholic, Protestant	Euro
Italian	Roman Catholic	Euro
Latvian, Russian	Protestant, Roman Catholic, Russian Orthodox	Lats
German	Roman Catholic, Protestant	Swiss franc
Lithuanian, Russian, Polish	Roman Catholic, Protestant, Russian Orthodox	Litas
Letzeburgish, German, French	Roman Catholic	Euro
Macedonian, Albanian, Turkish	Macedonian Orthodox, Sunni Muslim	Macedonian denar
Maltese, English	Roman Catholic	Maltese lira
Romanian, Ukrainian, Gagauz, Russian	Romanian Orthodox, Russian Orthodox	Moldovan leu
French, Monegasque, Italian	Roman Catholic	Euro
Dutch, Frisian	Roman Catholic, Protestant, Sunni Muslim	Euro
Norwegian	Protestant, Roman Catholic	Norwegian krone
Polish, German	Roman Catholic, Polish Orthodox	Złoty
Portuguese	Roman Catholic, Protestant	Euro
Romanian, Hungarian	Romanian Orthodox, Protestant, Roman Catholic	Romanian leu
Russian, Tatar, Ukrainian, local languages	Russian Orthodox, Sunni Muslim, Protestant	Russian rouble

EUROPE COUNTRIES (continued)		area sq km	area sq miles	population	capital
SAN MARINO		61	24	28 000	San Marino
SERBIA AND MONTENEGRO		102 173	39 449	10 527 000	Belgrade
SLOVAKIA		49 035	18 933	5 402 000	Bratislava
SLOVENIA		20 251	7 819	1 984 000	Ljubljana
SPAIN		504 782	194 897	41 060 000	Madrid
SWEDEN		449 964	173 732	8 876 000	Stockholm
SWITZERLAND		41 293	15 943	7 169 000	Bern
UKRAINE		603 700	233 090	48 523 000	Kiev
UNITED KINGDOM		243 609	94 058	58 789 194	London
VATICAN CITY		0.5	0.2	472	Vatican City

EUROPE DEPENDENT TERRITORIES			area sq km	area sq miles	populatio
Azores		Autonomous Region of Portugal	2 300	888	242 07
Faroe Islands		Self-governing Danish Territory	1 399	540	47 00
Gibraltar		United Kingdom Overseas Territory	7	3	27 00
Guernsey		United Kingdom Crown Dependency	78	30	62 70
Isle of Man		United Kingdom Crown Dependency	572	221	75 00
Jersey		United Kingdom Crown Dependency	116	45	87 18

ASIA COUNTRIES		area sq km	area sq miles	population	capital
AFGHANISTAN		652 225	251 825	23 897 000	Kābul
ARMENIA		29 800	11 506	3 061 000	Yerevan
AZERBAIJAN		86 600	33 436	8 370 000	Baku
BAHRAIN		691	267	724 000	Manama
BANGLADESH		143 998	55 598	146 736 000	Dhaka
BHUTAN		46 620	18 000	2 257 000	Thimphu
BRUNEI		5 765	2 226	358 000	Bandar Seri Begawan
CAMBODIA		181 000	69 884	14 144 000	Phnom Penh
CHINA		9 584 492	3 700 593	1 289 161 000	Beijing
CYPRUS		9 251	3 572	802 000	Nicosia
EAST TIMOR		14 874	5 743	778 000	Dili
GEORGIA		69 700	26 911	5 126 000	T'bilisi

...nguages	religions	currency
...lian	Roman Catholic	Euro
...erbian, Albanian, Hungarian	Serbian Orthodox, Montenegrin Orthodox, Sunni Muslim	Serbian dinar, Euro
...ovak, Hungarian, Czech	Roman Catholic, Protestant, Orthodox	Slovakian koruna
...ovene, Croatian, Serbian	Roman Catholic, Protestant	Tólar
...astilian, Catalan, Galician, Basque	Roman Catholic	Euro
...vedish	Protestant, Roman Catholic	Swedish krona
...erman, French, Italian, Romansch	Roman Catholic, Protestant	Swiss franc
...krainian, Russian	Ukrainian Orthodox, Ukrainian Catholic, Roman Catholic	Hryvnia
...glish, Welsh, Gaelic	Protestant, Roman Catholic, Muslim	Pound sterling
...lian	Roman Catholic	Euro

...pital	languages	religions	currency
...nta Delgada	Portuguese	Roman Catholic, Protestant	Euro
...rshavn	Faroese, Danish	Protestant	Danish krone
...braltar	English, Spanish	Roman Catholic, Protestant, Sunni Muslim	Gibraltar pound
... Peter Port	English, French	Protestant, Roman Catholic	Pound sterling
...ouglas	English	Protestant, Roman Catholic	Pound sterling
...Helier	English, French	Protestant, Roman Catholic	Pound sterling

...nguages	religions	currency
...ari, Pushtu, Uzbek, Turkmen	Sunni Muslim, Shi'a Muslim	Afghani
...menian, Azeri	Armenian Orthodox	Dram
...eri, Armenian, Russian, Lezgian	Shi'a Muslim, Sunni Muslim, Russian and Armenian Orthodox	Azerbaijani manat
...abic, English	Shi'a Muslim, Sunni Muslim, Christian	Bahrain dinar
...ngali, English	Sunni Muslim, Hindu	Taka
...ongkha, Nepali, Assamese	Buddhist, Hindu	Ngultrum, Indian rupee
...lay, English, Chinese	Sunni Muslim, Buddhist, Christian	Brunei dollar
...mer, Vietnamese	Buddhist, Roman Catholic, Sunni Muslim	Riel
...andarin, Wu, Cantonese, Hsiang, regional languages	Confucian, Taoist, Buddhist, Christian, Sunni Muslim	Yuan, Hong Kong dollar, Macau pataca
...eek, Turkish, English	Greek Orthodox, Sunni Muslim	Cyprus pound
...rtuguese, Tetun, English	Roman Catholic	US dollar
...orgian, Russian, Armenian, Azeri, Ossetian, Abkhaz	Georgian Orthodox, Russian Orthodox, Sunni Muslim	Lari

world states and territories
europe, asia

		area sq km	area sq miles	population	capital
INDIA		3 064 898	1 183 364	1 065 462 000	New Delhi
INDONESIA		1 919 445	741 102	219 883 000	Jakarta
IRAN		1 648 000	636 296	68 920 000	Tehrān
IRAQ		438 317	169 235	25 175 000	Baghdād
ISRAEL		20 770	8 019	6 433 000	Jerusalem *(De facto capl. Disputed)*
JAPAN		377 727	145 841	127 654 000	Tōkyō
JORDAN		89 206	34 443	5 473 000	'Ammān
KAZAKHSTAN		2 717 300	1 049 155	15 433 000	Astana
KUWAIT		17 818	6 880	2 521 000	Kuwait
KYRGYZSTAN		198 500	76 641	5 138 000	Bishkek
LAOS		236 800	91 429	5 657 000	Vientiane
LEBANON		10 452	4 036	3 653 000	Beirut
MALAYSIA		332 965	128 559	24 425 000	Kuala Lumpur/Putrajaya
MALDIVES		298	115	318 000	Male
MONGOLIA		1 565 000	604 250	2 594 000	Ulan Bator
MYANMAR		676 577	261 228	49 485 000	Rangoon
NEPAL		147 181	56 827	25 164 000	Kathmandu
NORTH KOREA		120 538	46 540	22 664 000	P'yŏngyang
OMAN		309 500	119 499	2 851 000	Muscat
PAKISTAN		803 940	310 403	153 578 000	Islamabad
PALAU		497	192	20 000	Koror
PHILIPPINES		300 000	115 831	79 999 000	Manila
QATAR		11 437	4 416	610 000	Doha
RUSSIAN FEDERATION		17 075 400	6 592 849	143 246 000	Moscow
SAUDI ARABIA		2 200 000	849 425	24 217 000	Riyadh
SINGAPORE		639	247	4 253 000	Singapore
SOUTH KOREA		99 274	38 330	47 700 000	Seoul
SRI LANKA		65 610	25 332	19 065 000	Sri Jayewardenepura Ko
SYRIA		185 180	71 498	17 800 000	Damascus
TAIWAN		36 179	13 969	22 548 000	T'aipei
TAJIKISTAN		143 100	55 251	6 245 000	Dushanbe
THAILAND		513 115	198 115	62 833 000	Bangkok
TURKEY		779 452	300 948	71 325 000	Ankara

languages	religions	currency
Hindi, English, many regional languages	Hindu, Sunni Muslim, Shi'a Muslim, Sikh, Christian	Indian rupee
Indonesian, local languages	Sunni Muslim, Protestant, Roman Catholic, Hindu, Buddhist	Rupiah
Farsi, Azeri, Kurdish, regional languages	Shi'a Muslim, Sunni Muslim	Iranian rial
Arabic, Kurdish, Turkmen	Shi'a Muslim, Sunni Muslim, Christian	Iraqi dinar
Hebrew, Arabic	Jewish, Sunni Muslim, Christian, Druze	Shekel
Japanese	Shintoist, Buddhist, Christian	Yen
Arabic	Sunni Muslim, Christian	Jordanian dinar
Kazakh, Russian, Ukrainian, German, Uzbek, Tatar	Sunni Muslim, Russian Orthodox, Protestant	Tenge
Arabic	Sunni Muslim, Shi'a Muslim, Christian, Hindu	Kuwaiti dinar
Kyrgyz, Russian, Uzbek	Sunni Muslim, Russian Orthodox	Kyrgyz som
Lao, local languages	Buddhist, traditional beliefs	Kip
Arabic, Armenian, French	Shi'a Muslim, Sunni Muslim, Christian	Lebanese pound
Malay, English, Chinese, Tamil, local languages	Sunni Muslim, Buddhist, Hindu, Christian, traditional beliefs	Ringgit
Divehi (Maldivian)	Sunni Muslim	Rufiyaa
Khalka (Mongolian), Kazakh, local languages	Buddhist, Sunni Muslim	Tugrik (tögrög)
Burmese, Shan, Karen, local languages	Buddhist, Christian, Sunni Muslim	Kyat
Nepali, Maithili, Bhojpuri, English, local languages	Hindu, Buddhist, Sunni Muslim	Nepalese rupee
Korean	Traditional beliefs, Chondoist, Buddhist	North Korean won
Arabic, Baluchi, Indian languages	Ibadhi Muslim, Sunni Muslim	Omani riyal
Urdu, Punjabi, Sindhi, Pushtu, English	Sunni Muslim, Shi'a Muslim, Christian, Hindu	Pakistani rupee
Palauan, English	Roman Catholic, Protestant, traditional beliefs	US dollar
English, Pilipino, Cebuano, local languages	Roman Catholic, Protestant, Sunni Muslim, Aglipayan	Philippine peso
Arabic	Sunni Muslim	Qatari riyal
Russian, Tatar, Ukrainian, local languages	Russian Orthodox, Sunni Muslim, Protestant	Russian rouble
Arabic	Sunni Muslim, Shi'a Muslim	Saudi Arabian riyal
Chinese, English, Malay, Tamil	Buddhist, Taoist, Sunni Muslim, Christian, Hindu	Singapore dollar
Korean	Buddhist, Protestant, Roman Catholic	South Korean won
Sinhalese, Tamil, English	Buddhist, Hindu, Sunni Muslim, Roman Catholic	Sri Lankan rupee
Arabic, Kurdish, Armenian	Sunni Muslim, Shi'a Muslim, Christian	Syrian pound
Mandarin, Min, Hakka, local languages	Buddhist, Taoist, Confucian, Christian	Taiwan dollar
Tajik, Uzbek, Russian	Sunni Muslim	Somoni
Thai, Lao, Chinese, Malay, Mon-Khmer languages	Buddhist, Sunni Muslim	Baht
Turkish, Kurdish	Sunni Muslim, Shi'a Muslim	Turkish lira

world states and territories
asia

ASIA
COUNTRIES (continued)

		area sq km	area sq miles	population	capital
TURKMENISTAN		488 100	188 456	4 867 000	Ashgabat
UNITED ARAB EMIRATES		77 700	30 000	2 995 000	Abu Dhabi
UZBEKISTAN		447 400	172 742	26 093 000	Tashkent
VIETNAM		329 565	127 246	81 377 000	Ha Nôi
YEMEN		527 968	203 850	20 010 000	Şan'ā'

ASIA
DEPENDENT AND DISPUTED TERRITORIES

			area sq km	area sq miles	population
Christmas Island		Australian External Territory	135	52	1 560
Cocos Islands		Australian External Territory	14	5	632
Gaza		Semi-autonomous region	363	140	1 203 591
Jammu and Kashmir		Disputed territory (India/Pakistan)	222 236	85 806	13 000 000
West Bank		Disputed territory	5 860	2 263	2 303 660

AFRICA
COUNTRIES

		area sq km	area sq miles	population	capital
ALGERIA		2 381 741	919 595	31 800 000	Algiers
ANGOLA		1 246 700	481 354	13 625 000	Luanda
BENIN		112 620	43 483	6 736 000	Porto-Novo
BOTSWANA		581 370	224 468	1 785 000	Gaborone
BURKINA		274 200	105 869	13 002 000	Ouagadougou
BURUNDI		27 835	10 747	6 825 000	Bujumbura
CAMEROON		475 442	183 569	16 018 000	Yaoundé
CAPE VERDE		4 033	1 557	463 000	Praia
CENTRAL AFRICAN REPUBLIC		622 436	240 324	3 865 000	Bangui
CHAD		1 284 000	495 755	8 598 000	Ndjamena
COMOROS		1 862	719	768 000	Moroni
CONGO		342 000	132 047	3 724 000	Brazzaville
CONGO, DEMOCRATIC REP. OF		2 345 410	905 568	52 771 000	Kinshasa
CÔTE D'IVOIRE		322 463	124 504	16 631 000	Yamoussoukro
DJIBOUTI		23 200	8 958	703 000	Djibouti
EGYPT		1 000 250	386 199	71 931 000	Cairo
EQUATORIAL GUINEA		28 051	10 831	494 000	Malabo
ERITREA		117 400	45 328	4 141 000	Asmara

languages	religions	currency
Turkmen, Uzbek, Russian	Sunni Muslim, Russian Orthodox	Turkmen manat
Arabic, English	Sunni Muslim, Shi'a Muslim	United Arab Emirates dirham
Uzbek, Russian, Tajik, Kazakh	Sunni Muslim, Russian Orthodox	Uzbek som
Vietnamese, Thai, Khmer, Chinese, local languages	Buddhist, Taoist, Roman Catholic, Cao Dai, Hoa Hao	Dong
Arabic	Sunni Muslim, Shi'a Muslim	Yemeni rial

capital	languages	religions	currency
The Settlement	English	Buddhist, Sunni Muslim, Protestant, Roman Catholic	Australian dollar
West Island	English	Sunni Muslim, Christian	Australian dollar
Gaza	Arabic	Sunni Muslim, Shi'a Muslim	Israeli shekel
Srinagar			
	Arabic, Hebrew	Sunni Muslim, Jewish, Shi'a Muslim, Christian	Jordanian dinar, Israeli shekel

languages	religions	currency
Arabic, French, Berber	Sunni Muslim	Algerian dinar
Portuguese, Bantu, local languages	Roman Catholic, Protestant, traditional beliefs	Kwanza
French, Fon, Yoruba, Adja, local languages	Traditional beliefs, Roman Catholic, Sunni Muslim	CFA franc*
English, Setswana, Shona, local languages	Traditional beliefs, Protestant, Roman Catholic	Pula
French, Moore (Mossi), Fulani, local languages	Sunni Muslim, traditional beliefs, Roman Catholic	CFA franc*
Kirundi (Hutu, Tutsi), French	Roman Catholic, traditional beliefs, Protestant	Burundian franc
French, English, Fang, Bamileke, local languages	Roman Catholic, traditional beliefs, Sunni Muslim, Protestant	CFA franc*
Portuguese, creole	Roman Catholic, Protestant	Cape Verde escudo
French, Sango, Banda, Baya, local languages	Protestant, Roman Catholic, traditional beliefs, Sunni Muslim	CFA franc*
Arabic, French, Sara, local languages	Sunni Muslim, Roman Catholic, Protestant, traditional beliefs	CFA franc*
Comorian, French, Arabic	Sunni Muslim, Roman Catholic	Comoros franc
French, Kongo, Monokutuba, local languages	Roman Catholic, Protestant, traditional beliefs, Sunni Muslim	CFA franc*
French, Lingala, Swahili, Kongo, local languages	Christian, Sunni Muslim	Congolese franc
French, creole, Akan, local languages	Sunni Muslim, Roman Catholic, traditional beliefs, Protestant	CFA franc*
Somali, Afar, French, Arabic	Sunni Muslim, Christian	Djibouti franc
Arabic	Sunni Muslim, Coptic Christian	Egyptian pound
Spanish, French, Fang	Roman Catholic, traditional beliefs	CFA franc*
Tigrinya, Tigre	Sunni Muslim, Coptic Christian	Nakfa

world states and territories
africa

AFRICA
COUNTRIES (continued)

	area sq km	area sq miles	population	capital
ETHIOPIA	1 133 880	437 794	70 678 000	Addis Ababa
GABON	267 667	103 347	1 329 000	Libreville
THE GAMBIA	11 295	4 361	1 426 000	Banjul
GHANA	238 537	92 100	20 922 000	Accra
GUINEA	245 857	94 926	8 480 000	Conakry
GUINEA-BISSAU	36 125	13 948	1 493 000	Bissau
KENYA	582 646	224 961	31 987 000	Nairobi
LESOTHO	30 355	11 720	1 802 000	Maseru
LIBERIA	111 369	43 000	3 367 000	Monrovia
LIBYA	1 759 540	679 362	5 551 000	Tripoli
MADAGASCAR	587 041	226 658	17 404 000	Antananarivo
MALAWI	118 484	45 747	12 105 000	Lilongwe
MALI	1 240 140	478 821	13 007 000	Bamako
MAURITANIA	1 030 700	397 955	2 893 000	Nouakchott
MAURITIUS	2 040	788	1 221 000	Port Louis
MOROCCO	446 550	172 414	30 566 000	Rabat
MOZAMBIQUE	799 380	308 642	18 863 000	Maputo
NAMIBIA	824 292	318 261	1 987 000	Windhoek
NIGER	1 267 000	489 191	11 972 000	Niamey
NIGERIA	923 768	356 669	124 009 000	Abuja
RWANDA	26 338	10 169	8 387 000	Kigali
SÃO TOMÉ AND PRÍNCIPE	964	372	161 000	São Tomé
SENEGAL	196 720	75 954	10 095 000	Dakar
SEYCHELLES	455	176	81 000	Victoria
SIERRA LEONE	71 740	27 699	4 971 000	Freetown
SOMALIA	637 657	246 201	9 890 000	Mogadishu
SOUTH AFRICA, REPUBLIC OF	1 219 090	470 693	45 026 000	Pretoria/Cape Town
SUDAN	2 505 813	967 500	33 610 000	Khartoum
SWAZILAND	17 364	6 704	1 077 000	Mbabane
TANZANIA	945 087	364 900	36 977 000	Dodoma
TOGO	56 785	21 925	4 909 000	Lomé
TUNISIA	164 150	63 379	9 832 000	Tunis
UGANDA	241 038	93 065	25 827 000	Kampala

nguages	religions	currency
romo, Amharic, Tigrinya, local languages	Ethiopian Orthodox, Sunni Muslim, traditional beliefs	Birr
ench, Fang, local languages	Roman Catholic, Protestant, traditional beliefs	CFA franc*
nglish, Malinke, Fulani, Wolof	Sunni Muslim, Protestant	Dalasi
nglish, Hausa, Akan, local languages	Christian, Sunni Muslim, traditional beliefs	Cedi
ench, Fulani, Malinke, local languages	Sunni Muslim, traditional beliefs, Christian	Guinea franc
ortuguese, crioulo, local languages	Traditional beliefs, Sunni Muslim, Christian	CFA franc*
vahili, English, local languages	Christian, traditional beliefs	Kenyan shilling
esotho, English, Zulu	Christian, traditional beliefs	Loti, S. African rand
nglish, creole, local languages	Traditional beliefs, Christian, Sunni Muslim	Liberian dollar
abic, Berber	Sunni Muslim	Libyan dinar
alagasy, French	Traditional beliefs, Christian, Sunni Muslim	Malagasy franc
hichewa, English, local languages	Christian, traditional beliefs, Sunni Muslim	Malawian kwacha
ench, Bambara, local languages	Sunni Muslim, traditional beliefs, Christian	CFA franc*
abic, French, local languages	Sunni Muslim	Ouguiya
nglish, creole, Hindi, Bhojpurī, French	Hindu, Roman Catholic, Sunni Muslim	Mauritius rupee
abic, Berber, French	Sunni Muslim	Moroccan dirham
ortuguese, Makua, Tsonga, local languages	Traditional beliefs, Roman Catholic, Sunni Muslim	Metical
glish, Afrikaans, German, Ovambo, local languages	Protestant, Roman Catholic	Namibian dollar
ench, Hausa, Fulani, local languages	Sunni Muslim, traditional beliefs	CFA franc*
glish, Hausa, Yoruba, Ibo, Fulani, local languages	Sunni Muslim, Christian, traditional beliefs	Naira
hyarwanda, French, English	Roman Catholic, traditional beliefs, Protestant	Rwandan franc
ortuguese, creole	Roman Catholic, Protestant	Dobra
ench, Wolof, Fulani, local languages	Sunni Muslim, Roman Catholic, traditional beliefs	CFA franc*
glish, French, creole	Roman Catholic, Protestant	Seychelles rupee
nglish, creole, Mende, Temne, local languages	Sunni Muslim, traditional beliefs	Leone
mali, Arabic	Sunni Muslim	Somali shilling
rikaans, English, nine official local languages	Protestant, Roman Catholic, Sunni Muslim, Hindu	Rand
abic, Dinka, Nubian, Beja, Nuer, local languages	Sunni Muslim, traditional beliefs, Christian	Sudanese dinar
vazi, English	Christian, traditional beliefs	Emalangeni, S. African rand
vahili, English, Nyamwezi, local languages	Shi'a Muslim, Sunni Muslim, traditional beliefs, Christian	Tanzanian shilling
ench, Ewe, Kabre, local languages	Traditional beliefs, Christian, Sunni Muslim	CFA franc*
abic, French	Sunni Muslim	Tunisian dinar
glish, Swahili, Luganda, local languages	Roman Catholic, Protestant, Sunni Muslim, traditional beliefs	Ugandan shilling

world states and territories
africa

AFRICA COUNTRIES (continued)		area sq km	area sq miles	population	capital
ZAMBIA		752 614	290 586	10 812 000	Lusaka
ZIMBABWE		390 759	150 873	12 891 000	Harare

AFRICA DEPENDENT AND DISPUTED TERRITORIES			area sq km	area sq miles	populatio
Canary Islands		Autonomous Community of Spain	7 447	2 875	1 694 4
Madeira		Autonomous Region of Portugal	779	301	242 6
Mayotte		French Territorial Collectivity	373	144	171 0
Réunion		French Overseas Department	2 551	985	756 0
St Helena and Dependencies		United Kingdom Overseas Territory	121	47	5 6
Western Sahara		Disputed territory (Morocco)	266 000	102 703	308 0

OCEANIA COUNTRIES		area sq km	area sq miles	population	capital
AUSTRALIA		7 692 024	2 969 907	19 731 000	Canberra
FIJI		18 330	7 077	839 000	Suva
KIRIBATI		717	277	88 000	Bairiki
MARSHALL ISLANDS		181	70	53 000	Delap-Uliga-Djarrit
MICRONESIA, FED. STATES OF		701	271	109 000	Palikir
NAURU		21	8	13 000	Yaren
NEW ZEALAND		270 534	104 454	3 875 000	Wellington
PAPUA NEW GUINEA		462 840	178 704	5 711 000	Port Moresby
SAMOA		2 831	1 093	178 000	Apia
SOLOMON ISLANDS		28 370	10 954	477 000	Honiara
TONGA		748	289	104 000	Nuku'alofa
TUVALU		25	10	11 000	Vaiaku
VANUATU		12 190	4 707	212 000	Port Vila

OCEANIA DEPENDENT TERRITORIES			area sq km	area sq miles	populati
American Samoa		United States Unincorporated Territory	197	76	67 0
Cook Islands		Self-governing New Zealand Territory	293	113	18 0
French Polynesia		French Overseas Territory	3 265	1 261	244 0
Guam		United States Unincorporated Territory	541	209	163 0
New Caledonia		French Overseas Territory	19 058	7 358	228 0

languages	religions	currency
English, Bemba, Nyanja, Tonga, local languages	Christian, traditional beliefs	Zambian kwacha
English, Shona, Ndebele	Christian, traditional beliefs	Zimbabwean dollar

capital	languages	religions	currency
Santa Cruz de Tenerife, Las Palmas	Spanish	Roman Catholic	Euro
Funchal	Portuguese	Roman Catholic, Protestant	Euro
Dzaoudzi	French, Mahorian	Sunni Muslim, Christian	Euro
St-Denis	French, creole	Roman Catholic	Euro
Jamestown	English	Protestant, Roman Catholic	St Helena pound
Laâyoune	Arabic	Sunni Muslim	Moroccan dirham

*Communauté Financière Africaine franc

languages	religions	currency
English, Italian, Greek	Protestant, Roman Catholic, Orthodox	Australian dollar
English, Fijian, Hindi	Christian, Hindu, Sunni Muslim	Fiji dollar
Gilbertese, English	Roman Catholic, Protestant	Australian dollar
English, Marshallese	Protestant, Roman Catholic	US dollar
English, Chuukese, Pohnpeian, local languages	Roman Catholic, Protestant	US dollar
Nauruan, English	Protestant, Roman Catholic	Australian dollar
English, Maori	Protestant, Roman Catholic	New Zealand dollar
English, Tok Pisin (creole), local languages	Protestant, Roman Catholic, traditional beliefs	Kina
Samoan, English	Protestant, Roman Catholic	Tala
English, creole, local languages	Protestant, Roman Catholic	Solomon Islands dollar
Tongan, English	Protestant, Roman Catholic	Pa'anga
Tuvaluan, English	Protestant	Australian dollar
English, Bislama (creole), French	Protestant, Roman Catholic, traditional beliefs	Vatu

capital	languages	religions	currency
Pagotogo	Samoan, English	Protestant, Roman Catholic	US dollar
Avarua	English, Maori	Protestant, Roman Catholic	New Zealand dollar
Papeete	French, Tahitian, Polynesian languages	Protestant, Roman Catholic	CFP franc*
Agåtña	Chamorro, English, Tapalog	Roman Catholic	US dollar
Nouméa	French, local languages	Roman Catholic, Protestant, Sunni Muslim	CFP franc*

world states and territories
africa, oceania

OCEANIA
DEPENDENT TERRITORIES (continued)

			area sq km	area sq miles	population
Niue		Self-governing New Zealand Territory	258	100	2 000
Norfolk Island		Australian External Territory	35	14	2 037
Northern Mariana Islands		United States Commonwealth	477	184	79 000
Pitcairn Islands		United Kingdom Overseas Territory	45	17	51
Tokelau		New Zealand Overseas Territory	10	4	2 000
Wallis and Futuna Islands		French Overseas Territory	274	106	15 000

NORTH AMERICA
COUNTRIES

		area sq km	area sq miles	population	capital
ANTIGUA AND BARBUDA		442	171	73 000	St John's
THE BAHAMAS		13 939	5 382	314 000	Nassau
BARBADOS		430	166	270 000	Bridgetown
BELIZE		22 965	8 867	256 000	Belmopan
CANADA		9 984 670	3 855 103	31 510 000	Ottawa
COSTA RICA		51 100	19 730	4 173 000	San José
CUBA		110 860	42 803	11 300 000	Havana
DOMINICA		750	290	79 000	Roseau
DOMINICAN REPUBLIC		48 442	18 704	8 745 000	Santo Domingo
EL SALVADOR		21 041	8 124	6 515 000	San Salvador
GRENADA		378	146	80 000	St George's
GUATEMALA		108 890	42 043	12 347 000	Guatemala City
HAITI		27 750	10 714	8 326 000	Port-au-Prince
HONDURAS		112 088	43 277	6 941 000	Tegucigalpa
JAMAICA		10 991	4 244	2 651 000	Kingston
MEXICO		1 972 545	761 604	103 457 000	Mexico City
NICARAGUA		130 000	50 193	5 466 000	Managua
PANAMA		77 082	29 762	3 120 000	Panama City
ST KITTS AND NEVIS		261	101	42 000	Basseterre
ST LUCIA		616	238	149 000	Castries
ST VINCENT AND THE GRENADINES		389	150	120 000	Kingstown
TRINIDAD AND TOBAGO		5 130	1 981	1 303 000	Port of Spain
UNITED STATES OF AMERICA		9 826 635	3 794 085	294 043 000	Washington DC

capital	languages	religions	currency
Nuku'alofa	English, Polynesian	Christian	New Zealand dollar
Kingston	English	Protestant, Roman Catholic	Australian dollar
Capitol Hill	English, Chamorro, local languages	Roman Catholic	US dollar
Adamstown	English	Protestant	New Zealand dollar
	English, Tokelauan	Christian	New Zealand dollar
Matā'utu	French, Wallisian, Futunian	Roman Catholic	CFP franc*

*Franc des Comptoirs Français du Pacifique

languages	religions	currency
English, creole	Protestant, Roman Catholic	East Caribbean dollar
English, creole	Protestant, Roman Catholic	Bahamian dollar
English, creole	Protestant, Roman Catholic	Barbados dollar
English, Spanish, Mayan, creole	Roman Catholic, Protestant	Belize dollar
English, French	Roman Catholic, Protestant, Eastern Orthodox, Jewish	Canadian dollar
Spanish	Roman Catholic, Protestant	Costa Rican colón
Spanish	Roman Catholic, Protestant	Cuban peso
English, creole	Roman Catholic, Protestant	East Caribbean dollar
Spanish, creole	Roman Catholic, Protestant	Dominican peso
Spanish	Roman Catholic, Protestant	El Salvador colón, US dollar
English, creole	Roman Catholic, Protestant	East Caribbean dollar
Spanish, Mayan languages	Roman Catholic, Protestant	Quetzal, US dollar
French, creole	Roman Catholic, Protestant, Voodoo	Gourde
Spanish, Amerindian languages	Roman Catholic, Protestant	Lempira
English, creole	Protestant, Roman Catholic	Jamaican dollar
Spanish, Amerindian languages	Roman Catholic, Protestant	Mexican peso
Spanish, Amerindian languages	Roman Catholic, Protestant	Córdoba
Spanish, English, Amerindian languages	Roman Catholic, Protestant, Sunni Muslim	Balboa
English, creole	Protestant, Roman Catholic	East Caribbean dollar
English, creole	Roman Catholic, Protestant	East Caribbean dollar
English, creole	Protestant, Roman Catholic	East Caribbean dollar
English, creole, Hindi	Roman Catholic, Hindu, Protestant, Sunni Muslim	Trinidad and Tobago dollar
English, Spanish	Protestant, Roman Catholic, Sunni Muslim, Jewish	US dollar

world states and territories
oceania, north america

NORTH AMERICA
DEPENDENT TERRITORIES

			area sq km	area sq miles	population
Anguilla		United Kingdom Overseas Territory	155	60	12 000
Aruba		Self-governing Netherlands Territory	193	75	100 000
Bermuda		United Kingdom Overseas Territory	54	21	82 000
Cayman Islands		United Kingdom Overseas Territory	259	100	40 000
Greenland		Self-governing Danish Territory	2 175 600	840 004	57 000
Guadeloupe		French Overseas Department	1 780	687	440 000
Martinique		French Overseas Department	1 079	417	393 000
Montserrat		United Kingdom Overseas Territory	100	39	4 000
Netherlands Antilles		Self-governing Netherlands Territory	800	309	221 000
Puerto Rico		United States Commonwealth	9 104	3 515	3 879 000
St Pierre and Miquelon		French Territorial Collectivity	242	93	6 000
Turks and Caicos Islands		United Kingdom Overseas Territory	430	166	21 000
Virgin Islands (U.K.)		United Kingdom Overseas Territory	153	59	21 000
Virgin Islands (U.S.A.)		United States Unincorporated Territory	352	136	111 000

SOUTH AMERICA
COUNTRIES

		area sq km	area sq miles	population	capital
ARGENTINA		2 766 889	1 068 302	38 428 000	Buenos Aires
BOLIVIA		1 098 581	424 164	8 808 000	La Paz/Sucre
BRAZIL		8 514 879	3 287 613	178 470 000	Brasília
CHILE		756 945	292 258	15 805 000	Santiago
COLOMBIA		1 141 748	440 831	44 222 000	Bogotá
ECUADOR		272 045	105 037	13 003 000	Quito
GUYANA		214 969	83 000	765 000	Georgetown
PARAGUAY		406 752	157 048	5 878 000	Asunción
PERU		1 285 216	496 225	27 167 000	Lima
SURINAME		163 820	63 251	436 000	Paramaribo
URUGUAY		176 215	68 037	3 415 000	Montevideo
VENEZUELA		912 050	352 144	25 699 000	Caracas

SOUTH AMERICA
DEPENDENT TERRITORIES

			area sq km	area sq miles	population
Falkland Islands		United Kingdom Overseas Territory	12 170	4 699	3 000
French Guiana		French Overseas Department	90 000	34 749	178 000

apital	languages	religions	currency
ne Valley	English	Protestant, Roman Catholic	East Caribbean dollar
ranjestad	Papiamento, Dutch, English	Roman Catholic, Protestant	Arubian florin
amilton	English	Protestant, Roman Catholic	Bermuda dollar
eorge Town	English	Protestant, Roman Catholic	Cayman Islands dollar
uuk	Greenlandic, Danish	Protestant	Danish krone
asse-Terre	French, creole	Roman Catholic	Euro
rt-de-France	French, creole	Roman Catholic, traditional beliefs	Euro
ymouth	English	Protestant, Roman Catholic	East Caribbean dollar
illemstad	Dutch, Papiamento, English	Roman Catholic, Protestant	Netherlands guilder
an Juan	Spanish, English	Roman Catholic, Protestant	US dollar
-Pierre	French	Roman Catholic	Euro
and Turk	English	Protestant	US dollar
ad Town	English	Protestant, Roman Catholic	US dollar
arlotte Amalie	English, Spanish	Protestant, Roman Catholic	

nguages	religions	currency
anish, Italian, Amerindian languages	Roman Catholic, Protestant	Argentinian peso
anish, Quechua, Aymara	Roman Catholic, Protestant, Bahaʼí	Boliviano
rtuguese	Roman Catholic, Protestant	Real
anish, Amerindian languages	Roman Catholic, Protestant	Chilean peso
anish, Amerindian languages	Roman Catholic, Protestant	Colombian peso
anish, Quechua, other Amerindian languages	Roman Catholic	US dollar
glish, creole, Amerindian languages	Protestant, Hindu, Roman Catholic, Sunni Muslim	Guyana dollar
anish, Guaraní	Roman Catholic, Protestant	Guaraní
anish, Quechua, Aymara	Roman Catholic, Protestant	Sol
tch, Surinamese, English, Hindi	Hindu, Roman Catholic, Protestant, Sunni Muslim	Suriname guilder
anish	Roman Catholic, Protestant, Jewish	Uruguayan peso
anish, Amerindian languages	Roman Catholic, Protestant	Bolívar

ital	languages	religions	currency
nley	English	Protestant, Roman Catholic	Falkland Islands pound
yenne	French, creole	Roman Catholic	Euro

world states and territories
north america, south america

World extremes – capitals

Largest national capital (population)	Tōkyō, Japan	26 849 000
Smallest national capital (population)	Vatican City	472
Most northerly national capital	Reykjavík, Iceland	64° 08'N
Most southerly national capital	Wellington, New Zealand	41° 18'S
Highest capital	La Paz, Bolivia	3 630 m 11 909 ft

AL.	ALBANIA	JOR.	JORDAN
A.	ANDORRA	K.	KUWAIT
ARM.	ARMENIA	KYR.	KYRGYZSTAN
AUS.	AUSTRIA	LEB.	LEBANON
AZ.	AZERBAIJAN	LITH.	LITHUANIA
B.	BURUNDI	LUX.	LUXEMBOURG
BE.	BENIN	M.	MACEDONIA
BEL.	BELGIUM	MO.	MOLDOVA
B.H.	BOSNIA-HERZEGOVINA	NETH.	NETHERLANDS
BN.	BAHRAIN	NI.	NIGERIA
BUR.	BURKINA	POL.	POLAND
CAM.	CAMEROON	Q.	QATAR
C.A.R.	CENTRAL AFRICAN REPUBLIC	R.	RWANDA
C.D'I.	CÔTE D'IVOIRE	SLA.	SLOVAKIA
CR.	CROATIA	SL.	SLOVENIA
CYP.	CYPRUS	S.M.	SERBIA AND
CZ.R.	CZECH REPUBLIC		MONTENEGRO
DEN.	DENMARK	SUR.	SURINAME
EQ.G.	EQUATORIAL GUINEA	SW.	SWITZERLAND
FR.G.	FRENCH GUIANA	T.	TOGO
GEOR.	GEORGIA	TAJIK.	TAJIKISTAN
GER.	GERMANY	TURKM.	TURKMENISTAN
GH.	GHANA	U.A.E.	UNITED ARAB
GUY.	GUYANA		EMIRATES
HUN.	HUNGARY	UZBEK.	UZBEKISTAN
ISR.	ISRAEL		

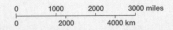

0	1000	2000	3000 miles
0	2000	4000 km	

World extremes – countries			
Largest country	Russian Federation	17 075 400 sq km	6 592 849 sq miles
Smallest country	Vatican City	0.5 sq km	0.2 sq miles
Largest population	China	1 289 161 000	
Smallest population	Vatican City	472	
Most densely populated country	Monaco	17 000 per sq km	34 000 per sq mile
Least densely populated country	Mongolia	2 per sq km	4 per sq mile

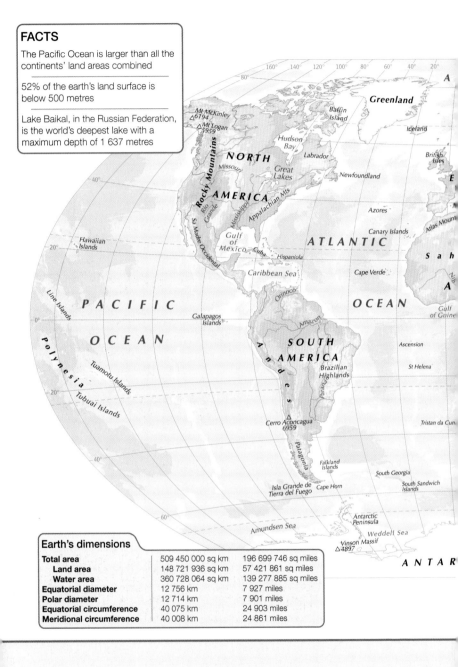

FACTS

The Pacific Ocean is larger than all the continents' land areas combined

52% of the earth's land surface is below 500 metres

Lake Baikal, in the Russian Federation, is the world's deepest lake with a maximum depth of 1 637 metres

Earth's dimensions

Total area	509 450 000 sq km	196 699 746 sq miles
Land area	148 721 936 sq km	57 421 861 sq miles
Water area	360 728 064 sq km	139 277 885 sq miles
Equatorial diameter	12 756 km	7 927 miles
Polar diameter	12 714 km	7 901 miles
Equatorial circumference	40 075 km	24 903 miles
Meridional circumference	40 008 km	24 861 miles

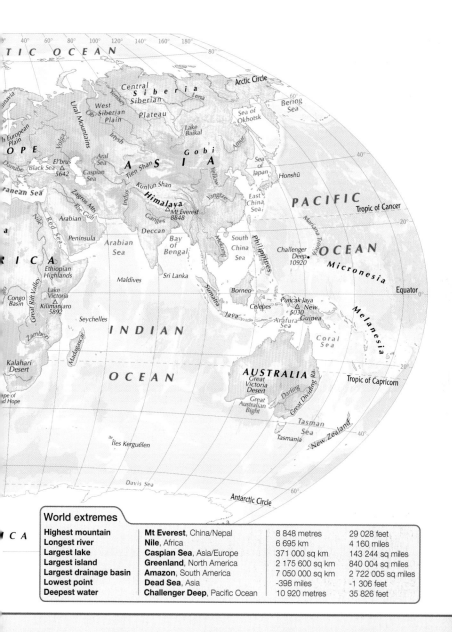

World extremes			
Highest mountain	**Mt Everest**, China/Nepal	8 848 metres	29 028 feet
Longest river	**Nile**, Africa	6 695 km	4 160 miles
Largest lake	**Caspian Sea**, Asia/Europe	371 000 sq km	143 244 sq miles
Largest island	**Greenland**, North America	2 175 600 sq km	840 004 sq miles
Largest drainage basin	**Amazon**, South America	7 050 000 sq km	2 722 005 sq miles
Lowest point	**Dead Sea**, Asia	-398 miles	-1 306 feet
Deepest water	**Challenger Deep**, Pacific Ocean	10 920 metres	35 826 feet

world
physical features

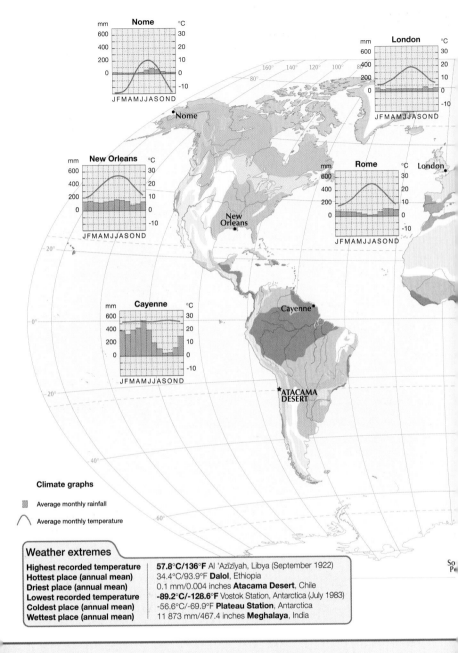

Nome

mm / °C

London

mm / °C

New Orleans

mm / °C

Rome

mm / °C

Cayenne

mm / °C

Climate graphs

Average monthly rainfall

Average monthly temperature

Weather extremes

Highest recorded temperature	**57.8°C/136°F** Al 'Azīzīyah, Libya (September 1922)
Hottest place (annual mean)	34.4°C/93.9°F **Dalol**, Ethiopia
Driest place (annual mean)	0.1 mm/0.004 inches **Atacama Desert**, Chile
Lowest recorded temperature	**-89.2°C/-128.6°F** Vostok Station, Antarctica (July 1983)
Coldest place (annual mean)	-56.6°C/-69.9°F **Plateau Station**, Antarctica
Wettest place (annual mean)	11 873 mm/467.4 inches **Meghalaya**, India

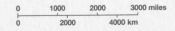

0	1000	2000	3000 miles
0	2000	4000 km	

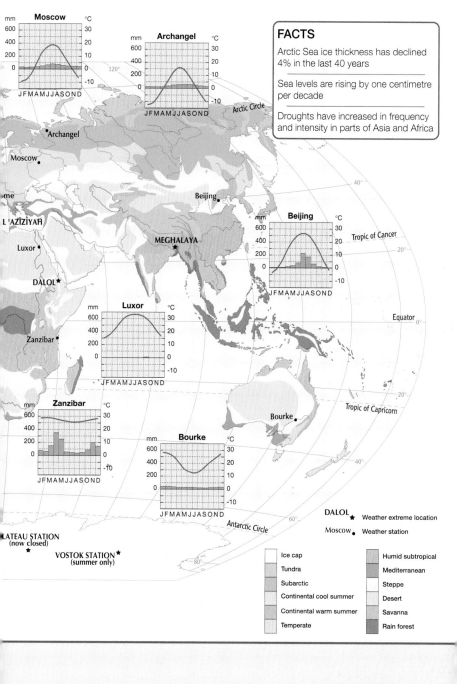

Moscow

Archangel

Archangel

Moscow

Arctic Circle

L 'AZĪZĪYAH

Luxor

Beijing

MEGHALAYA

Beijing

Tropic of Cancer

DALOL

Luxor

Luxor

Equator

Zanzibar

Zanzibar

Tropic of Capricorn

Bourke

Bourke

Antarctic Circle

DALOL ★ Weather extreme location

Moscow ● Weather station

PLATEAU STATION (now closed)

VOSTOK STATION ★ (summer only)

Ice cap	Humid subtropical
Tundra	Mediterranean
Subarctic	Steppe
Continental cool summer	Desert
Continental warm summer	Savanna
Temperate	Rain forest

world
climate

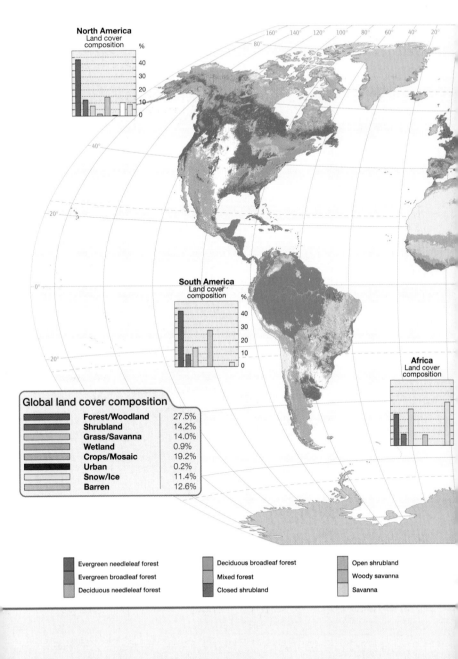

North America
Land cover composition

South America
Land cover composition

Africa
Land cover composition

Global land cover composition

Forest/Woodland	27.5%
Shrubland	14.2%
Grass/Savanna	14.0%
Wetland	0.9%
Crops/Mosaic	19.2%
Urban	0.2%
Snow/Ice	11.4%
Barren	12.6%

Evergreen needleleaf forest

Evergreen broadleaf forest

Deciduous needleleaf forest

Deciduous broadleaf forest

Mixed forest

Closed shrubland

Open shrubland

Woody savanna

Savanna

0   1000   2000   3000 miles
0   2000   4000 km

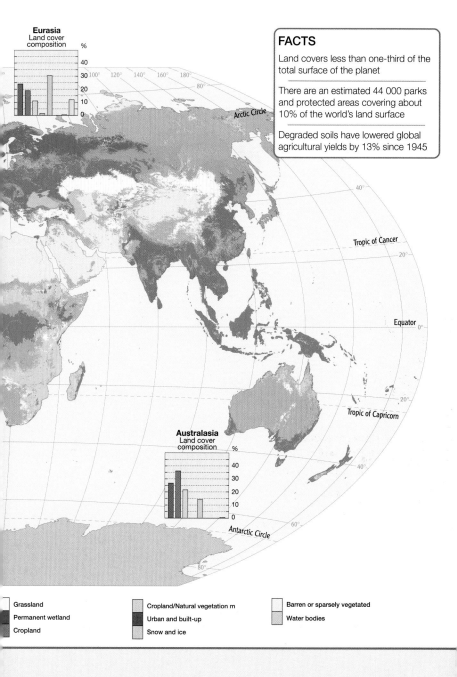

Eurasia
Land cover composition

Australasia
Land cover composition

FACTS

Land covers less than one-third of the total surface of the planet

There are an estimated 44 000 parks and protected areas covering about 10% of the world's land surface

Degraded soils have lowered global agricultural yields by 13% since 1945

Arctic Circle

Tropic of Cancer

Equator 0°

Tropic of Capricorn

Antarctic Circle

Grassland

Permanent wetland

Cropland

Cropland/Natural vegetation m

Urban and built-up

Snow and ice

Barren or sparsely vegetated

Water bodies

world
land cover

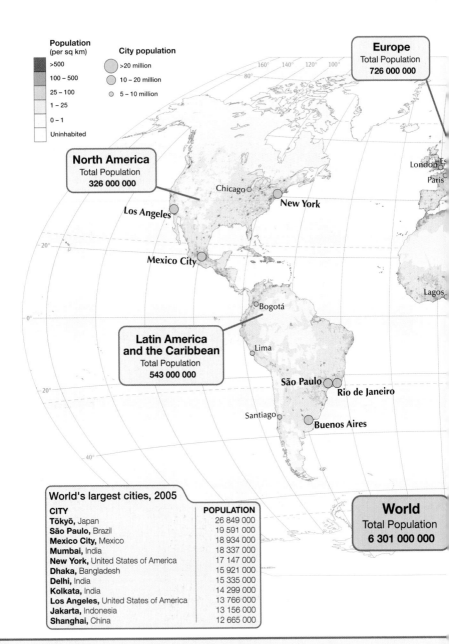

Population
(per sq km)

- >500
- 100 – 500
- 25 – 100
- 1 – 25
- 0 – 1
- Uninhabited

City population

- >20 million
- 10 – 20 million
- 5 – 10 million

Europe
Total Population
726 000 000

North America
Total Population
326 000 000

Chicago
New York
Los Angeles
Mexico City
London
Paris
Lagos

Bogotá

**Latin America
and the Caribbean**
Total Population
543 000 000

Lima

São Paulo
Rio de Janeiro

Santiago
Buenos Aires

World
Total Population
6 301 000 000

World's largest cities, 2005

CITY	POPULATION
Tōkyō, Japan	26 849 000
São Paulo, Brazil	19 591 000
Mexico City, Mexico	18 934 000
Mumbai, India	18 337 000
New York, United States of America	17 147 000
Dhaka, Bangladesh	15 921 000
Delhi, India	15 335 000
Kolkata, India	14 299 000
Los Angeles, United States of America	13 766 000
Jakarta, Indonesia	13 156 000
Shanghai, China	12 665 000

0	1000	2000	3000 miles
0	2000	4000 km	

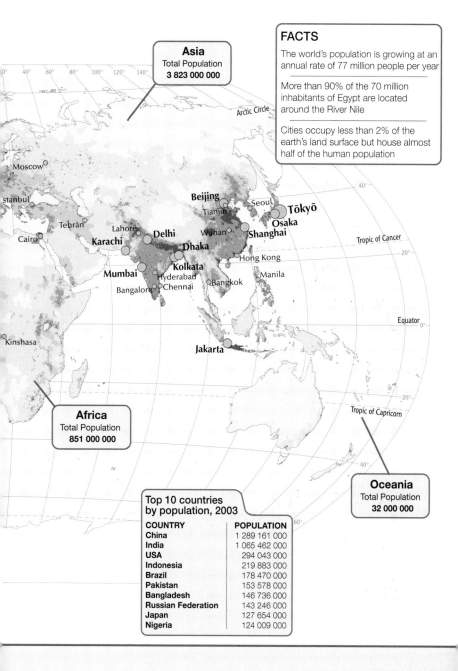

Asia
Total Population
3 823 000 000

Arctic Circle

Moscow

Istanbul

Tehrān

Cairo

Beijing

Tianjin

Seoul

Tōkyō

Osaka

Shanghai

Lahore

Delhi

Wuhan

Karachi

Dhaka

Hong Kong

Tropic of Cancer

Mumbai

Kolkata

Hyderabad

Bangalore

Chennai

Bangkok

Manila

Kinshasa

Equator

Jakarta

Tropic of Capricorn

Africa
Total Population
851 000 000

Oceania
Total Population
32 000 000

Top 10 countries by population, 2003

COUNTRY	POPULATION
China	1 289 161 000
India	1 065 462 000
USA	294 043 000
Indonesia	219 883 000
Brazil	178 470 000
Pakistan	153 578 000
Bangladesh	146 736 000
Russian Federation	143 246 000
Japan	127 654 000
Nigeria	124 009 000

world
population and cities

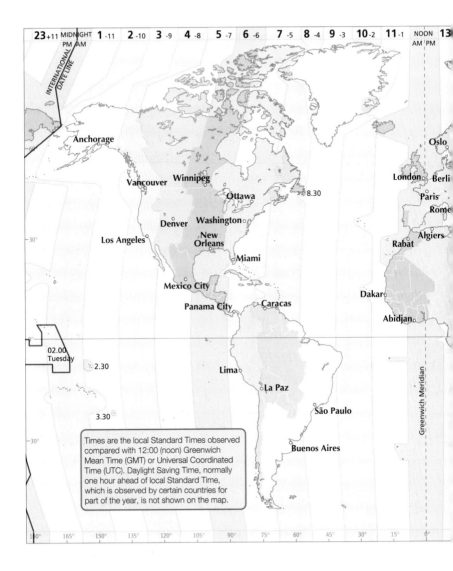

| 23 +11 | MIDNIGHT | 1 -11 | 2 -10 | 3 -9 | 4 -8 | 5 -7 | 6 -6 | 7 -5 | 8 -4 | 9 -3 | 10 -2 | 11 -1 | NOON | 13 |
| | PM AM | | | | | | | | | | | | AM PM | |

INTERNATIONAL DATE LINE

Anchorage

Oslo

Vancouver Winnipeg

London Berlin

Ottawa

Paris

8.30

Denver Washington

Rome

Los Angeles New Orleans

Algiers

Rabat

Miami

Mexico City

Dakar

Panama City Caracas

Abidjan

02.00 Tuesday

2.30

Lima

La Paz

Greenwich Meridian

3.30

São Paulo

Times are the local Standard Times observed compared with 12:00 (noon) Greenwich Mean Time (GMT) or Universal Coordinated Time (UTC). Daylight Saving Time, normally one hour ahead of local Standard Time, which is observed by certain countries for part of the year, is not shown on the map.

Buenos Aires

180° 165° 150° 135° 120° 105° 90° 75° 60° 45° 30° 15° 0°

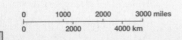

| 0 | 1000 | 2000 | 3000 miles |
| 0 | | 2000 | 4000 km |

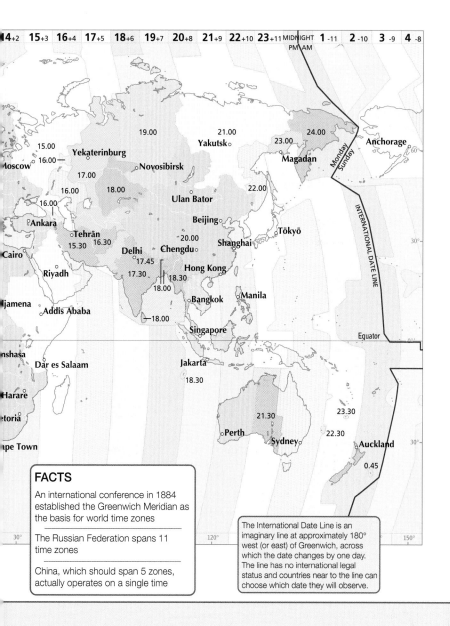

19.00

21.00

24.00

Yakutsk○

23.00

Anchorage

15.00

Yekaterinburg

16.00

Magadan

Moscow

Novosibirsk

17.00

22.00

16.00   18.00

Ulan Bator

16.00

Beijing○

Tōkyō

Ankara

Tehrān

20.00

15.30 16.30   Delhi   Chengdu○   Shanghai

Cairo   17.45

Riyadh   17.30   Hong Kong

18.30

18.00

jamena   Addis Ababa   Bangkok   Manila

18.00

Singapore

Equator

nshasa   Dar es Salaam   Jakarta

Harare   18.30

toria

23.30

21.30

pe Town   Perth   22.30

Sydney○   Auckland

0.45

Monday / Sunday

INTERNATIONAL DATE LINE

60°

30°

30°

FACTS

An international conference in 1884 established the Greenwich Meridian as the basis for world time zones

The Russian Federation spans 11 time zones

China, which should span 5 zones, actually operates on a single time

The International Date Line is an imaginary line at approximately 180° west (or east) of Greenwich, across which the date changes by one day. The line has no international legal status and countries near to the line can choose which date they will observe.

30°   120°   150°

world
timezones

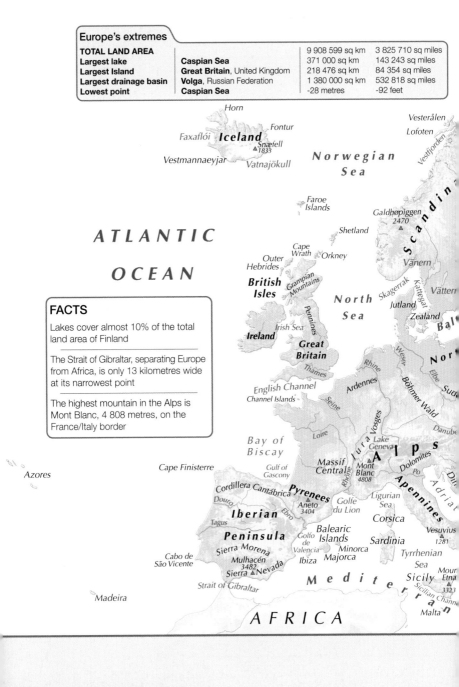

Europe's extremes

TOTAL LAND AREA		9 908 599 sq km	3 825 710 sq miles
Largest lake	Caspian Sea	371 000 sq km	143 243 sq miles
Largest Island	Great Britain, United Kingdom	218 476 sq km	84 354 sq miles
Largest drainage basin	Volga, Russian Federation	1 380 000 sq km	532 818 sq miles
Lowest point	Caspian Sea	-28 metres	-92 feet

Horn

Fontur

Vesterålen

Faxaflói **Iceland**

Lofoten

Snæfell
▲1833

Vestmannaeyjar Vatnajökull

Vestfjorden

N o r w e g i a n
S e a

Faroe
Islands

Galdhøpiggen
2470
▲

Shetland

S
c
a
n
d
i
n

ATLANTIC

Cape
Wrath Orkney
Outer
Hebrides

OCEAN

British
Isles Grampian
Mountains

N o r t h
S e a

Skagerrak

Vänern

Vänern

Jutland

Kattegat

Vättern

Zealand

Bal

FACTS

Lakes cover almost 10% of the total
land area of Finland

The Strait of Gibraltar, separating Europe
from Africa, is only 13 kilometres wide
at its narrowest point

The highest mountain in the Alps is
Mont Blanc, 4 808 metres, on the
France/Italy border

Irish Sea
Ireland

Pennines

**Great
Britain**

Thames

Weser

Rhine

N o r

Elbe

Böhmer Wald

Sude

English Channel
Channel Islands

Ardennes

Seine

Jura

Vosges

Loire

Lake
Geneva
▲ **A l p s**
Mont
Blanc
4808

Danube

Böhmer Wald

Dolomites

Po

Bay of
Biscay

Gulf of
Gascony

**Massif
Central**

Rhône

Adriat

Cape Finisterre

Cordillera Cantábrica **Pyrenees**

Aneto
3404

Golfe
du Lion

Ligurian
Sea

A p e n n i n e s

Din

Azores

Douro

Iberian

Ebro

Corsica

Tagus

Peninsula

Golfo
de
Valencia

Balearic
Islands

Minorca

Sardinia

Vesuvius
▲
1281

Tyrrhenian
Sea

Cabo de
São Vicente

Sierra Morena

Mulhacén
3482
Sierra ▲Nevada

Ibiza Majorca

Sicily

Moun

Etna
▲
3323

Madeira

Strait of Gibraltar

M e d i t e r

r
a
n

Sicilian Channel

Malta

AFRICA

0	150	300	450 miles
0	300	600 km	

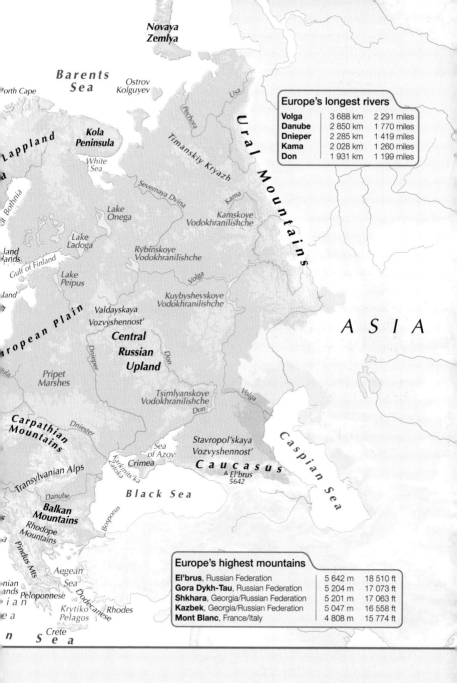

Novaya
Zemlya

Barents
Sea

orth Cape   Ostrov
           Kolguyev

Usa

Pechora

U r a l   M o u n t a i n s

Lappland

**Kola
Peninsula**

White
Sea

Timanskiy Kryazh

Severnaya Dvina

Kama

Bothnia

Lake
Onega

Kamskoye
Vodokhranilishche

land
ands

Lake
Ladoga

Rybinskoye
Vodokhranilishche

Gulf of Finland

Lake
Peipus

Volga

land

Kuybyshevskoye
Vodokhranilishche

A S I A

ropean Plain

Valdayskaya
Vozvyshennost'

**Central
Russian
Upland**

Dnieper

Don

Volga

Pripet
Marshes

ula

Tsimlyanskoye
Vodokhranilishche

Don

**Carpathian
Mountains**

Dniester

Sea
of Azov

Stavropol'skaya
Vozvyshennost'

C a s p i a n   S e a

Kerkinits'ka
Zatoka

Crimea

C a u c a s u s

▲ El'brus
5642

Transylvanian Alps

Danube

B l a c k   S e a

**Balkan
Mountains**

Rhodope
Mountains

Bosporus

Pindus Mts

Aegean
Sea

nian
ands   Peloponnese
i a n

Dodecanese

Rhodes

Krytiko
Pelagos

e a

Crete

n   S e a

europe
physical features

Europe's countries

Largest country	Russian Federation	17 075 400 sq km	6 592 812 sq miles
Smallest country	Vatican City	0.5 sq km	0.2 sq miles
Largest population	Russian Federation	143 246 000	
Smallest population	Vatican City	472	
Most densely populated country	Monaco	17 000 per sq km	34 000 per sq mile
Least densely populated country	Iceland	3 per sq km	7 per sq mile

Reykjavík ICELAND

Norwegian Sea

N O R W A Y

S W E D E

Tórshavn Faroe Islands (Denmark)

ATLANTIC

OCEAN

Bergen Oslo

Stockho

Aalborg

Glasgow Edinburgh *North* DENMARK Malmö

Belfast UNITED *Sea* Copenhagen Bal

REPUBLIC KINGDOM Hamburg

OF Dublin Manchester

IRELAND Birmingham NETH. Berlin Pozna

Cardiff The Hague Amsterdam

London *English Channel* Brussels Essen GERMANY

Channel Islands (U.K.) BELGIUM Frankfurt Prague

Nantes Paris LUX. am Main CZ.R.

Seine Luxembourg *Danube* Vienna

Loire Orléans Strasbourg Munich Bratisla

Bay of Biscay FRANCE Bern SW. Vaduz LIE. AUSTRIA

Bordeaux Lyon Geneva Ljubljana SLOVEN

AL. ALBANIA
B.H. BOSNIA-HERZEGOVINA
CR. CROATIA
CZ.R. CZECH REPUBLIC
HUN. HUNGARY
LIE. LIECHTENSTEIN
LUX. LUXEMBOURG
M. MACEDONIA
NETH. NETHERLANDS
S.M. SERBIA AND MONTENEGRO
SW. SWITZERLAND

Milan Zag

Turin Po SAN CR.

Azores (Portugal)

MARINO Sp

Andorra Marseille MONACO

Oporto la Vella ANDORRA Vatican City

Madrid Barcelona *Corsica* Rome

Lisbon SPAIN Palma Naples

PORTUGAL *Tagus* de Mallorca *Sardinia*

Valencia *Balearic Islands* *Tyrrhenian Sea*

Seville Cartagena *Medit e r*

Cádiz Gibraltar (U.K.) Palermo Sicily

Madeira (Portugal)

A F R I C A Valletta MALTA

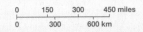

0	150	300	450 miles
0		300	600 km

Novaya
Zemlya

Vorkuta

*Barents
Sea*

*Ostrov
Kolguyev*

Pechora

appland

**Kola
Peninsula**

*White
Sea*

Archangel

R U S S I A N

Severnaya Dvina

Bothnia

FINLAND *Lake
Ladoga*

F E D E R A T I O N

Perm'

Helsinki

St Petersburg

Izhevsk

Ufa

Gulf of Finland
Tallinn

Yaroslavl'

Volga

Nizhniy
Novgorod

Kazan'

ESTONIA

A S I A

LATVIA

Moscow

Ul'yanovsk

Samara

Riga

Tula

Orenburg

LITHUANIA
.FED. **Vilnius**

Saratov

Kaliningrad

Minsk

BELARUS

Voronezh

Homyel'

Volgograd

Varsaw Brest

Dnieper

Kiev

Kharkiv

Volga

Astrakhan'

LAND

Rivne

U K R A I N E Donets'k

Don

atowice

L'viv

Dniester

Dnipropetrovs'k

Rostov-
na-Donu

VAKIA

MOLDOVA

Budapest **Chişinău**

Odesa

Krasnodar

Groznyy

N.

C a u c a s u s

ROMANIA

Caspian Sea

Belgrade **Bucharest** Constanța

rajevo Niš

Danube

B l a c k   S e a

S.M.
gorica

ana M.

BULGARIA

Sofia

Skopje

İstanbul

AL.

T U R K E Y

Thessaloniki

*Aegean
Sea*

GREECE

Athens

ian

Crete

n   S e a

europe
countries

1 2 3 4 5 6 7 8 9

Golchikha
Gydan Peninsula (Gydanskiy Poluostrov)
Ust'-Port
Tazovskaya Guba
Ob' Hamburg
Taz
Nyda
Tazovskiy
Novyy Urengoy
Urengoy
Korotchaevo
Ob'skaya Guba
Novyy Port
Yamburg
Arctic Circle
Ozgovskaya Guba
Nadym
Pangody
Novyy Urengoy
Noyabr'sk
Netteyugansk
Surgut
Pereyaslovskoye
Lyantor
Khanty-Mansiysk
Mamontovo
Ob'
Yamal Tambey
Yamal Peninsula (Poluostrov Yamal)
Seyakha
Mys Kamennyy
Belovarskiy
Zapadno Sibirskaya Ravnina
(West Siberian Plain)
Nyagan
Igrim
Oktyabr'skoye
Yugorsk
Sovetskiy
Neftvugansk
Khantymansiysk
Ostrov Belyy
Marresale
Yar-Sale
Yaroogo
Labytnangi
Salekhard
Kaz'ymskiy Mys
Berezovo
Til'tim
Nyagan'
RUSSIAN FEDERATION
Kondinskoye
Tobol'sk
Tyumen'
Irtysh

Kara Sea (Karskoye More)
Bajdarabskaya Guba
Kara
Khoy
Ostrov Vaygach
Guba Dolgaya
Kharasavey
Khrebet Pay-Khoy
Tundra
Vorkuta
Abez'
Usinsk
Inta
Pechora
Kyrta
Gora 1617
Gora Tel'pos-Iz
VukTyl'
Ust'-Pechorsk
Nizhniy Odes
Sosnogorsk
Sosva
Nerokhi
Igrim
Ust'-Kulom
Gavny
Konzhakovskiy Kamen'
Kizel
Berezniki
Solikamsk
Nyrob
Gora
Kizel
Chusovoy
Ural'skiy Khrebet)
Kushva
Nizhniy Tagil
Yekaterinburg
Serov
Irbit
Turinsk
Tavda

Stolbovoy
Novaya Zemlya
Krasino
Ostrov Mezhdusharskiy
Proliv Karskiye Vorota
Bol'shezemel'skaya Tundra
Khoreyver
Nar'yan-Mar
Nosovaya
Charkayuom
Izhma
Tsil'ma
Ust'-Tsil'ma
Kadzherom
Nizhniy Odes
Troitsko-Pechorsk
Ukhta
Kozhva
Sindor
Yemva
Zheshart
Koryazhma
Storozhevsk
Sharya
Syktyvkar
Ob'yachevo
Kirs
Kirovo-Chepetsk
Glazov
Vyatka
Omutninsk
Shabalino
Perm'
Ocher
Votkinsk
Izhevsk
Igra

Barents Sea
Ostrov Kolguyev
Severnyy
Chyoshskaya Guba
Indiga
Novvy Bor
Myla
Timanskiy Kryazh
Ugorsk
Ust'-Ura
Oluza
Kotlas
Velikiy Ustyug
Sharya
Galich
Manturovo
Kostroma
Kirov
Slobodskoy
Shabalino
Orlov
Kotel'nich
Kirov

North Cape (Nordkapp)
Havøysund
Hammerfest
Tromsø
Vadsø
Kirkenes
Vardø
Varzino
Kanin Nos
Poluostrov Kanin
Koyda
Mezen'
Leshukonskoye
Kyssa
Karpogory
Poluostrov Kanin
White Sea (Beloye More)
Mezen'
Shilega
Pinega
Arkhangel'sk
Archangel (Arkhangel'sk)
Severodvinsk
Novodvinsk
Severnaya Dvina
Krasnoborsk
Vel'sk
Nyandoma
Totma
Vologda
Gryazovets
Cherepovets
Rybinsk
Yaroslavl'
Kostroma

Mehamn
NORWAY
Alta
Karasjok (Kárášjohka)
Kautokeino
Enontekiö
Poluostrov Rybachiy
Nikel'
Murmansk
Severomorsk
Kola
Monchegorsk
Olenegorsk
Kirovsk
Apatity
Kol'skiy Poluostrov (Kola Peninsula)
Umba
Sosnovka
Kandalaksha
Kovdor
Kem'
Belomorsk
Onega
Lake Onega (Ozero Onezhskoye)
Medvezh'yegorsk
Segezha
Nadvoitsy
Povenets
Pudozh
Vytegra
Ozero Beloye
Belozersk
Kirillov
Danilov
Lyubim

Tromsø
Kiruna
SWEDEN
Gällivare
Jokkmokk
Arvidsjaur
Boden
Luleå
Gulf of Bothnia (Bottenviken)
Skellefteå
Kalix
Tornio
Haparanda
Kemi
Oulu
Raahe
Kajaani
Kuusamo
Salla
Rovaniemi
Kemijärvi
Sodankylä
Ivalo
Inari
Karigasniemi
Utsjoki
Karasjok
FINLAND
Kuhmo
Kostomuksha
Muyezerskiy
Reboly
Suoyarvi
Petrozavodsk
Kondopoga
Lake Ladoga (Ladozhskoye Ozero)
Olonets
Lodeynoye Pole
Tikhvin
Cherepovets
Babayevo
Ustyuzhna

Mo i Rana
Östersund
Sundsvall
Umeå
Vaasa
Seinäjoki
Ylivieska
Iisalmi
Nurmes
Joensuu
Lieksa
Sortavala
Pitkyaranta
Priozersk
Vyborg
St Petersburg (Sankt-Peterburg)
Gatchina
Luga
Novgorod
Staraya Russa
Valday
Vyshniy Volochek
Bologoye
Torzhok
Tver'
Vyshny Volochek

TALLINN
ESTONIA
Tartu
Pärnu
Narva
Kingisepp
Kohtla-Järve
Pskov
Ostrov
Valga
Võru
Gulf of Finland (Suomenlahti)
Helsinki
HELSINKI
Espoo
Tampere
Kotka
Lahti
Kouvola
Lappeenranta
Savonlinna
Mikkeli
Jyväskylä
Kuopio
Varkaus
Turku
Pori

Sosnovyy Bor

LATVIA
Aluksne
Rezekne
Cesis
Valmiera

0   100   200   300 miles

0   200   400 km

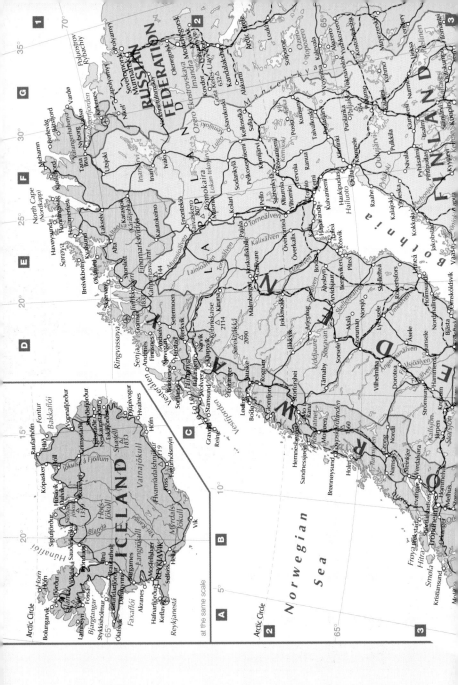
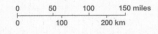

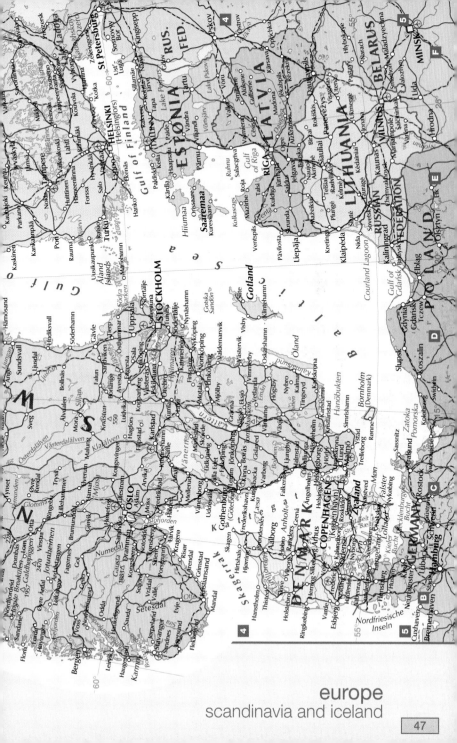

europe
scandinavia and iceland

47

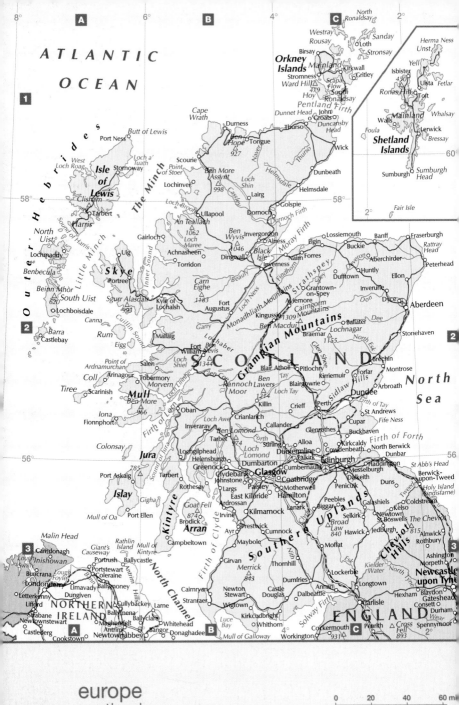

ATLANTIC OCEAN

North Sea

North Channel

SCOTLAND

ENGLAND

NORTHERN IRELAND

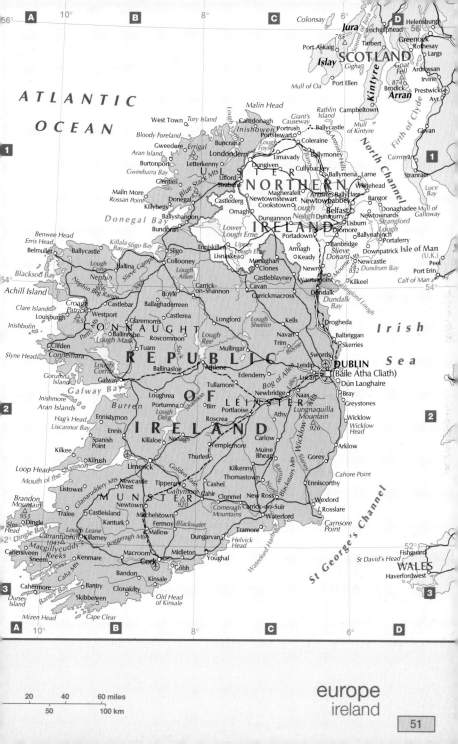

europe
ireland

UNITED

KINGDOM

North Sea

Irish Sea

North Channel

SCOTLAND

NORTHERN IRELAND

ENGLAND

Pennines

Southern Uplands

Cheviot Hills

The Wash

Firth of Forth

Glasgow
Edinburgh
Newcastle upon Tyne
Sunderland
Middlesbrough
Leeds
Manchester
Liverpool
Kingston upon Hull
York
Sheffield
Belfast

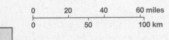

| 0 | 20 | 40 | 60 miles |
| 0 | 50 | | 100 km |

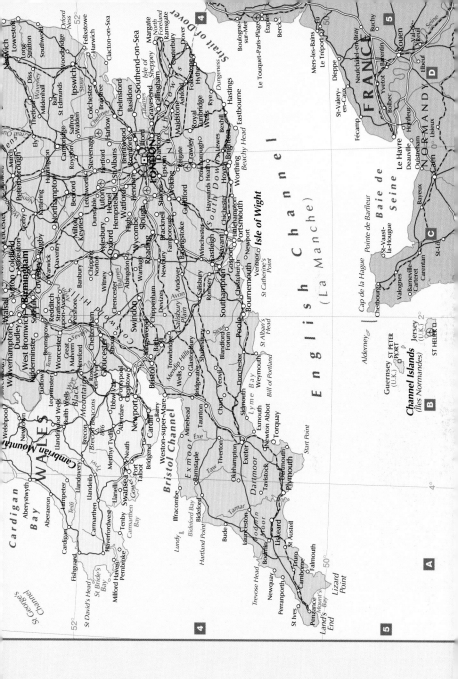

North Sea

NETHERLANDS
AMSTERDAM

BELGIUM
BRUSSELS
Bruxelles

FRANCE

LUXEMBOURG

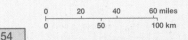

0	20	40	60 miles
0	50	100 km

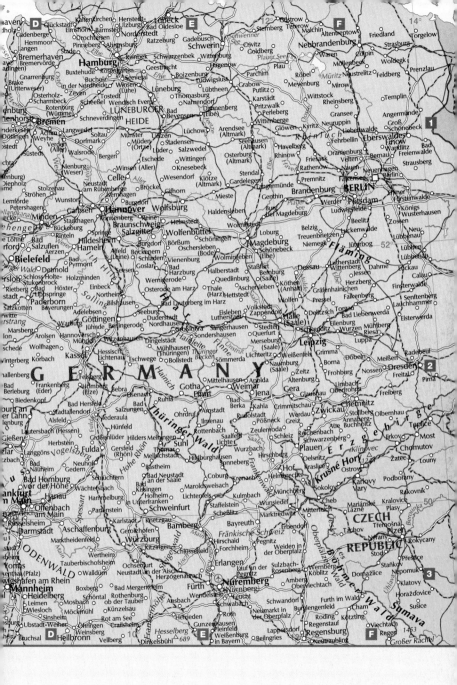

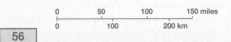

1

A   **B**   **C**

Bude Tiverton Yeovil Winchester Crawley Folkestone Dover Calais
Newquay Exeter Dorchester Southampton Worthing Brighton Hastings Dunkirk
Bodmin Dartmoor Exmouth Poole Bournemouth Portsmouth Le Touquet- Étaples Li
St Ives Truro Torquay Lyme Isle of Wight Paris-Plage Bruay-la-
Penzance Plymouth Bay UNITED KINGDOM Berck Bussière Arras
Land's End Falmouth Start Point English Channel Abbeville Roullens
Isles Lizard (La Manche) Dieppe Péronne
of Scilly Point Cap de la Fécamp Neufchâtel- Amiens Montdidier Compiègne
Hague Cherbourg Le Havre en-Bray Yvetot Beauvais Mante
Alderney Deauville Bolbec Rouen Versailles Chantilly Ver
Guernsey ST PETER Baie de Seine Honfleur PAR
(U.K.) PORT Carentan Lisieux Évreux Dreux Mennecy
Channel Islands ST HÉLIER St-Lô Caen Argentan L'Aigle Chartres Étampes
(Îles Normandes) (U.K.) Coutances NORMANDY Sées Nogent- Neml
Île d'Ouessant Roscoff Granville Vire le-Rotrou Montargis
Lesneven Lannion Avranches Flers Alençon Mayenne Châteaudun Orléans
Guipavas Morlaix Dol-de-Bretagne Mayenne Le Mans Vendôme Châteauneuf-
Plouzané Guingamp St-Brieuc BRITTANY Fougères La Flèche Château- sur-Loire
Brest St-Malo Dinan Vitré Laval Baugé du-Loir Cosne-
Douarnenez Châteaulin Pontivy Loudéac Rennes Angers Tours St-Avertin sur-L
Pte du Raz Quimper Quimperlé Vannes Châteaubriant Ancenis Saumur Chinon Loches Vierzon
Ploemeur Lorient Belle-Île Quiberon La Baule-Escoublac Nantes Cholet Thouars Châtellerault Le Blanc
Île de Groix Carnac St-Nazaire Vertou La Roche- Bressuire Poitiers Montmorillon
Noirmoutier-en-l'Île Pornic sur-Yon Parthenay Le Dorat Commentry
Île de Noirmoutier Challans Fontenay- Niort Civray Bellac Bourganeuf
St-Jean-de-Monts La Roche- le-Comte Limoges
Île d'Yeu Talmont- La Rochelle Confolens St-Junien
Les Sables-d'Olonne St-Hilaire Rochefort St-Jean-d'Angély St-Yrieix-
Île de Ré Pte de Chassiron Saintes la-Perche Ussel
St-Pierre-d'Oléron Cognac Angoulême Brive-la- Tulle
Pte de la Coubre Royan Barbezieux- Gaillarde Aurillac
Pte de Grave Soulac-sur-Mer St-Hilaire Uzerche
Montendre Ribérac Montignac Égletons
Pauillac Coutras Périgueux Le Bugue Souillac
Mérignac Libourne Gourdon Figeac
Arcachon Pessac Bordeaux Bergerac Cahors Espalion
La Teste-de-Buch Langon Marmande Lot
Bazas Villeneuve-sur-Lot Rodez
Mimizan Casteljaloux Agen Moissac Carmau
Morcenx Labouheyre Nérac Lectoure Montauban Albi
Soustons Tartas Aire-sur- Condom Grenade- Gaillac
Mont-de-Marsan l'Adour Auch Colomiers Toulouse Castres
Bayonne Dax Orthez Maubourguet Muret Carcassonne
Biarritz Peyrehorade Pau Tarbes Bagnères- Foix Durban-Corbières
Irún Saint-Jean- Lourdes de-Luchon Pamiers Quillan
St-Jean-Pied-de-Port Pied-de-Port Soulom

2

A T L A N T I C
O C E A N

Golfe de
St-Malo

Cap
Fréhel

B a y
o f
B i s c a y

G u l f   o f
G a s c o n y

Mar Cantábrico

Luarca Avilés Cabo de Peñas
Ribadeo Gijón Xixón Ribadesella Santander
Salas Oviedo Torrecerredo Laredo Donostia-San
Cangas Mieres Torrelavega Algorta Sebastián
del Narcea Pola Peña Bilbao Biarritz
Villablino de Lena Ubiña Llodio Durango Tolosa Oloron-
Ponferrada Guardo Aguilar Vitoria-Gasteiz Extarri- Ste-Marie
Astorga León de Campoo Miranda de Ebro Aranatz
Truchas Saldaña Osorno Briviesca Estella Pamplona
Sierra Benavente Sahagún Burgos Logroño Tafalla
de la Cabrera Medina de Palencia Nájera Calahorra Aldaba
Bragança Ríoseco Lerma Sierra de la Demanda Alfaro Ejea de los
Zamora Valladolid Duero Aranda Tudela Caballeros Huesca
Fermoselle Toro Tordesillas de Duero Soria Tarazona Barbastro
Medina del Cuéllar Ayllón Alagón Zaragoza Binéfar
Campo Quinto Fraga

C o r d i l l e r a   C a n t á b r i c a
Sierra de la Demanda
Alto del
Moncayo

S P A I N

P y r e n e e s

ANDORRA
LA VELLA

ANDORRA

CATALUÑA Vic Girona
Tremp Berga Ripoll Olot
Torelló Bany
Graus Monzón Barbastro Tàrrega Manresa Igualada Mataró
Almazán Lleida Sabadell

50 miles markers

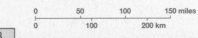

0   50   100   150 miles
0   100   200 km

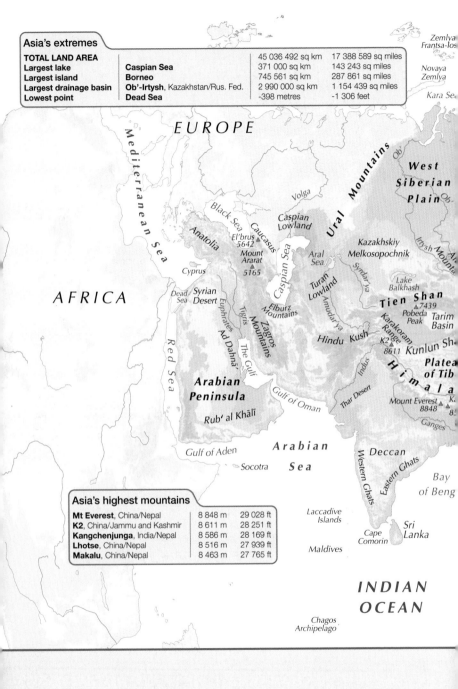

Asia's extremes

TOTAL LAND AREA		45 036 492 sq km	17 388 589 sq miles
Largest lake	Caspian Sea	371 000 sq km	143 243 sq miles
Largest island	Borneo	745 561 sq km	287 861 sq miles
Largest drainage basin	Ob'-Irtysh, Kazakhstan/Rus. Fed.	2 990 000 sq km	1 154 439 sq miles
Lowest point	Dead Sea	-398 metres	-1 306 feet

EUROPE

Zemlya
Frantsa-Iosifa

Novaya
Zemlya

Kara Sea

Mediterranean Sea

West
Siberian
Plain

Ob'

Ob'

Volga

Ural Mountains

Black Sea

Caspian
Lowland

Kazakhskiy
Melkosopochnik

Irtysh Mountains

Anatolia

Caucasus

El'brus
5642

Mount
Ararat
5165

Aral
Sea

Turan
Lowland

Syrdar'ya

Lake
Balkhash

AFRICA

Cyprus

Caspian Sea

Dead
Sea

Syrian
Desert

Elburz
Mountains

Amudar'ya

Tien Shan

▲7439
Pobeda
Peak

Tarim
Basin

Ad Dahnā

Euphrates

Tigris

Zagros Mountains

Hindu Kush

Karakoram Range

K2
8611

Kunlun Sh

Red Sea

The Gulf

Indus

Platea
of Tib
H i m a l a

**Arabian
Peninsula**

Gulf of Oman

Thar Desert

Mount Everest ▲
8848

Ka
8!

Rub' al Khālī

Ganges

Gulf of Aden

Socotra

**A r a b i a n
S e a**

Deccan

Western Ghats

Eastern Ghats

Bay
of Beng

Asia's highest mountains

Mt Everest, China/Nepal	8 848 m	29 028 ft
K2, China/Jammu and Kashmir	8 611 m	28 251 ft
Kangchenjunga, India/Nepal	8 586 m	28 169 ft
Lhotse, China/Nepal	8 516 m	27 939 ft
Makalu, China/Nepal	8 463 m	27 765 ft

Laccadive
Islands

Cape
Comorin

Sri
Lanka

Maldives

INDIAN

OCEAN

Chagos
Archipelago

0	500	1000	1500 miles
0	1000	2000 km	

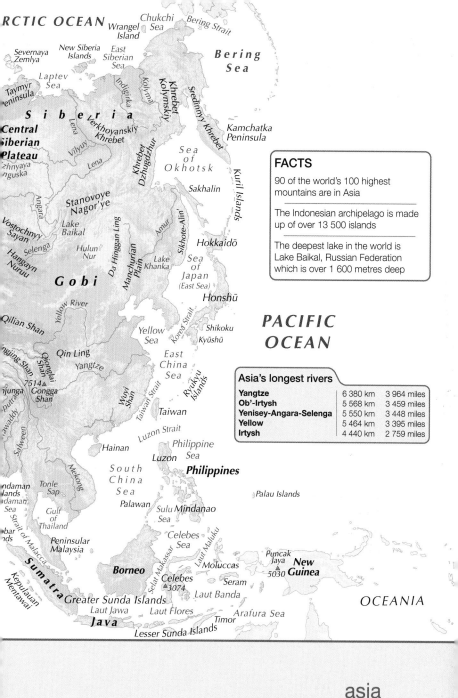

Asia's longest rivers

Yangtze	6 380 km	3 964 miles
Ob'-Irtysh	5 568 km	3 459 miles
Yenisey-Angara-Selenga	5 550 km	3 448 miles
Yellow	5 464 km	3 395 miles
Irtysh	4 440 km	2 759 miles

asia
physical features

Asia's countries

Largest country	**Russian Federation**	17 075 400 sq km	6 592 812 sq miles
Smallest country	**Maldives**	298 sq km	115 sq miles
Largest population	**China**	1 289 161 000	
Smallest population	**Palau**	20 000	
Most densely populated country	**Singapore**	6 656 per sq km	17 219 per sq mile
Least densely populated country	**Mongolia**	2 per sq km	4 per sq mile

EUROPE

Mediterranean Sea

Moscow

Nizhniy Novgorod

Samara

Volga

Yekaterinburg

RUSSIAN

Ural Mountains

Ural'sk

Ob'

Omsk

Novosibir

Ankara

Black Sea

Astana

KAZAKHSTAN

TURKEY GEORGIA

T'bilisi

Adana

ARMENIA

Nicosia

CYPRUS

Yerevan

AZERBAIJAN

Aral Sea

Lake Balkhash

Beirut

LEBANON SYRIA

Baku

UZBEKISTAN

Bishkek

Almaty

Jerusalem

Damascus

Tabriz

Caspian Sea

TURKMENISTAN

Tien Shan

Urüm

ISRAEL

Amman

JORDAN

Tashkent

KYRGYZSTAN

AFRICA

Baghdad

Tehrān

Ashgabat

Dushanbe

TAJIKISTAN

IRAQ

KUWAIT

IRAN

Herāt

Kābul

Islamabad

Plate of Tib

Kuwait

The Gulf

Shīrāz

AFGHANISTAN

H i m a l a

Red Sea

Jeddah

BAHRAIN

Riyadh

Manama

QATAR

Doha

Dubai

Kandahar

Lahore

PAKISTAN

Delhi

Mecca

Abu Dhabi

New Delhi

Mount Everest

SAUDI ARABIA

U.A.E.

Muscat

Hyderabad

NEPAL 8848

Agra

Kathmandu

Ganges BANG

Karachi

Allahabad

Patna

OMAN

Ahmadabad

INDIA

Dhak.

Şan'ā'

YEMEN

Kolkata

Aden

Arabian

Mumbai

Socotra

Sea

Hyderabad

Bay of Beng

Bangalore

Chennai

Laccadive Islands

Madurai

Sri Jayewardenep Kotte

Colombo

SRI LANKA

MALDIVES

Male

INDIAN

OCEAN

British Indian Ocean Territory

Asia's capitals

Largest capital (population)	**Tōkyō**, Japan	26 849 000	
Smallest capital (population)	**Koror**, Palau	14 000	
Most northerly capital	**Astana**, Kazakhstan	51° 10'N	
Most southerly capital	**Dili**, East Timor	8° 35'S	
Highest capital	**Thimphu**, Bhutan	2 423 metres	7 949 feet

0	500	1000	1500 miles
0	1000		2000 km

RCTIC OCEAN

*Bering
Sea*

Magadan

~ril'sk

*Sea
of
Okhotsk*

Petropavlovak-
Kamchatskiy

EDERATION

FACTS

Over 60% of the world's
population live in Asia

Asia has 12 of the world's
20 largest cities

East Timor is Asia's newest
independent country –
founded in May 2002

Irkutsk *Lake
Baikal*

Harbin   Sapporo
Ulan Bator   Vladivostock   Hakodate
MONGOLIA   *Sea
of*
Shenyang   NORTH   *Japan*   **JAPAN**
KOREA   *(East Sea)*
Beijing Dalian   P'yŏngyang   Tōkyō
Tianjin   **Seoul** SOUTH   Ōsaka
KOREA   Hiroshima
Lanzhou   *Yellow*   Fukuoka
Sea

C H I N A Xi'an   Nanjing Shanghai *East*
Yangtze Hangzhou   *China*
Chengdu   Wuhan   *Sea*
Chongqing

*PACIFIC

OCEAN*

T'aipei

Kunming   Liuzhou   Guangzhou   TAIWAN
Nanning   Hong Kong   Kaoshiung
Ha Nôi   *Luzon Strait*
~ANMAR   LAOS Hai Phong
ein **Vientiane**   VIETNAM   Quezon City   **PHILIPPINES**
~goon   **THAILAND**   *South*
Bangkok   *China*   **Manila**
~daman   CAMBODIA   *Sea*   PALAU
ands **Phnom**   **Koror**
dia) **Penh** Hồ Chi Minh
icobar   Kota   Davao
lands   Bandar Seri   Kinabalu
India) **MALAYSIA** Begawan   *Celebes*
BRUNEI   *Sea*   Jayapura
Medan **Kuala Lumpur**
Putrajaya Kuching   *New
Guinea*
SINGAPORE   *Borneo*
Singapore   Pontianak
I N D O N E S I A

Jakarta   Palembang Banjarmasin   *Laut Banda*   *OCEANIA*
Laut Jawa   Makassar
Bandung Surabaya   EAST TIMOR
Semarang   **Dili**
Java

Sumatra

asia
countries

C · 135° · D · 150° · E

1

VAN

Philippine

Sea

P A C I F I C

O C E A N

Northern
Mariana
Islands
(U.S.A.)

Pagan

15°

CAPITOL HILL · Saipan
· Tinian

Rota

Guam ⊕HAGÅTÑA
(U.S.A.)

llo
nds

PHILIPPINES

aet · Catanduanes
· Sorsogon
osin · Catarman
bion · **Samar**
Masbate · Catbalogan
Bacolod · Tacloban
nay · **Cebu**
Tagbilaran · Surigao
gros · Butuan
Bohol Sea · Cagayan de Oro
· Oroquieta · **Mindanao**
abato · Pagadian · **Davao**
nboanga · Mati
Moro Gulf · General Santos

Ulithi · Fais

⊕Yap

FEDERATED STATES
OF MICRONESIA

2

Ngulu · Sorol

Eauripik

C a r o l i n e
I s l a n d s

PALAU
KOROR ⊕

Kepulauan
Talaud

ebes
Kepulauan
e a Sangir·

Morotai

Equator 0°

St Matthias
Group

Manado
ahasa · Tobelo
Tondano · Ternate· **Halmahera**
epulauan ·Gorontalo · Sao-Siu
·uwuk
ogian
Banggai Peleng · Obi · Labuna · Waigeo · Kwoka · Jazirah Manokwari · Biak
·Taliabu Mangole · Bacan · Salawati · Sorong · Doberai · Numfoor · Selat Yapen · Tanjung d'Urville
epulauan Kepulauan · Misool · Fafanlap · Innanwatan · Yapen · Teluk Wasir
Banggai Sula · **Seram** (Ceram Sea) · Babo · Nabire · Pegunungan Van Rees
Manui · Namlea Piru · G. Binaija · Fakfak · Cenderawasih · Sarmi · Jayapura · Vanimo
Kendari · **Ambon**○ 3019 · Kaimana · Pegunungan Trikora · Maoke Mandala · Sepik · Aitape · Wewak
·Wowoni · Ambon · Kepulauan Kepulauan · Adi · Enarotali 5030 4730 Pk · 4700 · Central Range 4000 4509
Raha · Buru · Banda Watubela · Amamapare · Pk Jaya · **New Guinea** · 4073
Buton · *Laut Banda* · Kepulauan Kai · Tual · Dobo Wokam · Tanjung · **PAPUA**
au· Tukangbesi · (Banda Sea) · Kai Kecil · Besar · Benjina · Deyong · Digul · **NEW GUINEA**
·es Kepulauan · Kepulauan · Kepulauan Aru · Sia · Trangan · Pulau

3

S U L A W E S I
(C E L E B E S)
M a l u k u (Moluccca Sea)
Laut Seram
Laut Maluku (Molucca Sea)

I S I A
3000
Selat Dampir

Pelleluhu Islands
Hermit Islands · Admiralty Islands
Manus I.
Rambutyo I.

Schouten Islands · Manam Island · Madang · Umbo
· Goroka · Huon · Long
Mount · Pen. · Island
Hagen · Lae○ · Mount
Kikori · Wau · Victoria

Bismarck
Archipelago

Bismarck
Sea

a Kalabahi · Roma · Damar · Wuliaru · Larat · Kepulauan Tanimbar · Tanjung Vals · Dolak · Merauke · Bereina
·es Kepulauan Kepulauan · Alor · Kaiwatu · Kepulauan · Selaru · Morehead · Daru · **Balimo**
a· Alor · Wetar · Leti · Sermata · Kerema · Morobeo
·OCUSSI · DILI · 2960 · *A r a f u r a S e a* · Gulf · PORT
·wu· Manatuto · of Papua · MORESBY
(ea) · **EAST** · Kefamenanu · Daru
·es Kepulauan · **TIMOR** · Cape York
a · Kupang · Melville · Croker I. · Wessel Is · Cape Wessel · Bamaga
Timor · Island · Nhulunbuy · Gulf · Weipa
Rote · Bathurst · Van Diemen · **AUSTRALIA** · of
·or Sea · Island · Gulf · Cape · Carpentaria · Coen○ · Cape Melville
Beagle Gulf ⊕Darwin · Jabiru 135° · Arnhem

D

C

Andaman
Sea

A

B

So
Chin

Banda Aceh
Sigli
Bireun
Calang
Lhokseumawe
Takengon Peureula
Gunung Abongabong Langsa
Blangkejeren △ 2985 Pangkalansusu
Gunung Leuser
△3145 Belawan
Tapaktuan Binjai
Medan
Tebingtinggi
Simeulue Pematangsiantar Kisaran
Sidikalang Tanjungbalai
Sinabang Singkil Prapat Danau
Balige Toba
Rantauprapat Labuhanbilik
Sibolga Bagansiapiapi
Gunungsitoli Gunungtua Dumai
Padangsidimpuan Duri
Nias Naludalu
Telukdalam Hutanopan Minas
Airbangis Talu Pekanbaru
Telo Payakumbuh Bangkinang
Equator Pulau-
pulau Batu Padangpanjang Kampar
Bukittinggi
Padang Solok Rengat
Siberut Sijunjung Gunung
Muarasiberut Kerinci
Sipura 3805 Muarabungo
Pagai Sungaipenuh Bangko Jambi
Utara Sarolangun Muaratembesi
Pagai Mukomuko
Selatan Surulangun
Sekayu
Lubuklinggau
Curup Tebingtinggi Prabumulih
Bengkulu Lahat
Gunung
Dempo △
3159
Bintuhan
Enggano Krui Kotaagung
Metro
Bandar Lampung
Krakatau

HAT
Yai Songkhla
Pattani
Satun Narathiwat
Kangar Yala Kota
Alor Setar Bharu
Sungai Petani Pasir
Putih
George Town Butterworth Kuala Kerai
Kuala
Terengganu
Taiping Gunung Dungun
Tahan
Ipoh △ Cukai
Kampar 2189 Kuala Lipis
Bagan Teluk Intan **Malaysia** Kuantan
Datuk
KUALA
LUMPUR Temerluh Pekan
Klang PUTRAJAYA
Bahau Padang Endau
Seremban
Melaka Segamat Mersing
Muar
Batu Pahat Keluang
SINGAPORE Johor Bahru
Tanjungpinang
Kepulauan Riau
Tembilahan Daik
Kepulauan
Kualatungal Lingga
Batanghari
Belinyu
Mentok Sungailiat
Pangkalpinang **Bangka**
Tanjungpandan
Musi **Palembang** Toboali
Menggala Manggar
Martapura **Belitung**
Menggala
Muaradua
Kotabumi

MALAY

Natuna Be

Panarik

*Kepulauan
Natuna*

*Kepulauan
Anambas*

*Kepulauan
Tambelan*

Lik

Sambas
Pemangkat
Singkawang

Bengkaya
Mempawah

Pontianak

*Pulau-pulau
Karimata*

Selat Kari

JAKARTA
Serang
Karawang Purwakarta
Bogor △ 3019 Cirebon
Sukabumi Te
Cianjur **Bandung**
Garut 1478
Ciamis
Cilac
Selat Sunda Tanjung
Panaitan Indramayu
Deli

Teluk Palabuhanratu

Ja
(Jawa

IND
La

I N D I A N

O C E A N

Kepulauan Mentawai

Peguhungan Barisan

S u m a t r a

0° Equator

10°

100°

| 0 | 100 | 200 | 300 miles |
| 0 | 150 | 300 | 450 km |

PHILIPPINES

Zamboanga
Moro
Gulf

Basilan
Isabela
Jolo
Jolo
*Sulu
Archipelago*

Balabac Strait
Banggi
Mapin
Kudat
Sulu
Kota Belud
Sea
Gunung
Kinabalu
Kota 4095
Ranau
Sandakan
Kinabalu
Beaufort
Lamag
Labuan
SABAH
Lahad
Datu
BANDAR SERI
Kuamut
BEGAWAN
Pensiangan
Tumindao
BRUNEI
Lawas
Semporna
Kuala Belait
Tawau
Lutong
Lumbis
Miri
Seria

C e l e b e s

1

Sea

Bintulu
Long
Kubuang
Akah
Tarakan
Igan Mukah
Sibu
Belaga
Tanjungselor
Sarikei
Rajang
Kapit
Datadian
Saratok
Debak
Tanjungredeb
Kuching
2988
Kota
Samarahan
Sri Aman
Putusibau
Sepinang
Semenanjung Minahasa
Lubok
Antu
B o r n e o
Sangkulirang
Tolitoli
Kwandang
Semitau
Kapuas
Sintang
Bontang
Moutong
Gorontalo
Nangahpinoh
Longiram
Sidoan
Balaiberkuak
Tenggarong
Teluk Tomini
Togian *Kepulauan*
Muaralaung
Batudaka
Togian
Nangatayap
Muarateweh
Samarinda
Donggala
Luwuk
Peleng
Rantaupanjang
K A L I M A N T A N
Palu
Poso
Tataba
Banggai
Mapane
Uekuli
Balikpapan
Tentena
Kolonedale
Kepulauan
Sukaraja
Palangkaraya
Tanahgrogot
Babana
Celebes
Teluk
Banggai
Sampit
Amuntai
Mamuju
Masamba
(Sulawesi)
Towori
Kualapembuang
Bukit
Rantepao
Wotu
Matili
Pangkalanbuun
Kandangan
Gandadiwata
Palopo
Kotabaru
3074
Malamala
Banjarmasin
Martapura
Polewali
Makale
Tanjung
Pagatan
Majene
Puting
Laut
Parepare
Anabanua
Kendari
Manui
Tanjung
Singkang
Teluk
Kolaka
Wowoni
Selatan
Watampone
Bone
2
Kepulauan
Makassar
Sinjai
Kabaena
Raha
Laut Kecil
2871
Bulukumba
Muna
Buton
O N E S I A
J a w a
G. Lompobatang
Baubau
Sea
Bontosunggu
Pulau-pulau
Kemujan
Bawean
Benteng
Salayar

Tanjung
Bugel
Bali
Madura
Kepulauan
Kudus
Tuban
Kangean
Sabalana
Tanahjampea
Kalao
Kalaotoa
Bangkalan
Sumenep
Surabaya
Raas
Laut Bali
Kepulauan
Kepulauan
Temanggung
Jombang
Pasuruan
Situbondo
(Bali Sea)
Tengah
Bonerate
Laut Flores
Madiun
Banyuwangi
(Flores Sea)
Surakarta
Malang
Sumbawa
Reo
Larantuka
yakarta
Lumajang
Jember
Singaraja
Mataram
Dompu
Raba
Labuhanbajo
Ruteng
Flores
Barung
Glagah
Alas
Maumere
3142
Praya
Sumbawabesar
Bajawa Ende
Bali
Taliwang
Selat Sumba
Denpasar
Selat Lombok
Lombok
Laut Sawu
Memboro
(Savu Sea)

Waikabubak
Waingapu

Sumba
120°
Savu

asia
malaysia and western indonesia

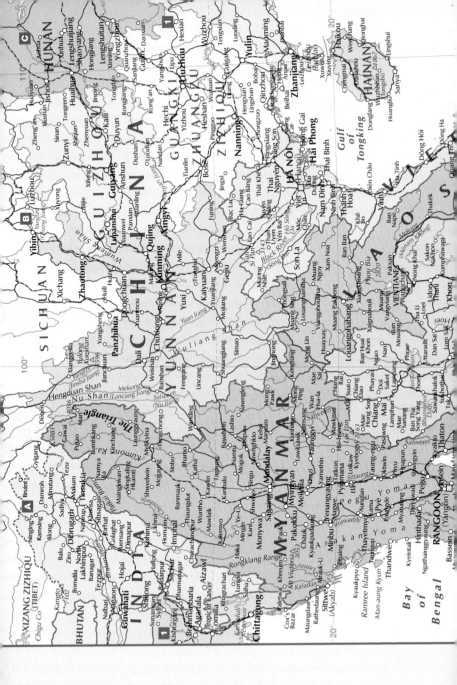

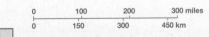

| 0 | 100 | 200 | 300 miles |
| 0 | 150 | 300 | 450 km |

asia
myanmar, thailand and indo-china

Babuyan
Calayan *Babuyan
            Islands*
Fuga Camiguin

Laoag Aparri *Philippine*

Banguied Tuguegarao *Sea*
Vigan Mount Chico
Tagudin Sapoday Bontoc Palanan
San Fernando Mount Ilagan
La Trinidad Pulog Santiago
Dagupan Baguio Bayombong *Luzon*
Lingayen San Carlos
Tarlac San Jose

2 Ibal Cabanatuan **2**
Scarborough Angeles San Fernando *Polillo Islands*
Shoal Olongapo Valenzuela
Balanga Santa Cruz Labo
MANILA Quezon City
Tagaytay City San Pablo Daet *Catanduanes*
Batangas Lucena Lopez Naga Virac
South Calapan Oas
Boac
China Mount Legaspi Sorsogon
Halcon Irosin
Sea 2585 *Mindoro* Catarman
Roxas *Sibuyan* Calbayog
San Jose Romblon Masbate *Samar*
Busuanga *Sibuyan Sea* Masbate Catbalogan
Calamian Pandan Roxas Tacloban
Group *Visayan* Ormoc Guiuan
Culion Linapacan *Panay* *Sea* *Leyte*
El Nido Pototan Bacolod Dinagat
Taytay *Cuyo* Iloilo Cebu Maasin
Islands San Jose de 2450 *Cebu* *Bohol* Siargao
Dumaran Buenavista *Negros* Talisay *Bohol Sea*
Roxas Cauayan Tagbilaran Surigao

3 *Palawan* Puerto Princesa Tanjay Dumaguete Tandag **3**
Bayawan
Quezon Aborlan Dipolog Cagayan
Mount Roxas de Oro Butuan
Mantalingajan Oroquieta Iligan Malaybalay
2054 Brooke's Point *Sulu* Liloy Ozamiz
Bugsuk *Sea* Pagadian Mount *Mindanao*
Balabac Apo 2815
Balabac *Zamboanga* Cotabato Tagum
Balabac Strait *Peninsula* Datu Piang Mount Davao
Kudat Banggi *Mapin* Zamboanga Apo Digos Mati
Kota Belud *Moro* 2954 *Davao*
Kota *Gunung* *Basilan* *Gulf* Banga *Gulf*
Kinabalu *Kinabalu* Isabela General Santos
Ranau Sandakan *Jolo* Jolo
Beaufort 4095 *Sulu*
Labuan Lamag *Archipelago* *Sarangani*
Lawas **MALAYSIA** Lahad *Islands*
BANDAR SERI **SABAH** Kuamut Datu *Kepulauan*
BEGAWAN Pensiangan *Tawitawi* *Nanusa*
Lumbis Semporna *Celebes* Karakelong *Kepulauan*
INDONESIA **A** Tawau *Sea* **B** **INDONESIA** *Talaud*
Tumindao 120° Sangir Kaburuang

0 100 200 300 mil
0 150 300 450 km

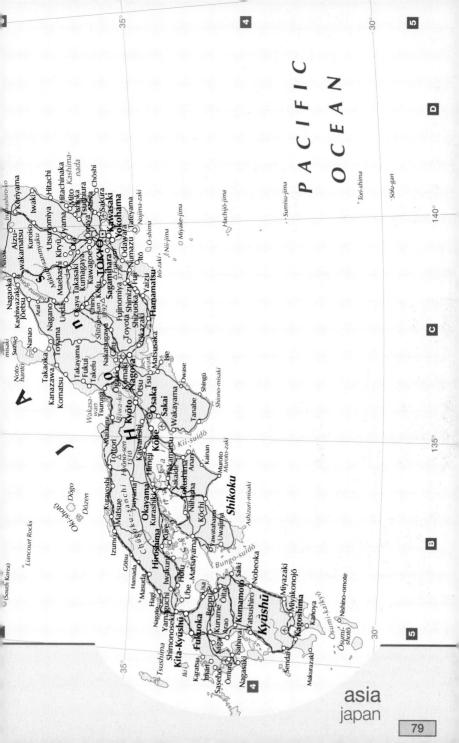

asia
japan

PACIFIC

OCEAN

Tori-shima

Sōfu-gan

Sumisu-jima

Hachijō-jima

Miyake-jima

Nii-jima

Ō-shima

Nojima-zaki

Tateyama

Chōshi

Kashima-nada

Sakura

Hitachinaka

Hitachi

Iwaki

Kōriyama

Aizu-wakamatsu

Kuroiso

Utsunomiya

Mito

Kashima

Tsuchiura

Mikuni-sanmyaku

Kiryū

Maebashi

Takasaki

Kumagaya

Kawagoe

TOKYO

Kawasaki

Yokohama

Odawara

Numazu

Itō

Irō-zaki

Shimizu

Shizuoka

Fuji 3776

Fujinomiya

Chino

Kōfu

Toyota

Okazaki

Yaizu

Hamamatsu

Nagaoka

Kashiwazaki

Jōetsu

Arai

Nagano

Ueda

Komoro

Shirane-san 3192

Nakatsugawa

Gifu

Komaki

Nagoya

Matsusaka

Ise

Tsu

Ōwase

Shingū

Shiono-misaki

Inubō-zaki

Sado

Mito

Suzu-misaki

Nanao

Noto-hantō

Takaoka

Kanazawa

Komatsu

Toyama

Takayama

Fukui

Taketu

Tsuruga

Wakasa-wan

Maizuru

Tottori

Hyōno-sen 1510

Chūgoku-sanchi

Matsue

Izumo

Kurayoshi

Tsuyama

Ōtsu

Kyōto

Kōbe

Ōsaka

Sakai

Wakayama

Tanabe

Kainan

Anan

Muroto

Muroto-zaki

Kii-suidō

Ōki-shotō

Dōgo

Dōzen

Liancourt Rocks

(South Korea)

Hamada

Masuda

Hagi

Nagato

Yamaguchi

Shimonoseki

Ube

Kita-Kyūshū

Fukuoka

Iki

Tsushima

Karatsu

Imari

Sasebo

Ōmura

Nagasaki

Isahaya

Saga

Tosu

Kurume

Ōmuta

Yatsushiro

Kumamoto

Kyūshū

Makurazaki

Sendai

Kagoshima

Kahoya

Ōsumi-kaikyō

Ōsumi-shotō

Nishino-omote

Miyakonojō

Miyazaki

Nobeoka

Saiki

Ōita

Beppu

Bungo-suidō

Ashizuri-misaki

Uwajima

Yawatahama

Kōchi

Shikoku

Matsuyama

Niihama

Saijō

Sakaide

Takamatsu

Marugame

Okayama

Kurashiki

Fukuyama

Onomichi

Kure

Hiroshima

Iwakuni

Hōfu

Himeji

Akashi

Kakogawa

Liancourt Rocks

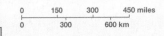

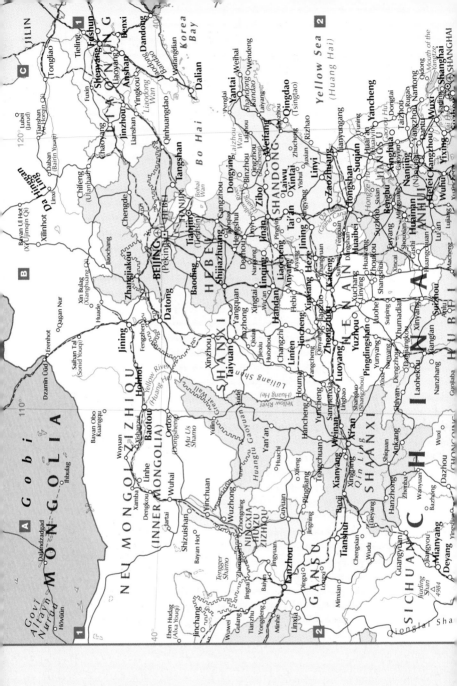

asia
central china

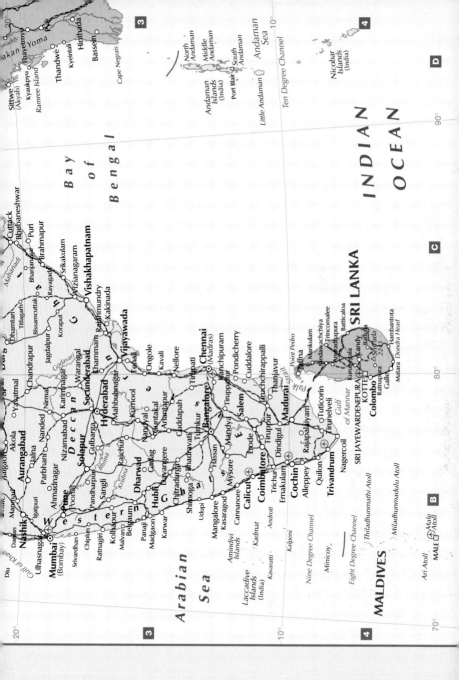

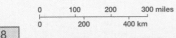

asia
arabian peninsula

91

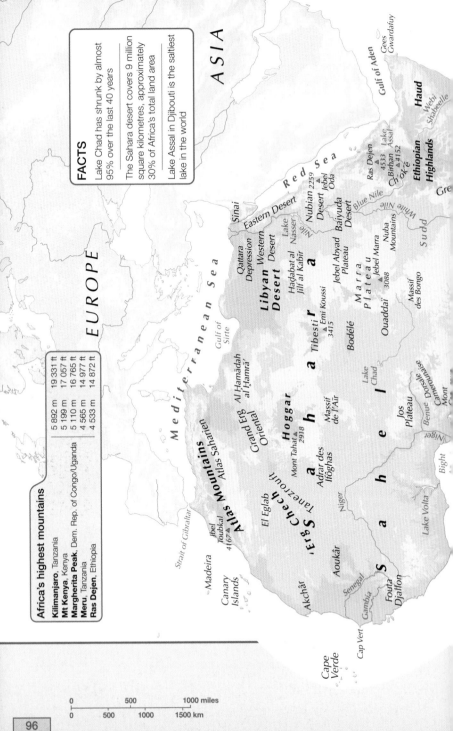

Africa's highest mountains

Kilimanjaro, Tanzania	5 892 m	19 331 ft
Mt Kenya, Kenya	5 199 m	17 057 ft
Margherita Peak, Dem. Rep. of Congo/Uganda	5 110 m	16 765 ft
Meru, Tanzania	4 565 m	14 977 ft
Ras Dejen, Ethiopia	4 533 m	14 872 ft

FACTS

Lake Chad has shrunk by almost 95% over the last 40 years

The Sahara desert covers 9 million square kilometres, approximately 30% of Africa's total land area

Lake Assal in Djibouti is the saltiest lake in the world

ATLANTIC

OCEAN

Guinea
São Tomé

Ascension

St Helena

Mount
Kenya
5199

Mount
Kilimanjaro
5892

Seychelles

Pemba Island
Zanzibar Island
Mafia Island

Cabo
Delgado

Comoro
Islands

Tanjona
Bobaomby

Aldabra
Islands

Maromokotro
2876

Mauritius

Réunion

Madagascar

Boby
2658

Tanjona
Vohimena

INDIAN

OCEAN

Valley

Meru
4565

Lake
Victoria

Lake
Tanganyika

Great Rift Valley

Mount
Mulanje
3002

Mozambique
Channel

Peak
5110

Great
Rift Valley

Chaîne des
Mitumba

Lake
Mweru

Lake
Bangweulu

Lake
Nyasa

Lake
Kariba

Thabana-
Ntlenyana
3482

Congo
Basin

Congo

Zambezi

Victoria
Falls

Limpopo

Drakensberg

Huíla
Plateau

Cubango

Okavango
Delta

Kalahari
Desert

Orange

Great
Karoo

Namib Desert

Cape of
Good Hope

Cape Agulhas

Africa's longest rivers

Nile	6 695 km	4 160 miles
Congo	4 667 km	2 900 miles
Niger	4 184 km	2 599 miles
Zambezi	2 736 km	1 700 miles
Webi Shabeelle	2 490 km	1 547 miles

Africa's extremes

TOTAL LAND AREA		30 343 578 sq km	11 715 655 sq miles
Largest lake	Lake Victoria	68 800 sq km	26 564 sq miles
Largest island	Madagascar	587 040 sq km	226 656 sq miles
Largest drainage basin	Congo, Congo/Dem. Rep. Congo	3 700 000 sq km	1 428 570 sq miles
Lowest point	Lake Assal, Djibouti	-152 metres	-499 feet

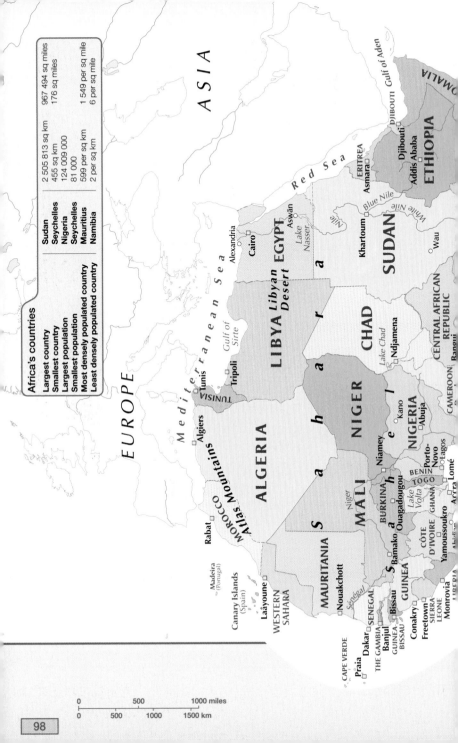

Africa's countries

Largest country	Sudan	2 505 813 sq km	967 494 sq miles
Smallest country	Seychelles	455 sq km	176 sq miles
Largest population	Nigeria	124 009 000	
Smallest population	Seychelles	81 000	
Most densely populated country	Mauritius	599 per sq km	1 549 per sq mile
Least densely populated country	Namibia	2 per sq km	6 per sq mile

EUROPE

ASIA

Mediterranean Sea

Gulf of Sirte

Madeira (Portugal)

Canary Islands (Spain)

Atlas Mountains

MOROCCO

Rabat

Laâyoune

WESTERN SAHARA

MAURITANIA

Nouakchott

CAPE VERDE
Praia

Dakar
THE GAMBIA
Banjul

SENEGAL

Sénégal

GUINEA-
BISSAU
Bissau

GUINEA

Conakry
Freetown
SIERRA
LEONE
Monrovia
LIBERIA

CÔTE
D'IVOIRE
Yamoussoukro

Abidjan

ALGERIA

Algiers

Tunis
TUNISIA
Tripoli

LIBYA

*Libyan
Desert*

S a h a r a

Niger

MALI

Bamako

BURKINA
Ouagadougou

Lake
Volta
GHANA
Accra
Lomé
TOGO
BENIN

NIGER

Niamey

S a h e l

Kano

NIGERIA

Abuja

Porto-
Novo
Lagos

Alexandria
Cairo

EGYPT

Aswan
Lake
Nasser

Nile

Red Sea

ERITREA
Asmara

Khartoum

Blue Nile

White Nile

SUDAN

Wau

Gulf of Aden

DJIBOUTI
Djibouti

Addis Ababa

ETHIOPIA

SOMALIA

CHAD

Ndjamena
Lake Chad

CENTRAL AFRICAN
REPUBLIC

Bangui

CAMEROON

0   500   1000 miles
0   500   1000   1500 km

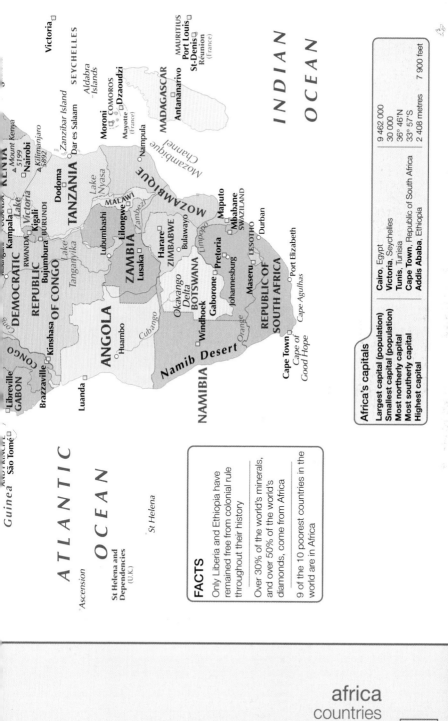

ATLANTIC OCEAN

INDIAN OCEAN

Ascension

St Helena

St Helena and Dependencies (U.K.)

Guinea São Tomé
Libreville GABON
CONGO
Brazzaville Kinshasa OF CONGO
DEMOCRATIC
REPUBLIC
Luanda
ANGOLA
Huambo
Cubango
Okavango Delta
NAMIBIA
Namib Desert
Windhoek
BOTSWANA
Gaborone Pretoria
Johannesburg
REPUBLIC OF
SOUTH AFRICA
Cape Town
Cape of Good Hope
Cape Agulhas
Port Elizabeth
Orange
Limpopo
Maseru LESOTHO
Durban
Mbabane SWAZILAND
Maputo
ZIMBABWE
Harare Bulawayo
ZAMBIA
Lusaka
Lubumbashi
Lilongwe
MALAWI
Zambezi
Lake Tanganyika
Kampala KENYA
Nairobi Mount Kenya 5199
Kilimanjaro 5892
RWANDA Kigali
BURUNDI Bujumbura
Lake Victoria
TANZANIA
Dodoma
Dar es Salaam
Zanzibar Island
Lake Nyasa
MOZAMBIQUE
Mozambique Channel
Nampula
Moroni COMOROS Dzaoudzi
Mayotte (France)
Aldabra Islands
SEYCHELLES
Victoria
MAURITIUS
Port Louis
St-Denis
Réunion (France)
MADAGASCAR
Antananarivo

FACTS

Only Liberia and Ethiopia have remained free from colonial rule throughout their history

Over 30% of the world's minerals, and over 50% of the world's diamonds, come from Africa

9 of the 10 poorest countries in the world are in Africa

Africa's capitals

Largest capital (population)	Cairo, Egypt	9 462 000
Smallest capital (population)	Victoria, Seychelles	30 000
Most northerly capital	Tunis, Tunisia	36° 46'N
Most southerly capital	Cape Town, Republic of South Africa	33° 57'S
Highest capital	Addis Ababa, Ethiopia	2 408 metres	7 900 feet

africa
countries

africa
northwest africa

0   150   300   450 miles
0   200   400   600 km

africa
northeast africa

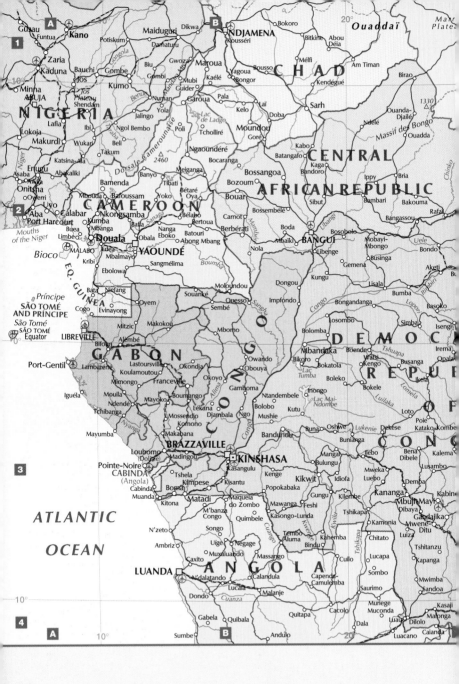

ATLANTIC

OCEAN

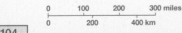

| 0 | 100 | 200 | 300 miles |
| 0 | 200 | 400 km | |

10°
Gabela A Quibala
Sumbe
Andulo
20
Luau Dilolo B Kolwezi DEMOCR
CONGO
Dala
Luacano
Caianda
Lubumbash
Camacupa
Luena
Lucusse
Cazombo
Mwinilunga
Solwezi
Chililabomb
Lobito
Benguela
Chinguar Kuito
Cuemba
Sachanga
Lumbala
Kaquengue
Mufumbwe
Chin
Zambezi
Kasempa
Cubal
Huambo
2620
Umpulo
ANGOLA
Cangamba
Lumbala
N'guimbo
Kabompo
Lubungu
Lucira
Caluquembe
Chipindo
Kalabo
Lukulu
ZAMB
Mumbwa
Bibala
Matala
Kuvango
Menongue
Chiume
Kaoma
1
Namibe
Lubango
Huíla
Plateau
Cuito
Cuanavale
Neriquinha
Senanga
Mongu
Namwala
Pemb
Tombua
Virei
Caiundo
Uamanda
Mulobezi
Kalomo
Oncócua
Nankova
Katima
Victoria
Oshakati
Xangongo
Ondjiva
Cunene
Chitado
Cuangar
Rundu
Dirico
Bagani
Mulilo
Luiana
Falls
Livingsto
Kasane
Hwang
Foz do Cunene
Kunene
Oshakati
CAPRIVI STRIP
Opuwo
Tsumeb
Okavango
Shumba
Lu
Sesfontein
Etosha
Grootfontein
Gumare
Okavango
Nata
Kamanjab
Pan
Outjo
Otavi
Tsumkwe
Delta
Maun
Tutun
20°
Kalkfeld
Otjiwarongo
Omatako
Eiseb
Sehithwa
Makgadikgadi
Francistown
Uis Mine
Okakarara
NAMIBIA
Omaruru
Steinhausen
Ghanzi
Orapa
Selebi-Phik
Hentiesbaai
Okahandja
Witvlei
Buitepos
BOTSWANA
Serowe
Swakopmund
WINDHOEK
Dordabis
Gobabis
Takatshwaane
Palapye
Walvis Bay
Rehoboth
Tsumis
Ncojane
Mahalapye
Be
Tropic of Capricorn
Nauchas
Park
Hoachanas
Kalahari
Kang
Molepolole
Lephal
Narib
Aranos
Tshane
Jwaneng
GABORONE
2
Maltahöhe
Mariental
Desert
Khakhea
Kanye
PRETO
Gochas
Lobatse
(Tshw
GREAT
Tses
Tshabong
Terra
Firma
Mbabane
Johannesbur
NAMAQUALAND
Keetmanshoop
Sowe
Lüderitz
Aus
Seeheim
Bokspits
Vryburg
Sasolbu
Aroab
REPUBLIC OF
Maake
Karasburg
2202
Kuruman
Tsweleleng
Thabo
SOUTH AFRICA
Oranjemund
Upington
Postmasburg
Galeshewe
Kimberley
MA
Alexander Bay
Orange
Pofadder
Bloemfontein
30°
Port Nolloth
Steinkopf
Kenhardt
Marydale
Hopetown
Mangaung
Mafeteng
LE
Brandvlei
Vanwyksvlei
De Aar
Oukamole
Bitterfontein
Calvinia
Carnarvon
Britstown
ORIQUAI
Williston
Victoria
Sada
Vanrhynsdorp
Fraserburg
West
Cradock
Lingenble
Queenstown
Vredenburg
Great Karoo
Graaf
Reinet
KwaNdubu
Mdantsane
Saldanha
Beaufort West
Touwsrivier
Willowmore
Oudtshoorn
Grahamstown
Lo
Malmesbury
Worcester
Little Karoo
Knysna
Port Elizabe
CAPE TOWN
Paarl
Cape
Khayelitsha
Swollendam
Mossel
Recife
Cape of Good Hope
Bredasdorp
Bay
Gansbaai
Cape Agulhas
10°
A
20°
B

ATLANTIC
OCEAN

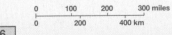

0   100   200   300 miles
0   200   400 km

africa
southern africa

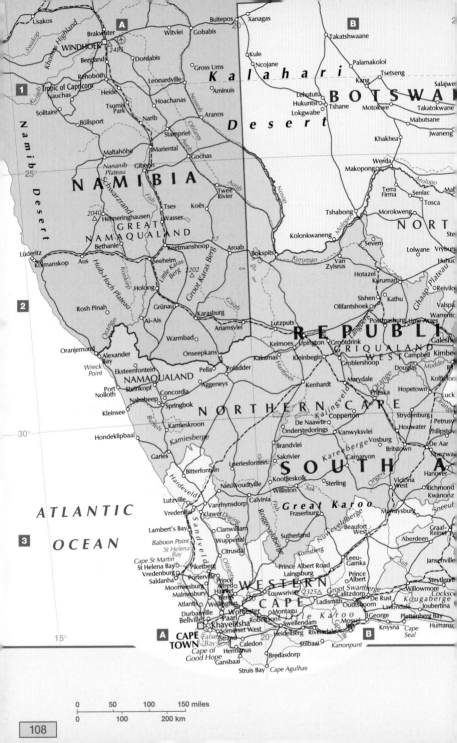

Wake Island

ASIA

Northern Mariana Islands
Pagan
Saipan

Guam

Marshall Islands

M i c r o n e s i a
Ralik Chain
Ratak Chain
Kwajalein
Majuro

Yap

Gaferut

Chuuk
Pohnpei
Kosrae

Caroline Islands

Gilbert Islands
Tarawa

M e l a n e s i a

Nauru

Onotoa
Kingsmill Group
Nanumea
Be

Oceania's longest rivers

Murray-Darling	3 750 km	2 330 miles
Darling	2 739 km	1 702 miles
Murray	2 589 km	1 608 miles
Murrumbidgee	1 690 km	1 050 miles
Lachlan	1 480 km	919 miles

Bismarck Archipelago
New Ireland
Bismarck Sea
New Britain

Bougainville I.
Choiseul
Santa Isabel
Malaita

Solomon Islands

Puncak Jaya
▲5030
New Guinea
Mount Wilhelm
▲4509
Mount Victoria
▲4073

Solomon Sea
Guadalcanal
San Cristobal

Santa Cruz Islands

Rotum

Arafura Sea

Torres Strait
Cape York

Louisiade Archipelago

Rennell

Banks Islands

Espíritu Santo

Fiji

Melville Island

Cape Londonderry

Cape Arnhem
Gulf of Carpentaria
Cape York Peninsula

Coral Sea

Malakula
Éfaté
Erromango
Tanna

Viti Lev
Kada

Hu

Timor Sea

Arnhem Land
Barkly Tableland

Great Barrier Reef

Îles Loyauté

Nouvelle Calédonie

Cape Lévêque

Kimberley Plateau

Lake Argyle

INDIAN OCEAN

Great Sandy Desert

Great Dividing Range

A u s t r a l i a

Norfolk Island

North West Cape

Gibson Desert

Macdonnell Ranges
867▲ Uluru
Musgrave Ranges

Simpson Desert

Lord Howe Island

North Cape

Great Victoria Desert

Lake Eyre

Darling

Nc
Isla

Nullarbor Plain

Lake Torrens

Murray

Mount Kosciuszko
▲2230

Tasman Sea

New Zealand

Great Australian Bight

Kangaroo Island

Bass Strait

Aoraki
3754▲
Southern Alps

Cape Leeuwin

Tasmania

South East Cape

South Island

Stewart Island

Antip
Is

Auckland Islands

Oceania's highest mountains

Puncak Jaya, Indonesia	5 030 m	16 502 ft
Puncak Trikora, Indonesia	4 730 m	15 518 ft
Puncak Mandala, Indonesia	4 700 m	15 420 ft
Puncak Yamin, Indonesia	4 595 m	15 075 ft
Mt Wilhelm, Papua New Guinea	4 509 m	14 793 ft

Campbell Island

Macquarie Island

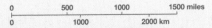

| 0 | 500 | 1000 | 1500 miles |
| 0 | 1000 | | 2000 km |

PACIFIC OCEAN

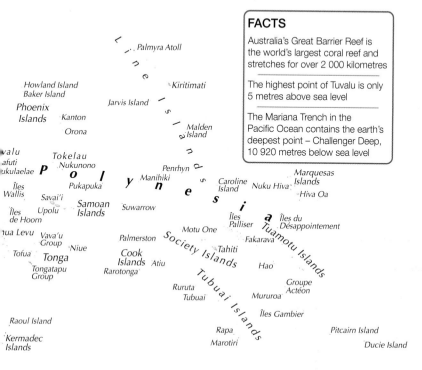

FACTS

Australia's Great Barrier Reef is the world's largest coral reef and stretches for over 2 000 kilometres

The highest point of Tuvalu is only 5 metres above sea level

The Mariana Trench in the Pacific Ocean contains the earth's deepest point – Challenger Deep, 10 920 metres below sea level

Oceania's extremes

TOTAL LAND AREA		8 844 516 sq km	3 414 868 sq miles
Largest lake	**Lake Eyre**, Australia	0–8 900 sq km	0–3 436 sq miles
Largest island	**New Guinea**, Indonesia/Papua New Guinea	808 510 sq km	312 166 sq miles
Largest drainage basin	**Murray-Darling**, Australia	1 058 000 sq km	408 494 sq miles
Lowest point	**Lake Eyre**, Australia	-16 metres	-53 feet

Wake Island
(U.S.A.)

Pagan
Northern
Mariana Islands
(U.S.A.)

MARSHALL
ISLANDS

Saipan □
□ Capitol Hill

Guam □
(U.S.A.) **Hagåtña**

Gaferut

□ Delap-Ulig
Majuro □ **Djarrit**

Yap'

Chuuk
Pohnpei □ **Palikir**

C a r o l i n e   I s l a n d s

Kosrae

Gilbert
Islands □ Tarawa
Bairiki

**FEDERATED STATES
OF MICRONESIA**

Yaren
NAURU

Kingsmill
Group

ASIA

TUVA

Funa

Rabaul
New Ireland

New Wilhelm **PAPUA**
Guinea ▲ 4509 **NEW**
GUINEA

Bougainville I.

New
Britain

SOLOMON ISLANDS

Mount

Solomon
Sea **Honiara** □

Malaita

Santa Cruz
Islands

Rotuma

*Arafura
Sea*

Torres Strait
□ **Port**
Moresby

VANUATU
Espíritu Santo

Banks
Islands

FIJI

C o r a l

Malakula
Éfaté

Su

Timor Sea

○ **Darwin**

Gulf
of
Carpentaria

○ **Cairns**

Coral Sea
Islands Territory
(Australia)

S e a

Port Vila
New
Caledonia
(France)

Viti Lev

Cape Lévêque

INDIAN
OCEAN

○ **Broome**

Lake
Argyle

○ **Townsville**

Nouméa □

○ Îles
Loyauté

A U S T R A L I A

Uluru
867 ▲

Alice Springs

Brisbane ○

Norfolk
Island
(Australia)

North West
Cape

Lake Eyre

Lord Howe
Island
(Australia)

North Cape

Lake
Torrens

Darling

Auckland ○
North
Island

○ **Kalgoorlie**

Great
Australian Bight

Adelaide

Murray

Mount
▲ 2229 Kosciuszko

Canberra □
○ Sydney

Wellington □

T a s m a n

○ **Perth**

Kangaroo
Island

Melbourne ○

S e a

Cape Leeuwin

Bass Strait

Aoraki
3754 ▲ Christchu

Tasmania

○ **Hobart**

South Island

NEW
ZEALA

Stewart Island

Oceania's capitals			
Largest capital (population)	**Canberra**, Australia	387 000	
Smallest capital (population)	**Vaiaku**, Tuvalu	5 100	
Most northerly capital	**Delap-Uliga-Djarrit**,
Marshall Islands	7° 7'N	
Most southerly capital	**Wellington**, New Zealand	41° 18'S	
Highest capital	**Canberra**, Australia	581 metres	1 906 feet

Auckland Islands
(N.Z.)

Campbell Island
(N.Z.)

Macquarie Island
(Australia)

0	500	1000	1500 miles
0	1000	2000 km	

PACIFIC OCEAN

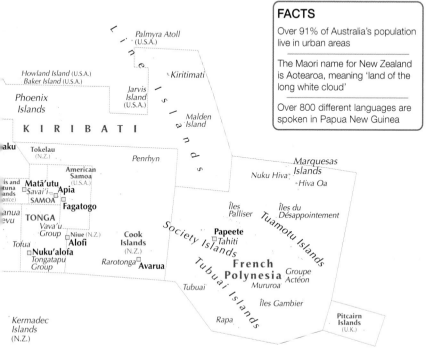

Oceania's countries			
Largest country	Australia	7 692 024 sq km	2 969 907 sq miles
Smallest country	Nauru	21 sq km	8 sq miles
Largest population	Australia	19 731 000	
Smallest population	Tuvalu	11 000	
Most densely populated country	Nauru	619 per sq km	1 625 per sq mile
Least densely populated country	Australia	3 per sq km	7 per sq mile

oceania
countries

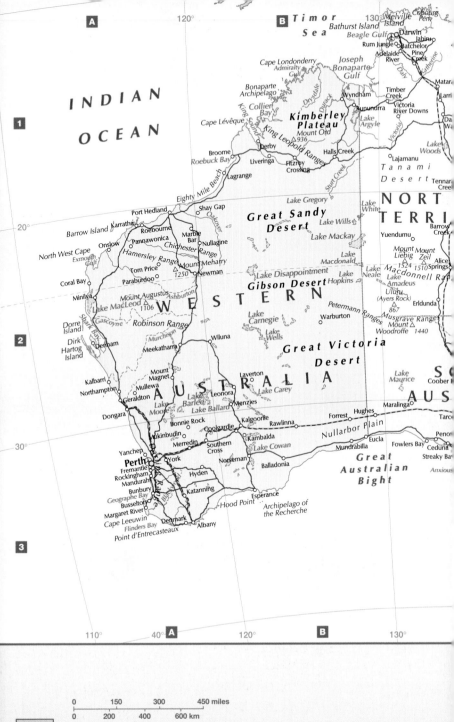

A 120° **B** Timor Sea

INDIAN

OCEAN

1

Cape Londonderry
Admiralty
Gulf

Bonaparte
Archipelago

Collier
Bay

Cape Lévêque

Broome

Roebuck Bay

Liveringa

Lagrange

Eighty Mile Beach

Timor Sea

Bathurst Island   Melville Island   Cobourg Pen

Darwin   Jabiru

Beagle Gulf

Rum Jungle   Batchelor   Pine Creek   Katherine

Adelaide River

Joseph
Bonaparte
Gulf

Wyndham   Timber Creek   Larri

Kununurra   Victoria River Downs   Da

Lake Argyle

Kimberley
Plateau
Mount Ord
△936

King Leopold Range

Halls Creek

Derby

Fitzroy Crossing

Stut Creek

Lajamanu

Lake Woods

Tanami
Desert   Tennar Cree

A 120° **B**

NOR

TERRI

Lake Gregory

Lake White

Great Sandy
Desert   Lake Wills

Lake Mackay

Yuendumu

Barrow Creek

20°

Port Hedland   Shay Gap

Barrow Island   Karratha

North West Cape   Onslow   Roebourne   Pannawonica   Marble Bar   Nullagine

Exmouth Gulf   Hamersley Range   Chichester Range

Coral Bay   Tom Price   Mount Meharry   Newman
Paraburdoo   △1250

Minilya   Mount Augustus   Ashburton
△1106

Dorre Island   Lake MacLeod   Robinson Range

Dirk Hartog Island   Denham   Gascoyne   Murchison

Shark Bay

Lake Disappointment

Gibson Desert   Lake Hopkins   Lake Neale

Lake Carnegie

Lake Wells

Great Victoria
Desert

Mount Liebig   Mount Zeil
△1524   △1510   Alice Springs

Macdonnell Ran

Lake Amadeus

Uluru
(Ayers Rock)
△867   Erldunda

Petermann Ranges   Warburton

Musgrave Range
Mount △
Woodroffe 1440

WESTERN

2

Kalbarri   Mount Magnet

Northampton   Mullewa   Meekatharra   Wiluna

Geraldton   Lake Moore   Laverton   Lake Carey
Lake Barlee   Leonora
Lake Ballard   Menzies

Dongara   Bonnie Rock   Coolgardie   Kalgoorlie

AUSTRALIA

Lake Maurice

Lake Cooper

SO

AUS

Maralinga

Forrest   Hughes

Rawlinna   Tarc

Nullarbor Plain

30°

Yanchep   Merredin   Southern Cross   Kambalda

Perth   Wkinbudin   York
Fremantle
Rockingham   Hyden
Mandurah
Bunbury
Busselton   Katanning
Margaret River
Cape Leeuwin   Denmark   Albany
Flinders Bay
Point d'Entrecasteaux

Norseman   Lake Cowan   Balladonia

Eucla   Mundrabilla   Fowlers Bay   Ceduna
Penon
Streaky Ba

Great
Australian
Bight

Anxious

Geographe Bay   Blackwood

Hood Point   Esperance
Archipelago of
the Recherche

3

110°   40° **A**   120°   **B**   130°

0   150   300   450 miles
0   200   400   600 km

135°   **B**   140°   **C**   QU

Alberga

Oodnadatta

Sturt
Stony
Desert

Cooper Creek

Noccundra   Thargomindal

Macumba

Warburton

Grey Range

1

Edward's
Creek

Mungeranie

Etadunna

Lake
Eyre
(North)

Cooper Creek

Bulloo
Downs

Hungerford

Coober Pedy

William
Creek

Lake
Blanche

Tibooburra

Milparinka

Wanaaring

Paroo

Marree

Lake Eyre
(South)

Tilcha

Lake Callabonna

Hawkers
Gate

Ingomar

Millers Creek

S O U T H

Leigh
Creek

Lake
Frome

Tongo

Darli

30°

Roxby
Downs

Balcanoona

White Cliffs

Momba

Tilpa

Tarcoola

A U S T R A L I A

Lake
Torrens

Parachilna

Frome Downs

Mootwingee

Wilcannia

Lake
Harris

Woomera

Hawker

Curnamona

Euriowie

Broken
Hill

Lake
Everard

Island
Lagoon

Pernatty
Lagoon

Woocalla

Lake
Macfarlane

Quorn

Wilmington

Yunta

Olary

Cockburn
Mingary

Menindee Lake

Menindee

N E W

Nonning

Port Augusta

Orroroo

Mount Manara

Poochera

Gawler Ranges

Iron Knob

Wirrabara

Peterborough

Coombah

Darnick

Ivanh

Streaky Bay

Buckleboo

Whyalla

Port
Pirie

Jamestown

Oakbank

Popiltah

Pooncarie

Mossgiel

Talia

Kyancutta

Kimba

Crystal Brook

Burra

Lake
Victoria

Garnpung
Lake

Booli

Anxious
Bay

Cleve

Lock

Snowtown

Wallaroo

Blyth

Clare

Murray

Wentworth

Hatfield

Oxley

Eyre

Arno
Bay

Moonta

Balaklava

Waikerie

Renmark

Merbein

Mildura

Peninsula

Ungarra

Maitland

Kapunda

Nuriootpa

Berri

Loxton

Red
Cliffs

Robinvale

Balranald

Murrumb

Tumby
Bay

Ardrossan

Gawler

Alawoona

Toolyb

Moulan

Port
Lincoln

Gambier
Islands

Spencer Gulf

Yorke Peninsula

Mannum

Adelaide

R I

Cape
Carnot

Gulf St
Vincent

Mount
Barker

Murray Bridge

Murrayville

Ouyen

Swan
Hill

Denilic

35°

Marion
Bay

Yorketown

Tailem Bend

Lameroo

Lake
Tyrrell

Ultima

Willunga

Goolwa

Coonalpyn

Sea Lake

Kerang

Cohu

Cape Borda

Kingscote

Victor
Harbor

Lake
Alexandrina

Meningie

Keith

Hopetoun

Wycheproof

Charlton

Echuca

Cape
de Coüedic

Kangaroo
Island

Youngshusband Peninsula

Warracknabeal

V I C

Investigator Strait

Bordertown

Nhill

Dimboola

Donald

Bendigo

Kingston South East

Padthaway

Horsham

St Arnaud

Cape Jaffa

Naracoorte

Stawell

Mt William
△ 1167

Ararat

Castlemaine

Myrce

Robe

Edenhope

Glenelg

Beaufort

Ballarat

Kyneton

Sunbur

3

Penola

Casterton

Coleraine

Skipton

Bacchus
Marsh

Millicent

Hamilton

Mortlake

Geelong

Mount Gambier

Heywood

Camperdown

Lake
Corangamite

Colac

Discovery
Bay

Portland

Port
Fairy

Warrnambool

Colac

Lorne

Cape Nelson

Port
Campbell

Apollo Bay

Cape
Otway

A   135°   **B**   140°   **C**

0   50   100   150 miles

0   100   200 km

oceania
southeast australia

oceania
new zealand

118

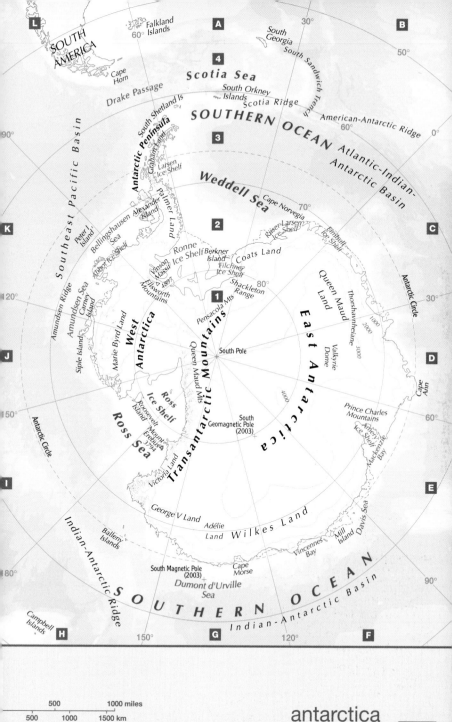

SOUTH AMERICA

Falkland Islands
Cape Horn
Drake Passage

L 60° **A** 30° **B** 50°

South Georgia
South Sandwich Trench

Scotia Sea

4

SOUTHERN OCEAN Atlantic-Indian-Antarctic Basin

South Orkney Islands
Scotia Ridge
American-Antarctic Ridge 0°

South Shetland Is

Antarctic Peninsula
Graham Land
Larsen Ice Shelf
Palmer Land

3

Weddell Sea

Cape Norvegia 70°

Southeast Pacific Basin

K 90°

Bellingshausen Sea
Alexander Island
Peter I Island
Abbot Ice Shelf

2

Ronne Ice Shelf
Berkner Island
Riiser-Larsen Ice Shelf
Filchner Ice Shelf
Coats Land
Ekström Ice Shelf

C 60°

Vinson Massif ▽ 4897
Ellsworth Mountains
Pensacola Mts
Shackleton Range
80°

Queen Maud Land

Thorshavnheiane
1000
3000

Antarctic Circle

Amundsen Ridge
Carney Island

J 120°

Siple Island
Marie Byrd Land

West Antarctica

1

Queen Maud Mts

South Pole

East Antarctica

Valkyrie Dome
Cape Ann

D 30°

60°

Ross Ice Shelf
Roosevelt Island

Ross Sea

Transantarctic Mountains

South Geomagnetic Pole (2003) ✚

Prince Charles Mountains
Amery Ice Shelf
Mackenzie Bay

4000

Antarctic Circle

I 150°

Mount Erebus 3794
Victoria Land

George V Land

Adélie Land Wilkes Land

Vincennes Bay
Mill Island
Davis Sea

E 60°

Balleny Islands

South Magnetic Pole (2003) ✚
Dumont d'Urville Sea

Cape Morse

90°

Indian-Antarctic Ridge

SOUTHERN OCEAN Indian-Antarctic Basin

Campbell Islands

H 150° **G** 120° **F** 90°

| 500 | 1000 miles |
| 500 | 1000 | 1500 km |

antarctica

119

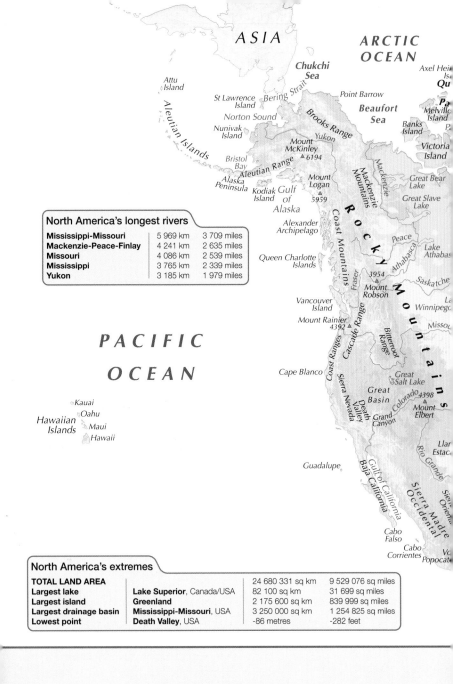

ASIA

ARCTIC OCEAN

Chukchi Sea

Axel Hei Is
Qu

Attu Island

St Lawrence Island

Point Barrow

Bering Strait

Beaufort Sea

Pa

Melville Island

Norton Sound

Brooks Range

Banks Island

P.

Nunivak Island

Yukon

Victoria Island

Mount McKinley ▲ 6194

Mackenzie Mountains

Great Bear Lake

Bristol Bay

Aleutian Range

Mount Logan

Great Slave Lake

Alaska Peninsula

Kodiak Island

Gulf of Alaska

5959

Coast Mountains

Mackenzie Mountains

R o c k y

Alexander Archipelago

Peace

Lake Athabas

Athabasca

North America's longest rivers

Mississippi-Missouri	5 969 km	3 709 miles
Mackenzie-Peace-Finlay	4 241 km	2 635 miles
Missouri	4 086 km	2 539 miles
Mississippi	3 765 km	2 339 miles
Yukon	3 185 km	1 979 miles

Queen Charlotte Islands

Fraser

3954
Mount Robson

Saskatche

La Winnipeg

M o u n t a i n s

Vancouver Island

Missou

Mount Rainier 4392 ▲

Coast Ranges

Cascade Range

Bitterroot Range

PACIFIC

OCEAN

Cape Blanco

Great Salt Lake

4398

Kauai

Oahu

Hawaiian Islands

Maui

Hawaii

Great Basin

Sierra Nevada

Death Valley

Grand Canyon

Colorado

Mount Elbert

Llar Estac

Rio Grande

Guadalupe

Gulf of California

Baja California

Sierra Madre Occidental

Sierre Orienta

Cabo Falso

Cabo Corrientes

Vo

Popocat

North America's extremes

TOTAL LAND AREA		24 680 331 sq km	9 529 076 sq miles
Largest lake	**Lake Superior**, Canada/USA	82 100 sq km	31 699 sq miles
Largest island	**Greenland**	2 175 600 sq km	839 999 sq miles
Largest drainage basin	**Mississippi-Missouri**, USA	3 250 000 sq km	1 254 825 sq miles
Lowest point	**Death Valley**, USA	-86 metres	-282 feet

0	500	1000	1500 miles
0	1000		2000 km

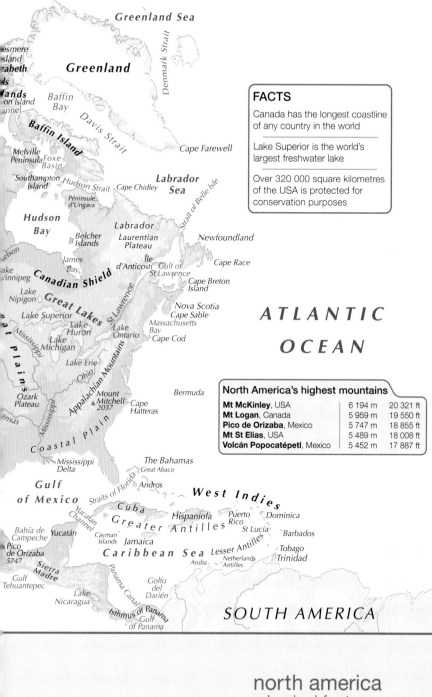

Greenland Sea

esmere
sland
rabeth
ls
lands
on Island
annel

Greenland

Baffin
Bay

Denmark Strait

Davis Strait

Baffin Island

Melville
Peninsula
Foxe
Basin

Cape Farewell

Southampton
Island

Hudson Strait

Cape Chidley

Labrador
Sea

Péninsule
d'Ungava

Hudson
Bay

Belcher
Islands

Laurentian
Plateau

Labrador

Newfoundland

Strait of Belle Isle

James
Bay

Île
d'Anticosti

Gulf of
St Lawrence

Cape Race

elson

Canadian Shield

St Lawrence

Cape Breton
Island

ake
/innipeg

Lake
Nipigon

Great Lakes

Nova Scotia
Cape Sable

Lake Superior

Lake
Huron

Lake
Ontario

Massachusetts
Bay

Mississippi

at plains

Lake
Michigan

Lake Erie

Cape Cod

Ohio

ATLANTIC

OCEAN

Ozark
Plateau

Appalachian Mountains

Mount
Mitchell
2037

Cape
Hatteras

Bermuda

ansas

Coastal Plain

Mississippi

Mississippi
Delta

The Bahamas
Great Abaco

Gulf
of Mexico

Straits of Florida

Andros

West Indies

Cuba

Yucatan
Channel

Greater Antilles

Hispaniola

Puerto
Rico

Dominica

Bahía de
Campeche

Yucatán

Cayman
Islands

Jamaica

St Lucia

Barbados

Pico
de Orizaba
5747

Caribbean Sea

Lesser Antilles

Netherlands
Antilles

Tobago

Sierra
Madre

Aruba

Trinidad

Gulf
Tehuantepec

Panama Canal

Golfo
del
Darién

Lake
Nicaragua

Isthmus of Panama

Gulf
of Panama

SOUTH AMERICA

North America's highest mountains		
Mt McKinley, USA	6 194 m	20 321 ft
Mt Logan, Canada	5 959 m	19 550 ft
Pico de Orizaba, Mexico	5 747 m	18 855 ft
Mt St Elias, USA	5 489 m	18 008 ft
Volcán Popocatépetl, Mexico	5 452 m	17 887 ft

north america
physical features

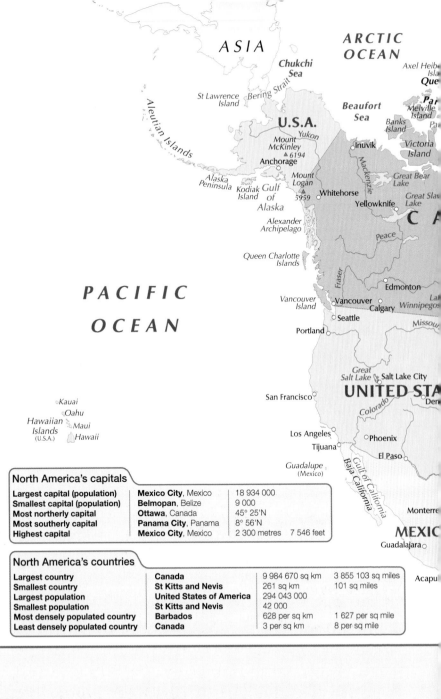

ASIA

ARCTIC OCEAN

Chukchi Sea

Axel Heib Isla
Que

St Lawrence
Island

Bering Strait

Beaufort Sea

Par
Melville
Island
Pa

Banks
Island

U.S.A.

Yukon

Inuvik

Victoria Island

Aleutian Islands

Mount
McKinley
▲ 6194

Anchorage

Mackenzie

Great Bear Lake

Mount
Logan
▲ 5959

Whitehorse

Yellowknife

Great Slav Lake

C A

Alaska Peninsula

Kodiak
Island

Gulf
of
Alaska

Peace

Alexander Archipelago

Fraser

Edmonton

La
Winnipegos

PACIFIC

OCEAN

Queen Charlotte Islands

Vancouver
Island

Vancouver

Calgary

Seattle

Missour

Portland

Great
Salt Lake

Salt Lake City

San Francisco

UNITED STA

Den

Colorado

○Kauai
○Oahu

Hawaiian Islands
(U.S.A.)

Maui

Hawaii

Los Angeles

Tijuana

Phoenix

El Paso

Gulf of California

Baja California

Guadalupe
(Mexico)

Monterre

MEXIC

Guadalajara

North America's capitals			
Largest capital (population)	**Mexico City**, Mexico	18 934 000	
Smallest capital (population)	**Belmopan**, Belize	9 000	
Most northerly capital	**Ottawa**, Canada	45° 25'N	
Most southerly capital	**Panama City**, Panama	8° 56'N	
Highest capital	**Mexico City**, Mexico	2 300 metres	7 546 feet

North America's countries			
Largest country	**Canada**	9 984 670 sq km	3 855 103 sq miles
Smallest country	**St Kitts and Nevis**	261 sq km	101 sq miles
Largest population	**United States of America**	294 043 000	
Smallest population	**St Kitts and Nevis**	42 000	
Most densely populated country	**Barbados**	628 per sq km	1 627 per sq mile
Least densely populated country	**Canada**	3 per sq km	8 per sq mile

Acapu

0	500	1000	1500 miles
0	1000	2000 km	

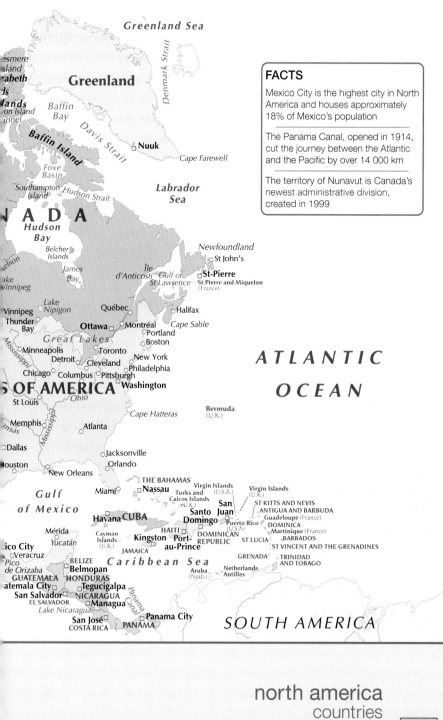

Greenland Sea

Greenland

Denmark Strait

esmere
sland
abeth
ds
lands
on Island
nnel

Baffin
Bay

Davis Strait

Nuuk

Cape Farewell

Baffin Island

Foxe
Basin

Southampton Island
Island

Hudson Strait

Labrador
Sea

A D A

Hudson
Bay

Belcher
Islands

James
Bay

elson

ake
Vinnipeg

Newfoundland
St John's

Île
d'Anticosti

Gulf of
St Lawrence

St-Pierre
St Pierre and Miquelon
(France)

Lake
Nipigon

Québec

Halifax

Vinnipeg
Thunder
Bay

Ottawa

Montréal

Cape Sable

Great Lakes

Portland

Minneapolis

Toronto

Boston

Detroit

Cleveland

New York

Chicago

Columbus

Pittsburgh

Philadelphia

S OF AMERICA

Ohio

Washington

St Louis

ATLANTIC

Memphis

nsas

Atlanta

Cape Hatteras

Bermuda
(U.K.)

OCEAN

Dallas

ouston

Jacksonville

Orlando

New Orleans

Gulf

of Mexico

Miami

THE BAHAMAS
Nassau

Virgin Islands
(U.S.A.)

Virgin Islands
(U.K.)

Turks and
Caicos Islands
(U.K.)

San
Juan

ST KITTS AND NEVIS
ANTIGUA AND BARBUDA
Guadeloupe (France)

Havana

CUBA

Santo
Domingo

Puerto Rico
(U.S.A.)

DOMINICA

Mérida

Cayman
Islands
(U.K.)

HAITI

Martinique (France)

Kingston

Port-
au-Prince

DOMINICAN
REPUBLIC

ST LUCIA

BARBADOS

ico City

Yucatán

JAMAICA

ST VINCENT AND THE GRENADINES

Veracruz

Caribbean Sea

GRENADA

TRINIDAD
AND TOBAGO

Pico
de Orizaba

BELIZE
Belmopan

Aruba
(Neth.)

Netherlands
Antilles

GUATEMALA

HONDURAS

atemala City

Tegucigalpa

San Salvador

NICARAGUA

EL SALVADOR

Managua

SOUTH AMERICA

Lake Nicaragua

San José

Panama City

COSTA RICA

PANAMA

Panama Canal

North America - West

165° · 75° · 150° · 135° · 120° · 105°

ARCTIC OCEAN

Beaufort Sea

RUS. FED.

St Lawrence Island
Providenya
Bering Strait
Gambell

Point Hope
Wainwright
Barrow
Point Barrow

Prince Patrick Island
Ellef Ringnes Island
Mackenzie King Island
Queen Elizabeth Islands
Heiberg

Cape Prince Alfred
McClure Strait
Parry Island
Bathurst Island
Cornwallis
Resolute

Sachs Harbour
Banks Island
Viscount Melville Sound
Stefansson Island
Prince Albert Peninsula
McClintock Channel
Prince of Wales Island
Some

Seward Peninsula
Nome
Kotzebue Sound
Kotzebue
Selawik
Noatak
Shishmaref

Brooks Range
Redstone Mountains
Colville
Kaktovik

Cape Parry
Amundsen Gulf
Holman

Victoria Island
Kugluktuk (Coppermine)
Coronation Gulf
Bao
Bathurst Inlet
Umingmaktok
Wollaston Peninsula
Queen Maud Gulf

St Michael
Unalakleet
Elim
Koyuk

U.S.A.
ALASKA
Wiseman
Bettles
Philip Smith Mountains
Anaktuvuk
Chandalar

Old Crow
Fort Yukon
Eagle Plain
Fort McPherson
Inuvik
Tuktoyaktuk

Anderson

Kotlik
Shageluk
Tuluksak
Emmonak
Kuskokwim Mountains

Galena
Koyukuk
Ruby
Tanana
Stevens Village
Fairbanks
Circle
Central

Ogilvie Mts
Dawson
Mayo

Fort Good Hope

Colville Lake
Great Bear Lake

McGrath
Mount McKinley 6194
Alaska Range
Nenana
Delta Junction
Tok

Stewart
Ross River

YUKON TERRITORY
Selwyn Mountains

Déline
Great Bear Lake

Bethel

Anchorage
Palmer
Glennallen
Beaver Creek

Whitehorse

Wrigley
Franklin Mountains

NORTHWEST TERRITORIES

Wekweti

N U N

Cook Inlet
Kenai
Seward
Valdez
Cordova
Yakutat
Mt Logan 5959

Haines
Skagway
Atlin

Teslin
Watson Lake

Fort Liard
Fort Simpson
Rae-Edzo
Yellowknife
Fort Providence
Hay River

Trout Lake
Great Slave Lake

Back

Baker Lake

Dubawnt Lake
Thelon

Kodiak Island
Cape Clear

Gulf of Alaska

St Elias Mountains

Juneau
Sitka

Alexander Archipelago
Prince of Wales Island

Dease Lake
Telegraph Creek
Stikine
Cassiar
Liard

C A N

Fort Nelson

Fort Liard
Wrigley

Pine Point
Fort Smith

Uranium City

Stony Rapids
Lake Athabasca
Fond-du-Lac
Wollaston Lake
Brochet
Nueltin Lake

Churc

60°
150°

PACIFIC OCEAN

Queen Charlotte Islands
Graham Island
Masset
Port Hardy
Sandspit
Moresby Island
Hecate Strait
Queen Charlotte Sound

Prince Rupert
Kitimat
Smithers
Burns Lake
Vanderhoof
Mackenzie

BRITISH COLUMBIA

Mount Robson 3954

COAST MOUNTAINS

Bella Coola
Bella Bella
Williams Lake
100 Mile House
Quesnel
Prince George
Mount Waddington 4042

ROCKY

Rainbow
High Level

Caribou Mountains
Fort Vermilion
Peace River

Fort Chipewyan

ALBERTA

La Loche
La Ronge
Buffalo Narrows

Reindeer Lake
Lynn Lake
Leaf Rapids

MANIT

Thompson
Snow Flin Flon

Campbell River
Powell River

Nanaimo
Vancouver Island
Victoria
Tacoma
Olympia

Vancouver
Kamloops
Salmon Arm
Kelowna
Penticton

Dawson Creek
Grande Prairie
Valleyview
Whitecourt
Slave Lake
Lac La Biche

Fort McMurray

SASKATCHEWAN

Nipawin
Prince Albert
Rosthern
Humboldt
Saskatoon

Swan River
Dauphin
Gypsumville

Lake Winnipeg

135°
45°

Mt Olympus 2428
Mt Baker 3285
Seattle
Bellingham

WASHINGTON

Spokane
Coeur d'Alene

Cranbrook
M O U N T A I N S

Jasper
Hinton
Edson
Wetaskiwin

Edmonton
Leduc
Red Deer
Airdrie

Calgary
Brooks
Medicine Hat
Lethbridge

North Battleford
Unity
Biggar
Kindersley
Moose Jaw
Melville
Yorkton
Moosomin

Regina
Weyburn
Estevan
Virden
Brandon
Portage la Prairie
Selkirk

Winni

Portland
Salem
Astoria
Olympia
Mt Rainier 4392
Mt St Helens
Richland
La Grande
Pendleton

OREGON
Eugene
Coos Bay
Bend

IDAHO
Snake
Boise Range

Helena
Butte
Bozeman
Billings
Great Falls
Havre
Shelby
Glasgow
Williston

M O N T A N A
U.S.A.
Missouri
Yellowstone

Minot
Devil's Lake
Grand Forks

N. DAKOTA
Bismarck
Jamestown
Bemidji

120° · 105°

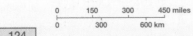

north america
canada

125

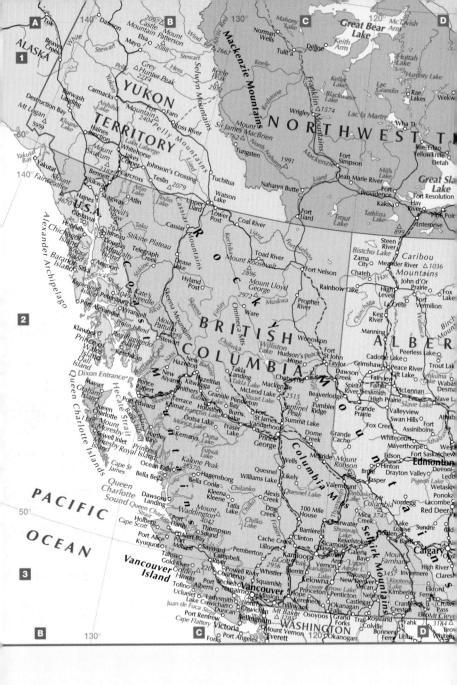

aktulik 110

90°

Contwoyto Lake
Garry Lake
Tehek Lake
Quoich
Evans Strait
Fisher Strait

Back
Southampton
Island
Coats
Island

Aberdeen Lake
Valley
Baker
Lake
Chesterfield
Inlet
Chesterfield Inlet
Cape Southampton

1

MacKay
Lake
Aylmer
Lake
Dubawnt
Lake
Tulemalu
Yathkyed
Lake
Qamanirjuaq
Banks
Lake
Rankin
Inlet
Baker Foreland
Whale Cove

Artillery
Lake
Angikuni
Lake
Kaminak
Lake

NUNAVUT

H u d s o n

tselk'e
Reliance
Snowdrift
Lynx
Lake
Kamilukuak
Lake
South
Henik Lake
Arviat

60°

Hjalmar
Lake
Rennie
Lake
Tha-anne
B a y

Taltson
Snowbird
Lake
Ennadai
Lake
Thlewiaza
Nejanilini
Lake
Button
Bay
Cape
Churchill

Fort Smith
594△
Selwyn
Lake
Kasba
Lake
Nueltin
Lake

Fitzgerald
Tazin
Phelps
Lake
Churchill
Cape
Churchill

Camsell Portage
Stony
Rapids
Black
Lake
Seal
Tadoule
Lake
North
Knife Lake

Uranium City
Fond-du-Lac
Black
Lake
Fond du Lac
Wollaston
Lake
Lac á
Brochet

**Lake
Athabasca**
Fort Chipewyan
Cluff
Lake Mine
Pasfield Lake
Cree
Lake
Wollaston
Lake
Brochet
Big Sand
Lake
Northern
Indian Lake
Gillam

Mackay
Fort
McMurray
la Loche
Turnor Lake
Lloyd
Lake
Clearwater
Geikie
Reindeer
Lake
Barrington
Lake
Southern
Indian Lake
Gauer Lake
Waskaiowaka
Lake
Split
Lake
Shamattawa

Buffalo Narrows
Peter Pond Lake
Churchill
Lake
Patuanak
Southend
Pukatawagan
Lynn
Lake
Granville
Lake
Leaf Rapids
Knee
Lake
Gods
Big Trout
Lake
Big Trout
Lake

la Biche
Cold
Lac
La Biche
Lac Ile-á-la-Crosse
Ile-á-la-Crosse
Canoe Lake
Pinehouse Lake
Sandy
Bay
Sisipuk Lake
Snow Lake
Nelson
House
Thompson
Thicket
Portage
Oxford
Lake
Gods
Lake
Beaver Hill
Stull Lake
Sachigo Lake
Big Trout
Lake

Bonnyville
Medley
Green
Lake
La Ronge
Lac la
Ronge
Deschambault
Lake
Flin Flon
Cranberry
Portage
Wabowden
Ponton
Garden Hill
Island Lake
ONTARIO

St Paul
Elk Point
Meadow Lake
Beauval
Dore Lake
Montreal Lake
Simonhouse
Norway House
St Theresa Point
Sandy Lake
North
Caribou
Lake

Vegreville
St Walburg
Big River
Weyakwin
Cumberland
Lake
The Pas
Stevenson
Sandy Lake
North Spirit
Lake
MacDowell
Lake
Cat Lake
St Joseph

Vermilion
Lloydminster
Maidstone
Smeaton
Nipawin
Westray
Gunisao
Lake
Grand
Rapids
Poplar
Berens River
Stout
Lake
Red
Lake
Ear
Falls
Bamaji
Lake
Lac
Seul
Sioux
Lookout

Wainwright
Unity
Wilkie
Prince Albert
Rosthern
Tisdale
Hudson Bay
Swan
River
Duck
Bay
Gypsumville
**Lake
Winnipeg**
Reindeer Island
North Spirit
Lake
Pakwash
Lake
Red
Lake
Trout
Lake
Vermilion
Kenora
Dryden

Provost
Macklin
Biggar
Saskatoon
Wakaw
Melfort
Blaine
Lake
Kelvington
Swan
River
Roblin
**Lake
Manitoba**
Bissett
Keewatin
**Lake
of the
Woods**
Fort
Frances

Coronation
Kerrobert
Rosetown
Kenaston
Wadena
Wynyard
Preeceville
Kamsack
Dauphin
Russell
Gimli
Selkirk
Lac du
Bonnet
Falcon
Lake

Oyen
Kindersley
Watrous
Foam
Lake
Yorkton
Neepawa
Stonewall
Winnipeg
Steinbach
Beausejour

Hanna
Leader
Riverhurst
Davidson
Lumsden
Fort Qu'Appelle
Indian
Head
Melville
Esterhazy
Minnedosa
Portage
la Prairie
Carman
Winkler
Morris
Emerson
Roseau
River
Vermilion
Baudette

Brooks
Medicine Hat
Swift Current
Kyle
Old Wives
Lake
Regina
Moosomin
Brandon
Souris
Altona
Hallock
Grafton
Thief
River
Falls
Red
Lakes
3

Redcliff
Maple Creek
Gull Lake
Gravelbourg
Assiniboia
Weyburn
Carlyle
Virden
Morden
Langdon
Grand
Forks
Bemidji
Grand Rapids
Hibbing

Bow Island
Eastend
Val Marie
Mankota
CANADA
Estevan
Deloraine
Carlyle
Bottineau
Devil's
Lake
Crookston
Park Rapids
Chisholm

Milk River
MONTANA
Scobey
Plentywood
U.S.A.
Crosby
NORTH DAKOTA
Rugby
Mayville
MINNESOTA

Havre
Malta
Glasgow
Wolf
Point
E
Williston
Stanley
New Town
Minot
Carrington
100
F
Park Rapids

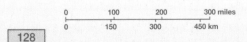

| 0 | 100 | 200 | 300 miles |
| 0 | 150 | 300 | 450 km |

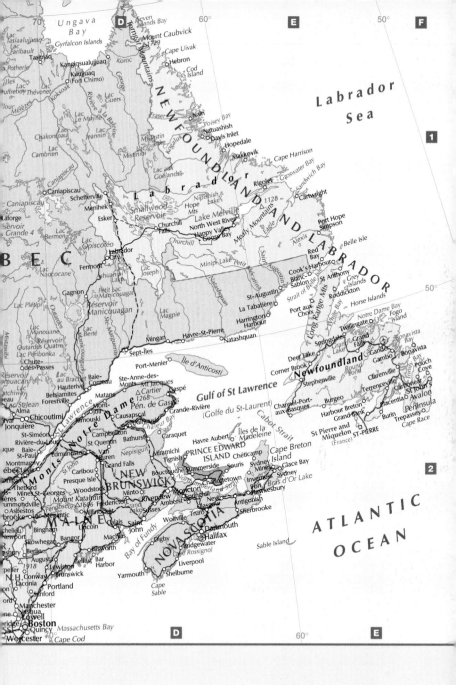

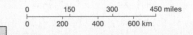

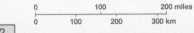

| 0 | | 100 | | 200 miles |
| 0 | 100 | 200 | 300 km |

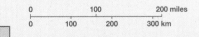

| 0 | | 100 | | 200 miles |
| 0 | 100 | 200 | 300 km |

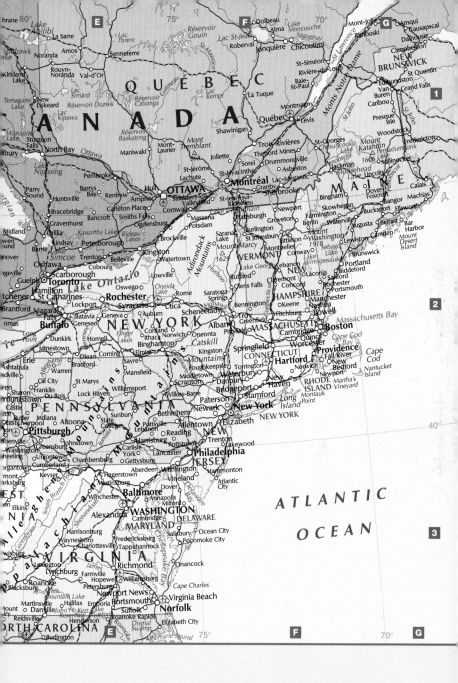

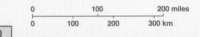

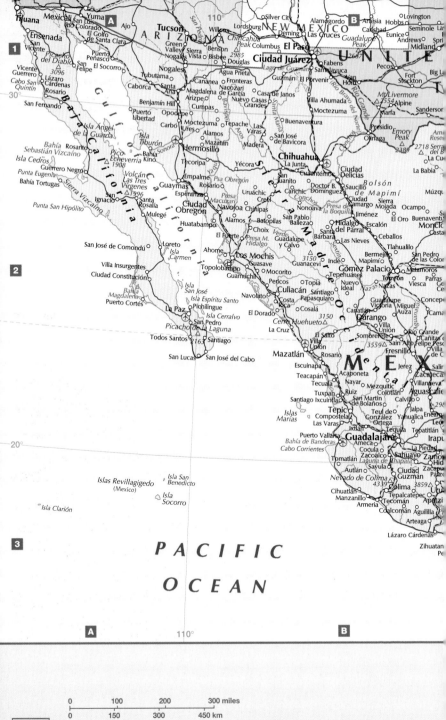

Tijuana Mexicali San Luis **A** Ajo Tucson Lordsburg NEW MEXICO **B** Artesia Hobbs Seminole La
Ensenada Rio Colorado El Golfo de Santa Clara Green Sierra Benson Chiricahua Deming Las Cruces Guadalupe Eunice Andrews Spri
San Vicente Puerto Peñasco Nogales Vista Bisbee Columbus El Paso Peak Midland
Vicente Guerrero San Felipe El Socorro Tubutama Canea Fronteras Guzmán El Porvenir Fabens Pecos
Cabo San Quintín Lázaro Cárdenas Caborca Santa Ana Casa de Janos Villa Ahumada Van Horn Fort Stockton Big Li
San Fernando Rosario Benjamín Hill Magdalena de García Nuevo Casas Grandes Moctezuma Marfa Sanderson
Puerto Libertad Opodepe Moctezuma Buenaventura Presidio Emory Peak Ami Rese
Isla Ángel de la Guarda Rosarito Ures Alamos Las Varas San José de Bavicora Ojinaga 2489 2718 del B
Sebastián Vizcaíno Isla Tiburón Hermosillo Madera Chihuahua La Junta La Babia
Isla Cedros Guerrero Negro Kino Tecoripa Yécora Cuauhtémoc Ciudad Delicias Bolsón Múzqu
Punta Eugenia Volcán Las Tres Vírgenes Empalme Psa Obregón San Juanito Ciudad Domínguez Saucillo de Mapimí Sierra Mojada Ocampo
Bahía Tortugas Guaymas Rosarito Creel Carichic Camargo Jiménez El Oro Buenaventu
Punta San Hipólito Santa Rosalía Ciudad Obregón Navojoa Chínipas San Pablo Ballezao Hidalgo Escalón Ceballos Moncl
San José de Comondú Mulegé Huatabampo Alamos Choix Guadalupe y Calvo Santa del Parral Bermejillo Tlahualilo Casta
Loreto Isla Carmen El Fuerte Ahome Las Nieves Gómez Palacio Mapimí San Pedro de las Color
Villa Insurgentes Topolobampo Los Mochis Guasave Guanacevi Inde Torreón Matamoros
Ciudad Constitución Isla San José Mocorito Tepehuanes Nazas Viesca Parras Ce
Bahía Magdalena Isla Espíritu Santo Culiacán Santiago Nuevo Ideal Guadalupe Victoria Miguel Concep Cama
Puerto Cortés Pichilingue Navolato Costa Rica Papasquiaro Canatlán Durango Villa Union Río Grande
La Paz San Pedro Isla Cerralvo El Dorado Cosalá Cerro Huehueto 3150 Sombrerete Cañitas de Felipe Fresnillo Villa de C
Picacho de la Laguna Todos Santos Santiago La Cruz El Salto Villa Unión 3559 San Alb Saltr Jerez Zaca
San Lucas San José del Cabo Mazatlán Rosario M E X Villanueva Aguasca
Escuinapa Acaponeta Nayar Mezquitic Colotlán Calvillo Salu
Teacapán Tecuala Ruiz San Martín de Bolaños Jalpa Ena
Tuxpan Santiago Ixcuintla Teul de González Yahualica Ene
Islas Marías Tepic Compostela Ortega Ixtlán Tequila Tepatitlán
Islas Revillagigedo Isla San Benedicto Las Varas Guadalajara Irap
(Mexico) Isla Socorro Puerto Vallarta Ameca Cocula La Piedad Zam
Bahía de Banderas Cabo Corrientes Zacoalco Sahuayo Hid
Tomatlán Sayula Ciudad Zapo
Isla Clarión Autlán Nevado de Colima 4339 Guzmán 3859 Colima Apatzi
Cihuatlán Tepalcatepec Coalcomán Aguililla
Manzanillo Tecomán Armería Arteaga
Lázaro Cárdenas
Zihuatan
Pe

P A C I F I C

O C E A N

| 0 | 100 | 200 | 300 miles |
| 0 | 150 | 300 | 450 km |

north america
the caribbean

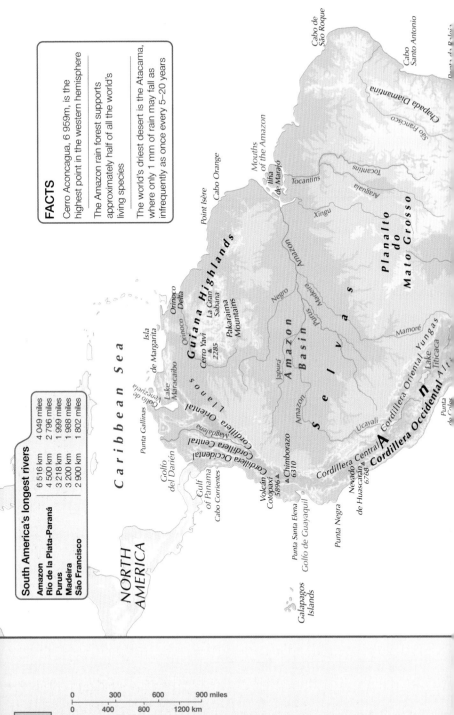

FACTS

Cerro Aconcagua, 6 959m, is the highest point in the western hemisphere

The Amazon rain forest supports approximately half of all the world's living species

The world's driest desert is the Atacama, where only 1 mm of rain may fall as infrequently as once every 5–20 years

South America's longest rivers		
Amazon	6 516 km	4 049 miles
Rio de la Plata-Paraná	4 500 km	2 796 miles
Purus	3 218 km	1 999 miles
Madeira	3 200 km	1 988 miles
São Francisco	2 900 km	1 802 miles

Caribbean Sea

NORTH AMERICA

Gulf of Panama
Cabo Corrientes
Golfo del Darién
Punta Gallinas
Golfo de Venezuela
Lake Maracaibo
Cordillera Occidental
Cordillera Central
Cordillera Oriental
Magdalena
Isla de Margarita
Orinoco Delta
Orinoco
La Gran Sabana
Guiana Highlands
Cerro Yaví 2285
Pakaraima Mountains
Llanos
Cabo Orange
Point Isère
Mouths of the Amazon
Ilha de Marajó
Tocantins
Tocantins
Araguaia
Xingu
Negro
Amazon
Japurá
Purus
Madeira
Amazon
Selvas
Amazon Basin
Mamoré
Planalto do Mato Grosso
São Francisco
Chapada Diamantina
Cabo de São Roque
Cabo Santo Antonio
Ponta da Baleia
Volcán Cotopaxi 5896
Chimborazo 6310
Punta Santa Elena
Golfo de Guayaquil
Punta Negra
Galapagos Islands
Ucayali
Nevada Central de Huascarán 6768
Cordillera Oriental
Yungas
Lake Titicaca
Andes
Cordillera Occidental
Altiplano
Punta de Coles

0	300	600	900 miles
0	400	800	1200 km

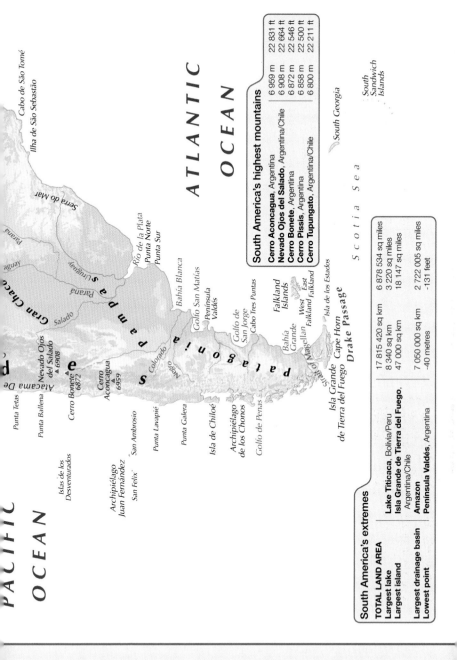

South America's highest mountains

Cerro Aconcagua, Argentina	6 959 m	22 831 ft
Nevado Ojos del Salado, Argentina/Chile	6 908 m	22 664 ft
Cerro Bonete, Argentina	6 872 m	22 546 ft
Cerro Pissis, Argentina	6 858 m	22 500 ft
Cerro Tupungato, Argentina/Chile	6 800 m	22 211 ft

South America's extremes

TOTAL LAND AREA		17 815 420 sq km	6 878 534 sq miles
Largest lake	**Lake Titicaca**, Bolivia/Peru	8 340 sq km	3 220 sq miles
Largest island	**Isla Grande de Tierra del Fuego**, Argentina/Chile	47 000 sq km	18 147 sq miles
Largest drainage basin	**Amazon**	7 050 000 sq km	2 722 005 sq miles
Lowest point	**Península Valdés**, Argentina	-40 metres	-131 feet

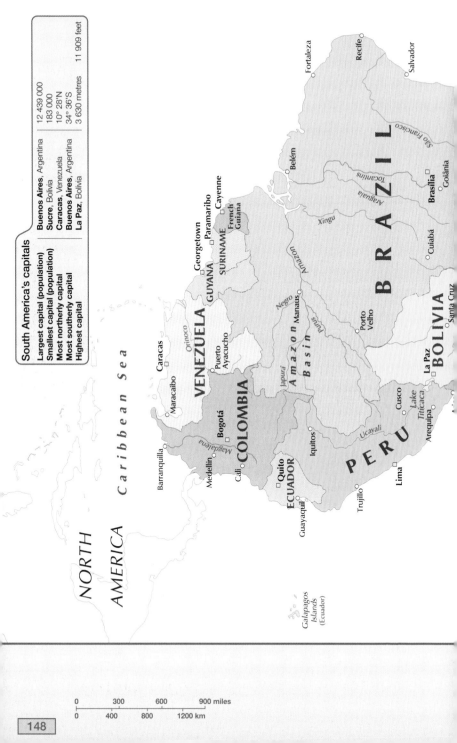

South America's capitals

Largest capital (population)	Buenos Aires, Argentina	12 439 000
Smallest capital (population)	Sucre, Bolivia	183 000
Most northerly capital	Caracas, Venezuela	10° 28'N
Most southerly capital	Buenos Aires, Argentina	34° 36'S
Highest capital	La Paz, Bolivia	3 630 metres 11 909 feet

NORTH

AMERICA

Caribbean Sea

Barranquilla

Maracaibo

Caracas

VENEZUELA

Orinoco

Puerto
Ayacucho

Georgetown

GUYANA

Paramaribo

SURINAME

Cayenne
French
Guiana

Medellín

Bogotá

Cali

COLOMBIA

Magdalena

Japurá

Negro

Manaus

Amazon

*Amazon
Basin*

Purus

Belém

Quito

ECUADOR

Guayaquil

Galapagos
Islands
(Ecuador)

Trujillo

Iquitos

Ucayali

PERU

Cusco

Lima

Arequipa

Lake
Titicaca

La Paz

BOLIVIA

Santa Cruz

Porto
Velho

B R A Z I L

Xingu

Tocantins

Araguaia

Cuiabá

Brasília

Goiânia

São Francisco

Fortaleza

Recife

Salvador

0	300	600	900 miles
0	400 800	1200 km	

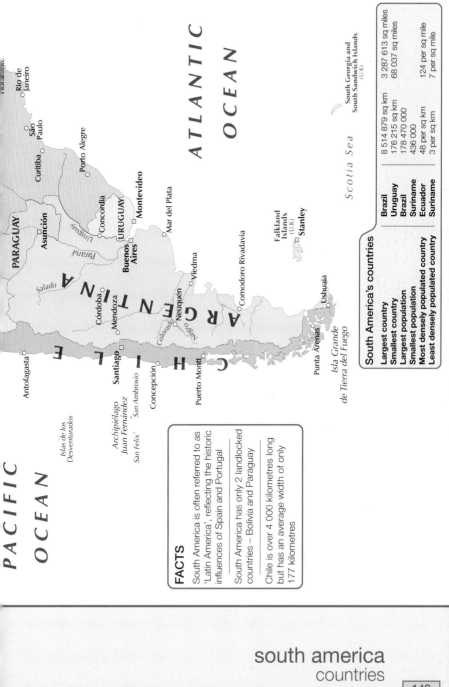

ATLANTIC OCEAN

ATLANTIC

OCEAN

South Georgia
(U.K.)
Grytviken
Cape Disappointment

Falkland Islands
(U.K.)
STANLEY
West-
Falkland
East
Falkland

Isla de los Estados

Estrecho
de Le Maire

MONTEVIDEO
URUGUAY
Rocha
Punta del Este
Florida
Bahía
Samborombón

Mar del Plata
Pinamar

Río de la Plata

ARGENTINA

Pergamino
Arroyos
Quilmes
BUENOS AIRES
Bilbar
Las Flores General
Belgrano
Pehuajó
Lomas de Zamora La Plata
Benito Juárez
Necochea
Azul
Olavarría
Coronel
Tres
Arroyos
Suárez
Tandil
Cuatro

Bahía Blanca

Bahía Blanca

Punta Rasa

Viedma

Stroeder

Punta
Bahía Blanca
Alta
Golfo San Matías

Peninsula
Valdés

Puerto
Madryn
Rawson

Cabo Dos Bahías

Comodoro Rivadavia
Golfo
de San Jorge
Caleta Olivia
Cabo Tres Puntas

Pico
Truncado
Deseado

Puerto
San Julián

Bahía
Grande

Río
Colorado
San Antonio
Oeste

Río Colorado
Choele Choel

Sierra Grande

Gangán
Las
Plumas
Chubut

PATAGONIA

Puerto Santa Cruz
Río Gallegos

Punta
Arenas

Río Grande

Ushuaia

Isla Navarino
Cape
Horn

Isla
Grande
de Tierra
del Fuego

Magallanes

Puerto
Natales

Archipiélago de la
Reina Adelaida

Golfo
de Penas

Isla
Campana

Isla Contreras

Isla Wellington

Golfo
Taitao
Península
de Taitao

Archipiélago
de los
Chonos

Puerto Aisén
Puerto
Cisnes

CHILE

SANTIAGO

Valparaíso

Mendoza
San Rafael

Rancagua
San Fernando
Curicó
Talca
Linares
Chillán
Los
Angeles
Concepción
Lebu
Carahue
Temuco
Valdivia
Osorno
Puerto
Montt
Ancud
Isla
de Chiloé
Castro

Volcán Lanín
San Martín de los Andes
San Carlos
de Bariloche

Nahuel Huapí

Neuquén
Plaza Huincul

Neuquén
General Roca

Santa
Isabel
Santa Rosa
Puelén
General
Acha

Colorado

40°

40°

50°

50°

80°
70°
60°
50°
40°

ATLANTIC

OCEAN

Tropic of Capricorn

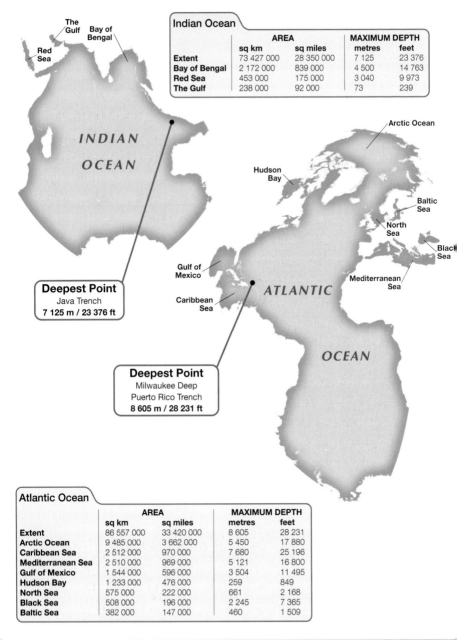

Indian Ocean

	AREA		MAXIMUM DEPTH	
	sq km	sq miles	metres	feet
Extent	73 427 000	28 350 000	7 125	23 376
Bay of Bengal	2 172 000	839 000	4 500	14 763
Red Sea	453 000	175 000	3 040	9 973
The Gulf	238 000	92 000	73	239

The Gulf
Bay of Bengal
Red Sea

INDIAN OCEAN

Arctic Ocean

Hudson Bay

Baltic Sea

North Sea

Black Sea

Gulf of Mexico

ATLANTIC

Mediterranean Sea

Caribbean Sea

Deepest Point
Java Trench
7 125 m / 23 376 ft

OCEAN

Deepest Point
Milwaukee Deep
Puerto Rico Trench
8 605 m / 28 231 ft

Atlantic Ocean

	AREA		MAXIMUM DEPTH	
	sq km	sq miles	metres	feet
Extent	86 557 000	33 420 000	8 605	28 231
Arctic Ocean	9 485 000	3 662 000	5 450	17 880
Caribbean Sea	2 512 000	970 000	7 680	25 196
Mediterranean Sea	2 510 000	969 000	5 121	16 800
Gulf of Mexico	1 544 000	596 000	3 504	11 495
Hudson Bay	1 233 000	476 000	259	849
North Sea	575 000	222 000	661	2 168
Black Sea	508 000	196 000	2 245	7 365
Baltic Sea	382 000	147 000	460	1 509

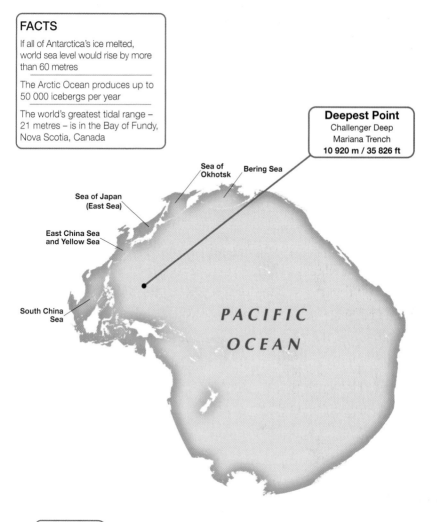

Deepest Point
Challenger Deep
Mariana Trench
10 920 m / 35 826 ft

Sea of Okhotsk

Bering Sea

Sea of Japan (East Sea)

East China Sea and Yellow Sea

South China Sea

PACIFIC OCEAN

Pacific Ocean

	AREA		MAXIMUM DEPTH	
	sq km	sq miles	metres	feet
Extent	166 241 000	64 186 000	10 920	35 826
Bering Sea	2 261 000	873 000	4 150	13 615
Sea of Okhotsk	1 392 000	537 000	3 363	11 033
Sea of Japan (East Sea)	1 013 000	391 000	3 743	12 280
East China Sea and Yellow Sea	1 202 000	464 000	2 717	8 913
South China Sea	2 590 000	1 000 000	5 514	18 090

A S I A

90°   A   B   120°   C   150°   D   180°   Bering Sea   E

Tropic of Cancer

Yellow River

Yangtze

Sakhalin

Sea of Japan

Hokkaido

Yellow Sea

Honshū

East China Sea

Shikoku

Kyūshū

Izu-Ogasawara Trench

8412

9780

Kuril Trench

5550

Aleutian Island

822

Aleutian Trench

Emperor Seamount Chain

1240

Emperor Trough

7900

Northwest Pacific Basin

6345

18

104

Hawaiia

Hawaiia

Mid - Pacific Mountains

Mapmakers Seamounts

3

15°

Bay of Bengal

South China Sea

Philippines

Ryukyu Trench

7181   7460

Kyushu – Palau Ridge

Philippine Trench

10057

Mariana Trench

10920 Challenger Deep   .1564

8054   .8967

MICRONESIA

PACIFIC

Central Pacific Basin

4

Sumatra

Borneo

Celebes Sea   5484

Sulawesi

West Caroline Basin

East Caroline Basin

Melanesian Basin

0°

Laut Java   Laut Banda   7288

Java

Arafura Sea

Timor Sea

New Guinea

New Britain   8940

Solomon Sea   8322

Solomon Islands

MELANESIA

POLY

5

INDIAN

Java Trench (Sunda Trench)

7125

Timor Sea

North Australian Basin

Great Barrier Reef

Coral Sea

Espíritu Santo

Nouvelle Calédonie

7633 New Hebrides Trench

Vanua Levu

Viti Levu

Horizon Deep 10800

Tonga Trench

N

OCEAN

15°

AUSTRALIA

South Fiji Basin

10047

Kermadec Trench

Sou

Pacifi

Tropic of Capricorn

Perth Basin

Great Australian Bight

South Australian Basin   .5670

Tasmania

Tasman Sea

5176

Tasman Basin

New Zealand

Chatham Rise

Chatham Islands

6

Broken Plateau

7102   6602   Diamantina Deep

Southeast Indian Ridge

60.

Campbell Plateau

7

A   90°   45°   B   120°   8

Indian - Antarctic Ridge

1646

60°   Ross S

Antarctic Circle   D   180°

C   150°   A N T A

0   1000 miles

0   1000   2000 km

158

pacific ocean

NORTH AMERICA

A · 30° · · 90° · 45° · **B** · 60° Labrador Sea **C** 60° · Reykjanes Ridge · 30° Iceland **D** · Norwegian Sea

Tropic of Cancer

4

Newfoundland .13
Grand Banks of Newfoundland

Iceland Basin

Rockall Bank · British Isles · North Sea

Celtic Shelf .38

EU

Gulf of Mexico

.4556

Bermuda

5943. · 4938.

Azores

Medit

Nares Deep

5508 Sargasso Sea

Monaco Basin

Canary Is

7535.

.6671

Cayman Trench

Greater Antilles

Milwaukee Deep .8605 Puerto Rico Trench

.5491

.6690

Mid-Atlantic Ridge

Caribbean Sea

Lesser Antilles

.5523

Cape Verde

Niger

5

Cocos Ridge

Guiana Basin

Cape Verde Basin

A F

Amazon Cone

Equator 0°

Amazon

ATLANTIC

Gulf of Guinea .5212

Guinea Basin

OCEAN

SOUTH

AMERICA

Ascension

.5391

6

St Helena

Brazil Basin

Angola Basin

15°

Peru - Chile Trench .8170

Tropic of Capricorn

.5460

Mid-Atlantic Ridge

Walvis Ridge .24

Co

Rio Grande Rise

Cape Bas

7 PACIFIC OCEAN

Paraná

Tristan da Cunha

.55

Argentine Basin

Atlantic-Indi

.6681

1530.

8 30° **A** 90°

Falkland Islands

Scotia Ridge

South Georgia

South Sandwich Trench

SOUTHER

8325.

0° .575

45° **9** **B** Cape Horn Drake Passage 60° Scotia Sea Scotia Ridge 60° **C** 30° Scotia Ridge **D** Atlantic-India

0 — 1000 miles
0 — 1000 km

30° F   60°   60° G   90°   H   45° 120°   I   30°

9695

ASIA

Irtysh

Aral Sea

Caspian Sea

Black Sea

Yellow River   Yellow Sea   4

9156

ean Sea

The Gulf

Red Sea

Nile

Indus

Ganges

Yangtze

East China Sea   .7460

CA

Gulf of Aden

Arabian Sea

Congo

Ganges Cone   Bay of Bengal

Andaman Islands   Andaman Basin   .4267

South China Sea   15°

Carlsberg Ridge

.5060   Somali Basin

Chagos-Laccadive Ridge   Chagos Trench

Mid-Indian Basin

Sumatra

Borneo

5

Zambezi

Mascarene Ridge

8. Vema Trench   .6402

Comoros

Mid-Indian Ridge

INDIAN   OCEAN

Laut Jawa

Java

Java Trench (Sunda Trench)   .7125   6

Madagascar

Mascarene Basin

West Australian Basin

North Australian Basin

15°

Madagascar Basin   6400.

Mozambique Channel

.1924

Broken Plateau

.549

.2067

Ninetyeast Ridge

Natal Basin   .1207

Mozambique Ridge

Southwest Indian Ridge

Perth Basin

AUSTRALIA   7

e Agulhas Plateau

.6195

Diamantina Deep   .6602   7102

Kerguelen Plateau

Southeast Indian Ridge

Great Australian Bight

ulhas asin

.230

îles Kerguélen

McDonald Islands   Heard Island

South Australian Basin

I   30°

dge   CEAN   .6972

30°   60°

186.

Australian-Antarctic Basin

9

45° H   120°

arctic Basin

NTARCTICA

Davis Sea

60° 90°

F   G   60°

atlantic and indian oceans

161

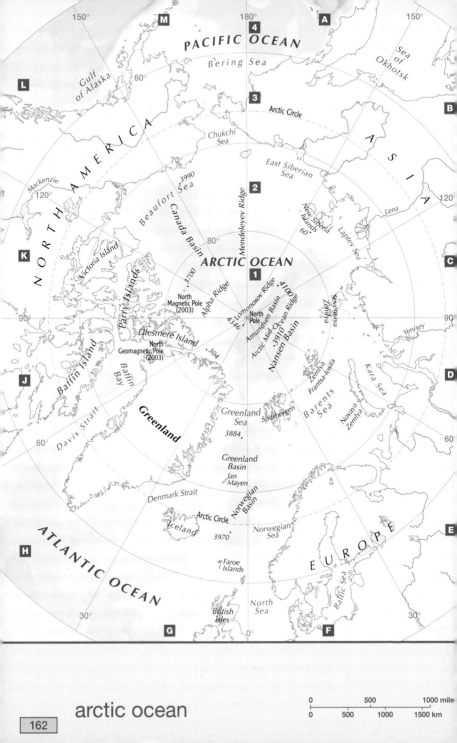

arctic ocean

0   500   1000 mile
0   500   1000   1500 km

Map labels:

PACIFIC OCEAN
Bering Sea
Sea of Okhotsk
Gulf of Alaska
Arctic Circle
Chukchi Sea
East Siberian Sea
NORTH AMERICA
Mackenzie
Beaufort Sea
Canada Basin
Mendeleyev Ridge
New Siberia Islands
ASIA
Lena
Laptev Sea
ARCTIC OCEAN
Lomonosov Ridge
North Pole
Alpha Ridge
North Magnetic Pole (2003)
Amundsen Basin
Arctic Mid Ocean Ridge
Nansen Basin
Severnaya Zemlya
Victoria Island
Parry Islands
Ellesmere Island
North Geomagnetic Pole (2003)
Baffin Island
Baffin Bay
Greenland
Zemlya Frantsa-Iosifa
Barents Sea
Kara Sea
Yenisey
Novaya Zemlya
Davis Strait
Greenland Sea
Spitsbergen
Greenland Basin
Jan Mayen
Denmark Strait
Norwegian Basin
Iceland
Arctic Circle
Norwegian Sea
ATLANTIC OCEAN
Faroe Islands
British Isles
North Sea
EUROPE
Baltic Sea

3990
3700
4546
304
4100
3910
3884
3970

INTRODUCTION TO THE INDEX

The index includes all names shown on the reference maps in the atlas. Names are referenced by page number and by a grid reference. The grid reference correlates to the alphanumeric values along the edges of each map which reflect the lines of latitude and longitude. Names are generally referenced to the largest scale map on which they appear. Each entry also includes the country or geographical area in which the feature is located. Where relevant, the index clearly indicates [inset] if a feature appears on an inset map.

Name forms are as they appear on the maps, with additional alternative names or name forms included as cross-references which refer the user to the entry for the map form of the name. Names beginning with Mc or Mac are alphabetized exactly as they appear. The terms Saint, Sainte, etc, are abbreviated to St, Ste, etc, but alphabetized as if in the full form.

Names of physical features beginning with generic geographical terms are permuted – the descriptive term is placed after the main part of the name. For example, Lake Superior is indexed as Superior, Lake; Mount Everest as Everest, Mount. This policy is applied to all languages.

Entries, other than those for towns and cities, include a descriptor indicating the type of geographical feature. Descriptors are not included where the type of feature is implicit in the name itself.

Administrative divisions are included to differentiate entries of the same name and feature type within the one country. In such cases duplicate names are alphabetized in order of administrative division. Additional qualifiers are also included for names within selected geographical areas.

INDEX ABBREVIATIONS

admin. div.	administrative division	**Ger.**	Germany	**Port.**	Portugal
Afgh.	Afghanistan	**Guat.**	Guatemala	**prov.**	province
Alg.	Algeria	**h.**	hill	**pt.**	point
Arg.	Argentina	**hd**	headland	**r.**	river
Austr.	Australia	**Hond.**	Honduras	**reg.**	region
aut. reg.	autonomous region	**i.**	island	**Rep.**	Republic
aut. rep.	autonomous republic	**imp. l.**	impermanent lake	**resr**	reservoir
Azer.	Azerbaijan	**Indon.**	Indonesia	**rf**	reef
b.	bay	**is**	islands	**Rus. Fed.**	Russian Federation
Bangl.	Bangladesh	**isth.**	isthmus	**S.**	South
B.I.O.T.	British Indian Ocean Territory	**Kazakh.**	Kazakhstan	**Serb. and Mont.**	Serbia and Montenegro
Bol.	Bolivia	**Kyrg.**	Kyrgyzstan	**str.**	strait
Bos.-Herz.	Bosnia Herzegovina	**l.**	lake	**Switz.**	Switzerland
Bulg.	Bulgaria	**lag.**	lagoon	**Tajik.**	Tajikistan
c.	cape	**Lith.**	Lithuania	**Tanz.**	Tanzania
Can.	Canada	**Lux.**	Luxembourg	**terr.**	territory
C.A.R.	Central African Republic	**Madag.**	Madagascar	**Thai.**	Thailand
Col.	Colombia	**Maur**.	Mauritania	**Trin. and Tob.**	Trinidad and Tobago
Czech Rep.	Czech Republic	**Mex.**	Mexico	**Turkm.**	Turkmenistan
Dem. Rep. Congo	Democratic Republic of Congo	**Moz.**	Mozambique	**U.A.E.**	United Arab Emirates
depr.	depression	**mt.**	mountain	**U.K.**	United Kingdom
des.	desert	**mts**	mountains	**Ukr.**	Ukraine
Dom. Rep.	Dominican Republic	**mun.**	municipality	**Uru.**	Uruguay
esc.	escarpment	**N.**	North	**U.S.A.**	United States of America
est.	estuary	**Neth.**	Netherlands	**Uzbek.**	Uzbekistan
Eth.	Ethiopia	**Nic.**	Nicaragua	**val.**	valley
Fin.	Finland	**N.Z.**	New Zealand	**Venez.**	Venezuela
for.	forest	**Pak.**	Pakistan	**vol.**	volcano
g.	gulf	**Para.**	Paraguay		
		pen.	peninsula		
		Phil.	Philippines		
		plat.	plateau		
		P.N.G.	Papua New Guinea		
		Pol.	Poland		

Aljezur Port. 60 B2
Al Jubayl Saudi Arabia 91 B2
Al Junaynah Saudi Arabia 90 B2
Aljustrel Port. 60 B2
Al Kahfah Saudi Arabia 90 B2
Al Kāmil Oman 91 C2
Al Karak Jordan 92 B2
Al Khābūrah Oman 91 C2
Al Khamāsīn Saudi Arabia 90 B2
Al Khārijah Egypt 102 B2
Al Khaṣab Oman 91 C2
Al Khawkhah Yemen 90 B3
Al Khawr Qatar 91 C2
Al Khufrah Libya 102 A2
Al Khums Libya 101 D1
Al Khunn Saudi Arabia 91 B2
Al Kir'ānah Qatar 91 C2
Alkmaar Neth. 54 B1
Al Kūt Iraq 93 C2
Al Kuwayt Kuwait see Kuwait
Al Lādhiqīyah Syria see Latakia
Allahabad India 87 C2
Allakh-Yun' Rus. Fed. 95 L2
'Allāqī, Wādī al watercourse Egypt
   90 A2
Allegheny r. U.S.A. 137 E2
Allegheny Mountains U.S.A. 137 D3
Allen, Lough l. Rep. of Ireland 51 B1
Allende Coahuila Mex. 143 B2
Allende Nuevo León Mex. 143 B2
Allentown U.S.A. 137 E2
Alleppey India 85 B4
Aller r. Ger. 55 D1
Alliance NE U.S.A. 134 C2
Alliance OH U.S.A. 136 D2
Al Līth Saudi Arabia 90 B2
Alloa U.K. 50 C2
Alma Can. 129 C2
Almada Port. 60 B2
Almadén Spain 60 C2
Al Madīnah Saudi Arabia see Medina
Al Maḥwīt Yemen 90 B3
Al Majma'ah Saudi Arabia 90 B2
Almanor, Lake U.S.A. 132 B2
Almansa Spain 61 C2
Al Manṣūrah Egypt 92 B2
Al Mariyyah U.A.E. 91 C2
Al Marj Libya 101 E1
Almaty Kazakh. 89 E2
Almazán Spain 60 C1
Almeirim Brazil 151 D3
Almelo Neth. 54 C1
Almenara Brazil 155 D1
Almendra, Embalse de resr Spain
   60 B1
Almendralejo Spain 60 B2
Almería Spain 60 C2
Almería, Golfo de b. Spain 60 C2
Al'met'yevsk Rus. Fed. 41 E3
Al Mindak Saudi Arabia 90 B2
Al Minyā Egypt 102 B2
Al Mish'āb Saudi Arabia 91 B2
Almodôvar Port. 60 B2
Almonte Spain 60 B2
Almora India 87 B2
Al Mubarrez Saudi Arabia 91 B2
Al Muḍaibī Oman 91 C2
Al Mudawwarah Jordan 92 B3
Al Mukallā Yemen see Mukalla
Al Mukhā Yemen see Mocha
Almuñécar Spain 60 C2
Al Muwayliḥ Saudi Arabia 90 A2
Almyros Greece 65 B3
Alness U.K. 50 B2
Alnwick U.K. 52 C2
Alofi Niue 113
Along India 74 A1
Alonnisos i. Greece 65 B3
Alor i. Indon. 71 C3
Alor, Kepulauan is Indon. 71 C3

Alor Setar Malaysia 72 B1
Alozero Rus. Fed. 46 G2
Alpena U.S.A. 136 D1
Alpine U.S.A. 141 D2
Alps mts Europe 59 D2
Al Qa'āmīyāt reg. Saudi Arabia 91 B3
Al Qaddāḥīyah Libya 101 D1
Al Qāhirah Egypt see Cairo
Al Qā'īyah Saudi Arabia 90 B2
Al Qāmishlī Syria 90 B2
Al Qaryatayn Syria 92 B2
Al Qaṭn Yemen 91 B3
Al Qunayṭirah Syria 92 B2
Al Qunfidhah Saudi Arabia 90 B3
Al Quṣayr Egypt 102 B2
Al Quwayīyah Saudi Arabia 90 B2
Alsfeld Ger. 55 D2
Alta Norway 46 E2
Altaelva r. Norway 46 E2
Altai Mountains Asia 89 F2
Altamaha r. U.S.A. 139 D2
Altamira Brazil 151 D3
Altamura Italy 63 C2
Altay China 89 F2
Altay Mongolia 80 C1
Altdorf Switz. 59 D2
Altea Spain 61 C2
Altenburg Ger. 55 F2
Altenkirchen (Westerwald) Ger. 54 C2
Altentreptow Ger. 55 F1
Altınoluk Turkey 65 C3
Altıntaş Turkey 65 D3
Altiplano plain Bol. 152 B2
Alto Araguaia Brazil 154 B1
Alto del Moncayo mt. Spain 61 C1
Alto Garças Brazil 154 B1
Alto Molócuè Moz. 107 C1
Altona Can. 127 F3
Altoona U.S.A. 137 E2
Alto Sucuriú Brazil 154 B1
Alto Taquarí Brazil 154 B1
Altötting Ger. 56 C3
Altun Shan mts China 89 F3
Alturas U.S.A. 132 B2
Altus U.S.A. 141 E2
Alūksne Latvia 42 C2
Al 'Ulā Saudi Arabia 90 A2
Al 'Uqaylah Libya 101 D1
Al Uqṣur Egypt see Luxor
Alushta Ukr. 45 D3
Alva U.S.A. 141 E1
Alvarado Mex. 143 C3
Älvdalen Sweden 47 C3
Älvdalen val. Sweden 47 C3
Ålvik Norway 48 E1
Älvsbyn Sweden 46 E2
Al Wajh Saudi Arabia 90 A2
Alwar India 86 B2
Al Widyān plat. Iraq/Saudi Arabia 93 C2
Alxa Youqi China see Ehen Hudag
Alyangula Austr. 115 C1
Alytus Lith. 42 B3
Alzada U.S.A. 134 C1
Alzey Ger. 54 D3
Amadeus, Lake salt flat Austr. 114 C2
Amadora Port. 60 B2
Amā'ir Saudi Arabia 90 B2
Åmål Sweden 47 C4
Amaliada Greece 65 B3
Amamapare Indon. 71 D3
Amambaí Brazil 154 A2
Amambaí r. Brazil 154 A2
Amambaí, Serra de hills Brazil/Para.
   154 A2
Amami-Ō-shima i. Japan 81 E3
Amami-shotō is Japan 81 E3
Amangel'dy Kazakh. 89 D1
Amantea Italy 63 C3
Amanzimtoti S. Africa 109 D3
Amapá Brazil 151 D2

Amareleja Port. 60 B2
Amarillo U.S.A. 141 D1
Amaro, Monte mt. Italy 62 B2
Amasya Turkey 92 B1
Amazon r. S. America 150 D2
Amazon, Mouths of the Brazil 151 E2
Amazonas r. S. America see Amazon
Ambala India 86 B1
Ambalavao Madag. 107 [inset] D2
Ambanja Madag. 107 [inset] D1
Ambato Ecuador 150 B3
Ambato Boeny Madag. 107 [inset] D1
Ambato Finandrahana Madag.
   107 [inset] D2
Ambatolampy Madag. 107 [inset] D1
Ambatomainty Madag. 107 [inset] D1
Ambatondrazaka Madag. 107 [inset]
   D1
Amberg Ger. 55 E3
Ambergris Cay i. Belize 144 B3
Ambikapur India 87 C2
Ambilobe Madag. 107 [inset] D1
Ambleside U.K. 52 B2
Amboasary Madag. 107 [inset] D2
Ambohimahasoa Madag. 107 [inset]
   D2
Ambon Indon. 71 C3
Ambon i. Indon. 71 C3
Ambositra Madag. 107 [inset] D2
Ambovombe Madag. 107 [inset] D2
Amboy U.S.A. 133 C4
Ambriz Angola 104 B3
Amdo China 87 D1
Amealco Mex. 143 B2
Ameca Mex. 142 B2
Ameland i. Neth. 54 B1
American Falls U.S.A. 132 D2
American Falls Reservoir U.S.A.
   132 D2
American Fork U.S.A. 132 D2
American Samoa terr.
   S. Pacific Ocean 113
Americus U.S.A. 139 D2
Amersfoort Neth. 54 B1
Amery Ice Shelf Antarctica 119 E3
Ames U.S.A. 135 E2
Amfissa Greece 65 B3
Amga Rus. Fed. 95 K2
Amgu Rus. Fed. 78 C1
Amguid Alg. 101 C2
Amgun' r. Rus. Fed. 95 L3
Amherst Can. 129 D2
Amiens France 58 C2
Amindivi Islands India 85 B3
Aminuis Namibia 108 A1
Amir Chah Pak. 86 A3
Amisk Lake Can. 127 E2
Amistad Reservoir Mex./U.S.A. 141 D
Amlwch U.K. 52 A3
'Ammān Jordan 92 B2
Ammassalik Greenland 125 J2
Am Nābiyah Yemen 90 B3
Amol Iran 93 D2
Amorgos i. Greece 65 C3
Amory U.S.A. 138 C2
Amos Can. 128 C2
Amoy China see Xiamen
Amparo Brazil 155 C2
Amparai India 137 G1
Amqui Can. 129 D2
Amravati India 87 B2
Amritsar India 86 B1
Amstelveen Neth. 54 B1
Amsterdam Neth. 54 B1
Amstetten Austria 56 C3
Am Timan Chad 101 E3
Amudar'ya r. Asia 88 C2
Amund Ringnes Island Can. 124 F1
Amundsen Gulf Can. 124 D2
Amuntai Indon. 73 C2
Amur r. China see Heilong Jiang

Araruama, Lago de *lag.* Brazil **155** D2
Arauca Col. **150** B2
Araxá Brazil **154** C1
Arbīl Iraq **93** C2
Arbroath U.K. **50** C2
Arbu Lut, Dasht-e *des.* Afgh. **86** A2
Arcachon France **58** B3
Arcadia U.S.A. **139** D3
Arcata U.S.A. **132** B2
Arcelia Mex. **143** B3
Archangel Rus. Fed. **40** D2
Archer *r.* Austr. **115** D1
Arco U.S.A. **132** D2
Arcos de la Frontera Spain **60** B2
Arctic Bay Can. **125** G2
Arctic Ocean **162**
Arctic Red *r.* Can. **126** B1
Ardabīl Iran **93** C2
Ardahan Turkey **93** C1
Årdalstangen Norway **47** B3
Ardennes *plat.* Belgium **54** B3
Ardestān Iran **93** D2
Ardlethan Austr. **117** D2
Ardmore U.S.A. **141** E2
Ardnamurchan, Point of *pt* U.K. **50** A2
Ardrossan Austr. **116** B2
Ardrossan U.K. **50** B3
Arena, Point *pt* U.S.A. **133** B3
Arendal Norway **47** B4
Arendsee (Altmark) Ger. **55** E1
Arequipa Peru **150** B4
Arere Brazil **151** D3
Arévalo Spain **60** C1
Arezzo Italy **62** B2
Argentan France **58** B2
Argentina *country* S. America **153** B4
Argentino, Lago *l.* Arg. **153** A6
Argenton-sur-Creuse France **58** C2
Argeş *r.* Romania **44** C3
Arghandab *r.* Afgh. **86** A1
Argolikos Kolpos *b.* Greece **65** B3
Argos Greece **65** B3
Argostoli Greece **65** B3
Arguís Spain **61** C1
Argun' *r.* China/Rus. Fed. **81** E1
Argyle, Lake Austr. **114** B1
Ar Horqin Qi China *see* Tianshan
Århus Denmark **47** C4
Ariamsvlei Namibia **108** A2
Ari Atoll Maldives **85** B4
Arica Chile **152** A2
Arinagour U.K. **50** A2
Arinos Brazil **155** C1
Aripuanã Brazil **150** D4
Aripuanã *r.* Brazil **150** C3
Ariquemes Brazil **150** C3
Ariranhá *r.* Brazil **154** B1
Arizona *state* U.S.A. **140** B2
Arizpe Mex. **142** A1
'Arjah Saudi Arabia **90** B2
Arjeplog Sweden **46** D2
Arkadelphia U.S.A. **138** B2
Arkalyk Kazakh. **89** D1
Arkansas *r.* U.S.A. **138** B2
Arkansas *state* U.S.A. **138** B1
Arkansas City U.S.A. **135** D3
Arkhangel'sk Rus. Fed. *see* Archangel
Arklow Rep. of Ireland **51** C2
Arkona, Kap *c.* Ger. **56** C2
Arkticheskogo Instituta, Ostrova *is* Rus. Fed. **94** H1
Arles France **59** C3
Arlit Niger **101** C3
Arlon Belgium **54** B3
Armagh U.K. **51** C1
Armant Egypt **102** B2
Armavir Rus. Fed. **45** F2
Armenia *country* Asia **93** C1
Armenia Col. **150** B2
Armeria Mex. **142** B3

Armidale Austr. **117** E2
Armstrong Can. **128** B1
Armyans'k Ukr. **92** B1
Arnaoutis, Cape Cyprus **92** B2
Arnaud *r.* Can. **129** D1
Arnhem Neth. **54** B2
Arnhem, Cape Austr. **115** C1
Arnhem Austr. **115** C1
Arnhem Land *reg.* Austr. **115** C1
Arno *r.* Italy **62** B2
Arno Bay Austr. **116** B2
Arnprior Can. **128** C2
Arnsberg Ger. **54** D2
Arnstadt Ger. **55** E2
Aroab Namibia **108** A2
Arolsen Ger. **55** D2
Aroma Sudan **90** A3
Arona Italy **62** A1
Aros *r.* Mex. **142** B2
Ar Ramādī Iraq **93** C2
Arran *i.* U.K. **50** B3
Ar Raqqah Syria **92** B2
Arras France **58** C1
Ar Rass Saudi Arabia **90** B2
Arriagá Mex. **143** C3
Ar Rimāl *reg.* Saudi Arabia **91** C2
Ar Riyāḍ Saudi Arabia *see* Riyadh
Arroyo Seco Mex. **143** C2
Ar Rustāq Oman **91** C2
Ar Ruṭbah Iraq **92** C2
Arsenaján Iran **93** D3
Arsen'yev Rus. Fed. **78** B2
Arta Greece **65** B3
Arteaga Mex. **142** B3
Artem Rus. Fed. **78** B2
Artemivs'k Ukr. **45** E2
Artenay France **58** C2
Artesia U.S.A. **140** D2
Arthur Point *pt* Austr. **115** E2
Arthur's Pass N.Z. **118** B3
Arthur's Town Bahamas **139** E4
Artigas Uru. **152** C4
Artillery Lake Can. **127** E1
Artsyz Ukr. **44** C2
Artux China **89** E3
Artvin Turkey **93** C1
Aru, Kepulauan *is* Indon. **71** C3
Arua Uganda **105** D2
Aruba *terr.* West Indies **145** D3
Arusha Tanz. **105** D3
Arvayheer Mongolia **80** C1
Arviat Can. **127** F1
Arvidsjaur Sweden **46** D2
Arvika Sweden **47** C4
Arzamas Rus. Fed. **41** D3
Arzew Alg. **61** C2
Arzfeld Ger. **54** C2
Aš Czech Rep. **55** F2
Asaba Nigeria **101** C4
Asahi-dake *vol.* Japan **78** D2
Asahikawa Japan **78** D2
Āsalē *l.* Eth. **90** B3
Asansol India **87** C2
Asbestos Can. **129** C2
Ascea Italy **62** C2
Ascensión Bol. **152** B2
Ascension *i.* S. Atlantic Ocean **97**
Ascensión, Bahía de la *b.* Mex. **143** D3
Aschaffenburg Ger. **55** D3
Ascheberg Ger. **55** D2
Aschersleben Ger. **55** E2
Ascoli Piceno Italy **62** B2
Åsele Sweden **46** D3
Asenovgrad Bulg. **64** B2
Ashburton *watercourse* Austr. **114** A2
Ashburton N.Z. **118** B3
Ashdown U.S.A. **138** B2
Asheville U.S.A. **139** D1

Ashford Austr. **117** E1
Ashford U.K. **53** D4
Ashgabat Turkm. **88** C3
Ashington U.K. **52** C2
Ashizuri-misaki *pt* Japan **79** B4
Ashkhabad Turkm. *see* Ashgabat
Ashland *KS* U.S.A. **134** D3
Ashland *KY* U.S.A. **136** D3
Ashland *OH* U.S.A. **136** D2
Ashland *OR* U.S.A. **132** B2
Ashland *WI* U.S.A. **136** B1
Ashmyany Belarus **42** C3
Ash Sharawrah Saudi Arabia **90** B3
Ash Shāriqah U.A.E. *see* Sharjah
Ash Sharqāt Iraq **93** C2
Ash Shaṭrah Iraq **93** C2
Ash Shiḥr Yemen **91** B3
Ash Shināṣ Oman **91** C2
Ash Shu'bah Saudi Arabia **90** B2
Ash Shumlūl Saudi Arabia **91** B2
Ashtabula U.S.A. **137** D2
Ashuanipi Lake Can. **129** D1
Asilah Morocco **60** B2
Asinara, Golfo dell' *b.* Italy **62** A2
Asino Rus. Fed. **94** H3
Asipovichy Belarus **42** C3
'Asīr *reg.* Saudi Arabia **90** B2
Askim Norway **47** C4
Askiz Rus. Fed. **80** C1
Asmara Eritrea **102** B3
Åsnen *l.* Sweden **47** C4
Asoteriba, Jebel *mt.* Sudan **102** B2
Aspang-Markt Austria **57** D3
Aspen U.S.A. **134** B3
Aspiring, Mount N.Z. **118** A3
Assab Eritrea **103** C3
Assal, Lake Djibouti **96**
As Salamiyah Saudi Arabia **91** B2
As Samāwah Iraq **93** C2
Aş Şanām *reg.* Saudi Arabia **91** C2
Aş Sarīr *reg.* Libya **101** E2
Assen Neth. **54** C1
Assesse Belgium **54** B2
As Sidrah Libya **101** D1
Assiniboia Can. **127** E3
Assis Brazil **154** B2
Assisi Italy **59** E3
Aş Şubayḩīyah Kuwait **91** B2
As Sulaymānīyah Iraq **93** C2
As Sulaymī Saudi Arabia **90** B2
As Sulayyil Saudi Arabia **90** B2
As Sūq Saudi Arabia **90** B2
As Suwaydā' Syria **92** B2
As Suwayq Oman **91** C2
As Suways Egypt *see* Suez
Astakos Greece **65** B3
Astana Kazakh. **89** E1
Astor Jammu and Kashmir **86** B1
Astorga Spain **60** B1
Astoria U.S.A. **132** B1
Astrakhan' Rus. Fed. **41** D4
Astravyets Belarus **42** C3
Astypalaia *i.* Greece **65** C3
Asunción Para. **152** C3
Aswān Egypt **102** B2
Asyūţ Egypt **102** B2
Atacama, Desierto de *des.* Chile *see* Atacama Desert
Atacama, Salar de *salt flat* Chile **152** B3
Atacama Desert Chile **152** B3
Atakpamé Togo **100** C4
Atalanti Greece **65** B3
Atalaya Peru **150** B4
Atamyrat Turkm. **89** D3
'Ataq Yemen **90** B3
Atâr Maur. **100** A2
Atascadero U.S.A. **133** B3

Baffin Island Can. **125** H2
Bafia Cameroon **104** B2
Bafing r. Guinea/Mali **100** A3
Bafoulabé Mali **100** A3
Bafoussam Cameroon **104** B2
Bāfq Iran **93** D2
Bafra Turkey **92** B1
Bāft Iran **91** C2
Bafwasende Dem. Rep. Congo **105** C2
Bagamoyo Tanz. **105** D3
Bagan Datuk Malaysia **72** B1
Bagani Namibia **106** B1
Bagansiapiapi Indon. **72** B1
Bagdad U.S.A. **140** B2
Bagé Brazil **152** C4
Baghdād Iraq **93** C2
Baghlān Afgh. **86** A1
Bagnères-de-Luchon France **58** C3
Bagrationovsk Rus. Fed. **42** B3
Bagrax China *see* **Bohu**
Baguio Phil. **76** B2
Bagzane, Monts mts Niger **101** C3
Baharampur India **87** C2
Bahau Malaysia **72** B1
Bahawalnagar Pak. **84** B2
Bahawalpur Pak. **86** B2
Bahía, Islas de la is Hond. **144** B3
Bahía Blanca Arg. **153** B4
Bahía Kino Mex. **142** A2
Bahía Negra Para. **152** C3
Bahía Tortugas Mex. **142** A2
Bahir Dar Eth. **103** B3
Bahraich India **87** C2
Bahrain country Asia **91** C2
Bahrīyah, Wāḩāt al oasis Egypt **102** A2
Bāhū Kālāt Iran **91** D2
Baia Mare Romania **44** B2
Baicheng China **81** E1
Baie-Comeau Can. **129** D2
Baie-St-Paul Can. **129** C2
Baihe China **77** B1
Baikal, Lake Rus. Fed. **81** D1
Baile Átha Cliath Rep. of Ireland *see* Dublin
Băileşti Romania **44** B3
Baima China **80** C2
Bainbridge U.S.A. **139** D2
Bairiki Kiribati **112**
Bairin Youqi China *see* **Daban**
Bairnsdale Austr. **117** D3
Baishan China **77** B1
Baishanzhen China **77** B1
Baiyin China **82** A2
Baiyuda Desert Sudan **102** B3
Baja Hungary **57** D3
Baja California pen. Mex. **142** A1
Bajawa Indon. **73** D2
Bājil Yemen **90** B3
Bakel Senegal **100** A3
Baker CA U.S.A. **133** C3
Baker MT U.S.A. **134** C1
Baker OR U.S.A. **132** C2
Baker, Mount vol. U.S.A. **132** B1
Baker Foreland hd Can. **127** F1
Baker Island terr.
   N. Pacific Ocean **113**
Baker Lake Can. **127** F1
Baker Lake l. Can. **127** F1
Bakersfield U.S.A. **133** C4
Bakhchysaray Ukr. **45** D3
Bakherden Turkm. **88** C3
Bakhmach Ukr. **45** D1
Bakı Azer. *see* **Baku**
Bakırköy Turkey **65** C2
Bakkaflói b. Iceland **46** [inset]
Bakouma C.A.R. **104** C2
Baku Azer. **93** C1
Balabac Phil. **76** A3
Balabac i. Phil. **76** A3

Balabac Strait Malaysia/Phil. **73** C1
Balaiberkuak Indon. **73** C2
Balaklava Austr. **116** B2
Balaklava Ukr. **45** D3
Balakliya Ukr. **45** E2
Balakovo Rus. Fed. **41** D3
Bālā Morghāb Afgh. **86** A1
Balancán Mex. **143** C3
Balan Dağı h. Turkey **65** C3
Balanga Phil. **76** B2
Balashov Rus. Fed. **41** D3
Balaton, Lake Hungary **57** D3
Balatonboglár Hungary **57** D3
Balbina, Represa de resr Brazil
   150 D3
Balbriggan Rep. of Ireland **51** C2
Balcanoona Austr. **116** B2
Balchik Bulg. **64** C2
Balclutha N.Z. **118** A4
Baldock Lake Can. **127** F2
Baldy Mountain h. Can. **127** E2
Baldy Peak U.S.A. **140** C2
Baleares, Islas is Spain *see*
   Balearic Islands
Balearic Islands is Spain **61** D2
Baleia, Ponta da pt Brazil **155** E1
Baleine, Grande Rivière de la r. Can.
   128 C1
Baleine, Rivière à la r. Can. **129** D1
Baleshwar India **87** C2
Bali i. Indon. **73** C2
Bali, Laut sea Indon. **73** C2
Balige Indon. **72** A1
Baliguda India **87** C2
Balıkesir Turkey **65** C3
Balikpapan Indon. **73** C2
Balimo P.N.G. **71** D3
Balingen Ger. **56** B3
Bali Sea Indon. *see* **Bali, Laut**
Balkanabat Turkm. **88** C3
Balkan Mountains Bulg./Serb. and
   Mont. **64** B2
Balkhash Kazakh. **89** E2
Balkhash, Lake Kazakh. **89** E2
Balladonia Austr. **114** B3
Ballaghaderreen Rep. of Ireland **51** B2
Ballangen Norway **46** D2
Ballarat Austr. **116** C3
Ballard, Lake salt flat Austr. **114** B2
Ballater U.K. **50** C2
Ballé Mali **100** B3
Ballena, Punta pt Chile **147**
Ballina Austr. **117** E1
Ballina Rep. of Ireland **51** B1
Ballinasloe Rep. of Ireland **51** B2
Ballinger U.S.A. **141** E2
Ballinrobe Rep. of Ireland **51** B2
Ballycastle Rep. of Ireland **51** B1
Ballycastle U.K. **51** C1
Ballyclare U.K. **51** D1
Ballymena U.K. **51** C1
Ballymoney U.K. **51** C1
Ballynahinch U.K. **51** D1
Ballyshannon Rep. of Ireland **51** B1
Balonne r. Austr. **115** D2
Balotra India **86** B2
Balrampur India **87** C2
Balranald Austr. **116** C2
Balş Romania **44** B3
Balsas Brazil **151** E3
Balsas Mex. **143** C3
Balta Ukr. **44** C2
Bălţi Moldova **44** C2
Baltic Sea g. Europe **47** D4
Balţīm Egypt **92** B2
Baltimore S. Africa **109** C1
Baltimore U.S.A. **137** E3
Baltiysk Rus. Fed. **42** A3
Balu India **74** A1
Balvi Latvia **42** C2

Balykchy Kyrg. **89** E2
Balykshi Kazakh. **88** C2
Bam Iran **91** C2
Bamaga Austr. **115** D1
Bamaji Lake Can. **128** A1
Bamako Mali **100** B3
Bambari C.A.R. **104** C2
Bamberg Ger. **55** E3
Bambili Dem. Rep. Congo **105** C2
Bambouti C.A.R. **105** C2
Bambuí Brazil **155** C2
Bamenda Cameroon **104** B2
Bāmiān Afgh. **86** A1
Bam Posht, Kūh-e mts Iran **86** A2
Bañados del Izozog swamp Bol.
   152 B2
Banalia Dem. Rep. Congo **105** C2
Bananal, Ilha do i. Brazil **151** D4
Banas r. India **86** B2
Banaz Turkey **65** C3
Ban Ban Laos **74** B2
Banbridge U.K. **51** C1
Banbury U.K. **53** C3
Bancroft Can. **128** C2
Banda Dem. Rep. Congo **105** C2
Banda India **87** C2
Banda, Kepulauan is Indon. **71** C3
Banda, Laut sea Indon. **71** C3
Banda Aceh Indon. **72** A1
Bandar-e 'Abbās Iran **91** C2
Bandar-e Anzalī Iran **93** C2
Bandar-e Chārak Iran **91** C2
Bandar-e Emām Khomeynī Iran **93** C2
Bandar-e Lengeh Iran **91** C2
Bandar-e Maqām Iran **91** C2
Bandar Lampung Indon. **72** B2
Bandar Seri Begawan Brunei **73** C1
Banda Sea Indon. *see* **Banda, Laut**
Bandeiras, Pico de mt. Brazil **155** D2
Bandelierkop S. Africa **109** C1
Banderas, Bahía de b. Mex. **142** B2
Bandiagara Mali **100** B3
Bandırma Turkey **65** C2
Bandon Rep. of Ireland **51** B3
Bandundu Dem. Rep. Congo **104** B3
Bandung Indon. **72** B2
Banff Can. **126** C2
Banff U.K. **50** C2
Banfora Burkina **100** B3
Banga Phil. **76** B3
Bangalore India **85** B3
Bangassou C.A.R. **104** C2
Banggai Indon. **73** D2
Banggai, Kepulauan is Indon. **73** D2
Banggi i. Malaysia **73** C1
Bangka i. Indon. **72** B2
Bangkalan Indon. **73** C2
Bangkinang Indon. **72** B1
Bangko Indon. **72** B2
Bangkok Thai. **75** B2
Bangladesh country Asia **87** C2
Bangor Northern Ireland U.K. **51** D1
Bangor Wales U.K. **52** A3
Bangor U.S.A. **137** G2
Bang Saphan Yai Thai. **75** A2
Bangued Phil. **76** B2
Bangui C.A.R. **104** B2
Bangweulu, Lake Zambia **107** B1
Ban Huai Khon Thai. **74** B2
Banī Mazār Egypt **92** B3
Banī Suwayf Egypt **102** B2
Banī Walīd Libya **101** D1
Bāniyās Syria **92** B2
Banja Luka Bos.-Herz. **63** C2
Banjarmasin Indon. **73** C2
Banjul Gambia **100** A3
Banks Island B.C. Can. **126** B2
Banks Island N.W.T. Can. **124** C1
Banks Islands Vanuatu **110**
Banks Lake Can. **127** F1

Banks Peninsula N.Z. **118** B3
Bankura India **87** C2
Banmauk Myanmar **74** A1
Ban Mouang Laos **74** B2
Bann r. U.K. **51** C1
Ban Napè Laos **74** B2
Ban Na San Thai. **75** A3
Bannerman Town Bahamas **139** E4
Bannu Pak. **86** B1
Banswara India **86** B2
Ban Tha Kham Thai. **75** A3
Ban Tha Song Yang Thai. **74** A2
Ban Tôp Laos **75** B2
Bantry Rep. of Ireland **51** B3
Bantry Bay Rep. of Ireland **51** B3
Banyo Cameroon **104** B2
Banyoles Spain **61** D1
Banyuwangi Indon. **73** C2
Baochang China **82** B1
Baoding China **82** B2
Baoji China **82** A2
Bao Lôc Vietnam **75** B2
Baoqing China **78** B1
Baoshan China **74** A1
Baotou China **82** B1
Baotou Shan mt. China/N. Korea **77** B1
Bapaume France **54** A2
Ba'qûbah Iraq **93** C2
Bar Serb. and Mont. **64** A2
Baraawe Somalia **103** C4
Baracoa Cuba **145** C2
Baradine Austr. **117** D2
Barahona Dom. Rep. **145** C3
Baraka watercourse Eritrea/Sudan **102** B3
Baram r. Malaysia **73** C1
Baranavichy Belarus **42** C3
Baranīs Egypt **90** A2
Baranivka Ukr. **44** C1
Barankul Kazakh. **88** C2
Baranof Island U.S.A. **126** B2
Barat Daya, Kepulauan is Indon. **71** C3
Barbacena Brazil **155** D2
Barbados country West Indies **145** E3
Barbastro Spain **61** D1
Barbezieux-St-Hilaire France **58** B2
Barcaldine Austr. **115** D2
Barcelona Spain **61** D1
Barcelona Venez. **150** C1
Barcelonnette France **59** D3
Barcelos Brazil **150** C3
Barcs Hungary **57** D3
Barddhaman India **87** C2
Bardejov Slovakia **57** E3
Bardsīr Iran **91** C2
Bareilly India **87** B2
Barentin France **53** C5
Barentu Eritrea **90** A3
Barfleur, Pointe de pt France **53** C5
Barh India **87** C2
Bar Harbor U.S.A. **137** G2
Bari Italy **63** C2
Barika Alg. **61** E2
Barikot Afgh. **86** B1
Barinas Venez. **150** B2
Baripada India **87** C2
Barisal Bangl. **87** D2
Barisan, Pegunungan mts Indon. **72** B2
Barito r. Indon. **73** C2
Barkā Oman **91** C2
Barkava Latvia **42** C2
Barkly Tableland reg. Austr. **115** C1
Barkol China **80** C2
Bârlad Romania **44** C2
Bar-le-Duc France **59** D2
Barlee, Lake salt flat Austr. **114** A2
Barletta Italy **63** C2

Barmedman Austr. **117** D2
Barmer India **86** B2
Barmouth U.K. **53** A3
Barmstedt Ger. **55** D1
Barnard Castle U.K. **52** C2
Barnato Austr. **117** C2
Barnaul Rus. Fed. **89** F1
Barneveld Neth. **54** B1
Barneville-Carteret France **53** C5
Barnsley U.K. **52** C3
Barnstaple U.K. **53** A4
Barnwell U.S.A. **139** D2
Barquisimeto Venez. **150** C1
Barra i. U.K. **50** A2
Barra do Corda Brazil **151** E3
Barra do Garças Brazil **154** B1
Barra do São Manuel Brazil **150** D3
Barranca Lima Peru **150** B4
Barranca Loreto Peru **150** B3
Barranqueras Arg. **152** C3
Barranquilla Col. **150** B1
Barreiras Brazil **151** E4
Barretos Brazil **154** C2
Barrie Can. **128** C2
Barrière Can. **126** C2
Barrier Range hills Austr. **116** C2
Barrington, Mount Austr. **117** E2
Barrington Lake Can. **127** E2
Barringun Austr. **117** D1
Barrow r. Rep. of Ireland **51** C2
Barrow U.S.A. **124** B2
Barrow, Point pt U.S.A. **124** B2
Barrow Creek Austr. **114** C2
Barrow-in-Furness U.K. **52** B2
Barrow Island Austr. **114** A2
Barrow Strait Can. **124** F2
Barry U.K. **53** B4
Barrys Bay Can. **128** C2
Barsalpur India **86** B2
Barstow U.S.A. **133** C4
Bar-sur-Aube France **59** D2
Bartın Turkey **92** B1
Bartle Frere, Mount Austr. **115** D1
Bartlesville U.S.A. **141** E1
Bartoszyce Pol. **57** E2
Barung i. Indon. **73** C2
Baruun-Urt Mongolia **81** D1
Barvinkove Ukr. **45** E2
Barysaw Belarus **42** C3
Barwon r. Austr. **117** D2
Basarabi Romania **44** C3
Basel Switz. **59** D2
Bashtanka Ukr. **45** D2
Basilan i. Phil. **76** B3
Basildon U.K. **53** D4
Basingstoke U.K. **53** C4
Başkale Turkey **93** C2
Baskatong, Réservoir resr Can. **128** C2
Basle Switz. see Basel
Basoko Dem. Rep. Congo **104** C2
Basra Iraq **93** C2
Bassano Can. **127** D2
Bassar Togo **100** C4
Bassein Myanmar **74** A2
Basse-Terre Guadeloupe **145** D3
Basseterre St Kitts and Nevis **145** D3
Bassikounou Maur. **100** B3
Bass Strait Austr. **115** D3
Bastak Iran **91** C2
Bastheim Ger. **55** E2
Basti India **87** C2
Bastia France **59** D3
Bastogne Belgium **54** B2
Bastrop U.S.A. **138** B2
Bata Equat. Guinea **104** A2
Batagay Rus. Fed. **95** K2
Bataguassu Brazil **154** B2
Batalha Port. **60** B2

Batan i. Phil. **76** B1
Batangafo C.A.R. **104** B2
Batangas Phil. **76** B2
Batanghari r. Indon. **72** B2
Batan Islands Phil. **76** B1
Batavia U.S.A. **137** E2
Bataysk Rus. Fed. **45** E2
Batchawana Mountain h. Can. **128** B2
Batchelor Austr. **114** C1
Bătdâmbâng Cambodia **75** B2
Batemans Bay Austr. **117** E3
Batesville U.S.A. **138** B1
Batetskiy Rus. Fed. **43** D2
Bath U.K. **53** B4
Bathinda India **86** B1
Bathurst Austr. **117** D2
Bathurst Can. **125** H3
Bathurst Inlet Can. **124** E2
Bathurst Inlet inlet Can. **124** E2
Bathurst Island Austr. **114** C1
Bathurst Island Can. **124** F1
Bāṭin, Wādī al watercourse Asia **90** B1
Batman Turkey **93** C2
Batna Alg. **101** C1
Baton Rouge U.S.A. **138** B2
Batopilas Mex. **142** B2
Batouri Cameroon **104** B2
Batovi Brazil **154** B1
Båtsfjord Norway **46** F1
Batticaloa Sri Lanka **85** C4
Battipaglia Italy **62** B2
Battle r. Can. **127** E2
Battle Creek U.S.A. **136** C2
Battle Mountain U.S.A. **132** C2
Batu mt. Eth. **103** B4
Batu, Pulau-pulau is Indon. **72** A2
Batudaka i. Indon. **73** D2
Bat'umi Georgia **93** C1
Batu Pahat Malaysia **72** B1
Baubau Indon. **73** D2
Bauchi Nigeria **101** C3
Baugé France **58** B2
Baume-les-Dames France **59** D2
Bauru Brazil **154** C2
Baús Brazil **154** B1
Bauska Latvia **42** B2
Bautzen Ger. **56** C2
Bavispe r. Mex. **142** B2
Bavly Rus. Fed. **41** E3
Bawdwin Myanmar **74** A1
Bawean i. Indon. **73** C2
Bawku Ghana **100** B3
Bayamo Cuba **145** C2
Bayanhongor Mongolia **80** C1
Bayan Hot China **82** A2
Bayan Obo Kuangqu China **82** A1
Bayan Ul Hot China **82** B1
Bayawan Phil. **76** B3
Bayburt Turkey **92** C1
Bay City MI U.S.A. **136** D2
Bay City TX U.S.A. **141** E3
Baydaratskaya Guba Rus. Fed. **40** F2
Baydhabo Somalia **103** C4
Bayeux France **53** C5
Bayjī Iraq **93** C2
Baykal, Ozero l. Rus. Fed. see Baikal, Lake
Baykal'skiy Khrebet mts Rus. Fed. **95** J3
Baykonyr Kazakh. **88** D2
Baymak Rus. Fed. **41** E3
Bayombong Phil. **76** B2
Bayonne France **58** B3
Bayramiç Turkey **65** C3
Bayreuth Ger. **55** E3
Bayt al Faqīh Yemen **90** B3
Baza Spain **60** C2
Baza, Sierra de mts Spain **60** C2
Bazardyuzyu, Gora mt. Azer./Rus. Fed. **93** C1

Bazas France **58** B3
Bazdar Pak. **86** A2
Bazhong China **82** A2
Bazmān Iran **91** D2
Bazmān, Kūh-e *mt.* Iran **91** D2
Bé, Nosy *i.* Madag. **107** [inset] D1
Beachy Head U.K. **53** D4
Beacon Bay S. Africa **109** C3
Beagle Gulf Austr. **114** B1
Bealanana Madag. **107** [inset] D1
Beardmore Can. **128** B2
Bear Paw Mountain U.S.A. **132** E1
Beata, Cabo *c.* Dom. Rep. **145** C3
Beata, Isla *i.* Dom. Rep. **145** C3
Beatrice U.S.A. **135** D2
Beatty U.S.A. **133** C3
Beaudesert Austr. **117** E1
Beaufort Austr. **116** C3
Beaufort Malaysia **73** C1
Beaufort U.S.A. **139** D2
Beaufort Sea Can./U.S.A. **124** C2
Beaufort West S. Africa **108** B3
Beauly *r.* U.K. **50** B2
Beaumont Belgium **54** B2
Beaumont N.Z. **118** A4
Beaumont U.S.A. **141** F2
Beaune France **59** C2
Beauraing Belgium **54** B2
Beauséjour Can. **127** E2
Beauvais France **58** C2
Beauval Can. **127** E2
Beaver *r.* Can. **127** E2
Beaver U.S.A. **133** D3
Beaver Creek Can. **126** A1
Beaver Dam U.S.A. **136** C2
Beaver Hill Lake Can. **127** F2
Beaver Island U.S.A. **136** C1
Beaverlodge Can. **126** D2
Beawar India **86** B2
Bebedouro Brazil **154** C2
Bebra Ger. **55** D2
Becerreá Spain **60** B1
Béchar Alg. **100** B1
Beckley U.S.A. **136** D3
Bedelē Eth. **103** B4
Bedford U.K. **53** C3
Bedford U.S.A. **136** C3
Bedum Neth. **54** C1
Beecroft Peninsula Austr. **117** E2
Beelitz Ger. **55** F1
Beenleigh Austr. **117** E1
Beersheba Israel **92** B2
Beeville U.S.A. **141** E3
Bega Austr. **117** D3
Begur, Cap de *c.* Spain **61** D1
Behshahr Iran **93** D2
Bei'an China **81** E1
Beihai China **83** A3
Beijing China **82** B2
Beilen Neth. **54** C1
Beilngries Ger. **55** E3
Beinn Mhòr *h.* U.K. **50** A2
Beira Moz. **107** C1
Beirut Lebanon **92** B2
Beja Port. **60** B2
Bejaïa Alg. **101** C1
Béjar Spain **60** B1
Beji *r.* Pak. **86** A2
Bekdash Turkm. **88** C2
Békés Hungary **57** E3
Békéscsaba Hungary **57** E3
Bekily Madag. **107** [inset] D2
Bela Pak. **86** A2
Bela-Bela S. Africa **109** C1
Bélabo Cameroon **104** B2
Bela Crkva Serb. and Mont. **64** B2
Belaga Malaysia **73** C1
Belarus *country* Europe **42** C3
Bela Vista Brazil **154** A2
Bela Vista Moz. **109** D2

Belawan Indon. **72** A1
Belaya *r.* Rus. Fed. **95** N2
Belaya Glina Rus. Fed. **45** F2
Belaya Kalitva Rus. Fed. **45** F2
Bełchatów Pol. **57** D2
Belcher Islands Can. **125** G3
Beledweyne Somalia **103** C4
Belém Brazil **151** E3
Belen U.S.A. **140** C2
Belev Rus. Fed. **43** E3
Belfast U.K. **51** D1
Belfast U.S.A. **137** G2
Belfort France **59** D2
Belgaum India **85** B3
Belgium *country* Europe **54** B2
Belgorod Rus. Fed. **45** E1
Belgrade Serb. and Mont. **64** B2
Belgrade U.S.A. **132** D1
Beli Nigeria **101** D4
Belinyu Indon. **72** B2
Belitung *i.* Indon. **72** B2
Belize Belize **144** B3
Belize *country* Central America **144** B3
Bel'kovskiy, Ostrov *i.* Rus. Fed. **95** L1
Bella Bella Can. **126** C2
Bellac France **58** C2
Bella Coola Can. **126** C2
Bellata Austr. **117** D1
Belle Fourche U.S.A. **134** C2
Belle Fourche *r.* U.S.A. **134** C2
Belle Glade U.S.A. **139** D3
Belle-Île *i.* France **58** B2
Belle Isle *i.* Can. **129** E1
Belle Isle, Strait of Can. **129** E1
Belleville Can. **128** C2
Belleville *IL* U.S.A. **136** C3
Belleville *KS* U.S.A. **135** D3
Bellevue U.S.A. **132** B1
Bellingham U.S.A. **132** B1
Bellinzona Switz. **59** D2
Belluno Italy **62** B1
Bellville S. Africa **108** A3
Belmonte Brazil **155** E1
Belmopan Belize **144** B3
Belmullet Rep. of Ireland **51** B1
Belogorsk Rus. Fed. **81** E1
Beloha Madag. **107** [inset] D2
Belo Horizonte Brazil **155** D1
Beloit U.S.A. **136** C2
Belomorsk Rus. Fed. **40** C2
Belorechensk Rus. Fed. **45** E3
Beloretsk Rus. Fed. **41** E3
Beloyarskiy Rus. Fed. **40** F2
Beloye, Ozero *l.* Rus. Fed. **43** E1
Beloye More *sea* Rus. Fed. *see*
  White Sea
Belozersk Rus. Fed. **43** E1
Belukha, Gora *mt.* Kazakh./Rus. Fed.
  89 F2
Belush'ye Rus. Fed. **40** D2
Belyy Rus. Fed. **43** D2
Belyy, Ostrov *i.* Rus. Fed. **40** G1
Belzig Ger. **55** F1
Bemidji U.S.A. **135** E1
Bena Dibele Dem. Rep. Congo **104** C3
Benalla Austr. **117** D3
Benavente Spain **60** B1
Benbecula *i.* U.K. **50** A2
Bend U.S.A. **132** B2
Bendearg *mt.* S. Africa **109** C3
Bendigo Austr. **116** C3
Bene Moz. **107** C1
Benešov Czech Rep. **56** C3
Benevento Italy **62** B2
Bengal, Bay of *sea* Indian Ocean **85** C3
Bengbu China **82** B2
Benghazi Libya **101** E1
Bengkayang Indon. **72** B1
Bengkulu Indon. **72** B2
Benguela Angola **106** A1

Ben Hope *h.* U.K. **50** B1
Beni *r.* Bol. **152** B2
Beni Dem. Rep. Congo **105** C2
Beni-Abbès Alg. **100** B1
Benidorm Spain **61** C2
Beni Mellal Morocco **100** B1
Benin *country* Africa **100** C4
Benin, Bight of *g.* Africa **100** C4
Benin City Nigeria **101** C4
Beni-Saf Alg. **61** C2
Benito Juárez Arg. **153** C4
Benjamim Constant Brazil **150** C3
Benjamín Hill Mex. **142** A1
Benjina Indon. **71** C3
Ben Lawers *mt.* U.K. **50** B2
Ben Lomond *h.* U.K. **50** B2
Ben Macdui *mt.* U.K. **50** C2
Ben More *h.* U.K. **50** A2
Benmore, Lake N.Z. **118** B3
Ben More Assynt *h.* U.K. **50** B1
Bennett Can. **126** B2
Bennetta, Ostrov *i.* Rus. Fed. **95** L1
Ben Nevis *mt.* U.K. **50** B2
Bennington U.S.A. **137** F2
Benoni S. Africa **109** C2
Bensheim Ger. **55** D3
Benson U.S.A. **140** B2
Benteng Indon. **73** D2
Benton Harbor U.S.A. **136** C2
Bentonville U.S.A. **138** B1
Benue *r.* Nigeria **101** C4
Benwee Head Rep. of Ireland **51** B1
Ben Wyvis *mt.* U.K. **50** B2
Benxi China **82** C1
Beograd Serb. and Mont. *see* **Belgrade**
Beohari India **87** C2
Beppu Japan **79** B4
Berane Serb. and Mont. **64** A2
Berat Albania **65** A2
Berau, Teluk *b.* Indon. **71** C3
Berber Sudan **102** B3
Berbera Somalia **103** C3
Berbérati C.A.R. **104** B2
Berck France **58** C1
Berdyans'k Ukr. **45** E2
Berdychiv Ukr. **44** C2
Berehove Ukr. **44** B2
Bereina P.N.G. **71** D3
Berens River Can. **127** F2
Berezhany Ukr. **44** B2
Berezivka Ukr. **44** D2
Berezne Ukr. **44** C1
Bereznik Rus. Fed. **40** D2
Berezniki Rus. Fed. **40** E3
Berezovo Rus. Fed. **40** F2
Berga Spain **61** D1
Bergama Turkey **65** C3
Bergamo Italy **62** A1
Bergen *Mecklenburg-Vorpommern* Ger.
  56 C2
Bergen *Niedersachsen* Ger. **55** D1
Bergen Norway **47** B3
Bergen op Zoom Neth. **54** B2
Bergerac France **58** C3
Bergheim (Erft) Ger. **54** C2
Bergisch Gladbach Ger. **54** C2
Bergland Namibia **108** A1
Bergsviken Sweden **46** E2
Bergues France **54** A2
Beringen Belgium **54** B2
Bering Sea N. Pacific Ocean **95** N3
Bering Strait Rus. Fed./U.S.A. **95** O2
Berkeley U.S.A. **133** B3
Berkner Island Antarctica **119** A2
Berkovitsa Bulg. **64** B2
Berlevåg Norway **46** F1
Berlin Ger. **55** F1
Berlin U.S.A. **137** F2
Berlingerode Ger. **55** E2

rmagui Austr. **117** E3
rmejíllo Mex. **142** B2
rmejo Bol. **152** B3
rmen, Lac *l.* Can. **129** D1
rmuda *terr.* N. Atlantic Ocean **160** B3
rn Switz. **59** D2
rnau Ger. **55** F1
rnburg (Saale) Ger. **55** E2
rnkastel-Kues Ger. **54** C3
roroha Madag. **107** [inset] D2
rounka *r.* Czech Rep. **55** G3
rri Austr. **116** C2
rrouaghia Alg. **61** D2
rry Islands Bahamas **145** C2
rsenbrück Ger. **54** C1
rshad' Ukr. **44** C2
rté, Lac *l.* Can. **129** D1
rtoua Cameroon **104** B2
ru *atoll* Kiribati **110**
ruri Brazil **150** C3
rwick-upon-Tweed U.K. **52** B2
ryslav Ukr. **45** D2
salampy Madag. **107** [inset] D1
sançon France **59** D2
snard Lake Can. **127** E2
ssemer U.S.A. **138** C2
sshoky, Gora *h.* Kazakh. **88** C2
tanzos Spain **60** B1
taré Oya Cameroon **104** B2
thanie Namibia **108** A2
thlehem S. Africa **109** C2
thlehem U.S.A. **137** E2
thune France **54** A2
tioky Madag. **107** [inset] D2
tpak-Dala *plain* Kazakh. **89** E2
troka Madag. **107** [inset] D2
tsiamites Can. **129** D2
tsiboka *r.* Madag. **107** [inset] D1
ttendorf U.S.A. **135** E2
tiah India **87** C2
tul India **87** B2
twa *r.* India **87** B2
tws-y-coed U.K. **52** B3
verley U.K. **52** C3
verungen Ger. **55** D2
verwijk Neth. **54** B1
xhill U.K. **53** D4
ykoz Turkey **65** C2
yla Guinea **100** B4
yneu Kazakh. **88** C2
ypazarı Turkey **92** B1
ysehir Turkey **92** B2
ysehir Gölü *l.* Turkey **92** B2
ysug *r.* Rus. Fed. **45** E2
zhanitsy Rus. Fed. **42** C2
ziers France **59** C3
adrak India **87** C2
adravati India **85** B3
agalpur India **87** C2
airi Hol *mt.* Pak. **86** A2
akkar Pak. **86** B1
amo Myanmar **74** A1
anjanagar India **87** C3
aratpur India **86** B2
avnagar India **86** B2
awanipatna India **87** C3
ekuzulu S. Africa **109** D2
lwara India **86** B2
ma *r.* India **85** B3
wani India **86** B2
ongweni S. Africa **109** C3
opal India **86** B2
ubaneshwar India **87** C2
uj India **86** A2
umiphol Dam Thai. **74** A2
usawal India **86** B2
utan *country* Asia **87** D2

Bia, Phou *mt.* Laos **74** B2
Biak Indon. **71** D3
Biak *i.* Indon. **71** D3
Biała Podlaska Pol. **57** E2
Białogard Pol. **57** D2
Białystok Pol. **57** E2
Bianco Italy **63** C3
Biarritz France **58** B3
Biasca Switz. **59** D2
Bibai Japan **78** D2
Bibala Angola **106** A1
Biberach an der Riß Ger. **56** B3
Bida Nigeria **101** C4
Biddeford U.S.A. **137** F2
Bideford U.K. **53** A4
Bideford Bay U.K. **53** A4
Biedenkopf Ger. **55** D2
Biel Switz. **59** D2
Bielefeld Ger. **55** D1
Biella Italy **62** A1
Bielsko-Biała Pol. **57** D3
Biên Hoa Vietnam **75** B2
Bienville, Lac *l.* Can. **128** C1
Bièvre Belgium **54** B3
Bifoun Gabon **104** B3
Biga Turkey **65** C2
Big Bend Swaziland **109** D2
Biggar Can. **124** E3
Biggar U.K. **50** C3
Big Hole *r.* U.S.A. **132** D1
Bighorn *r.* U.S.A. **134** B1
Bighorn Mountains U.S.A. **134** B2
Big Lake U.S.A. **141** D2
Big Rapids U.S.A. **136** C2
Big River Can. **127** E2
Big Sand Lake Can. **127** F2
Big Sioux *r.* U.S.A. **135** D2
Big Spring U.S.A. **141** D2
Big Timber U.S.A. **132** E1
Big Trout Lake Can. **128** B1
Big Trout Lake *l.* Can. **128** A1
Bihać Bos.-Herz. **63** C2
Bihar Sharif India **87** C2
Bihor, Vârful *mt.* Romania **44** B2
Bijagós, Arquipélago dos *is*
   Guinea-Bissau **100** A3
Bijär Iran **93** C2
Bijeljina Bos.-Herz. **63** C2
Bijelo Polje Serb. and Mont. **64** A2
Bijie China **83** A3
Bikaner India **86** B2
Bikin Rus. Fed. **78** B1
Bikin *r.* Rus. Fed. **78** B1
Bikoro Dem. Rep. Congo **104** B3
Bilãd Banī Bū 'Alī Oman **91** C2
Bilaspur India **87** C2
Bila Tserkva Ukr. **44** D2
Bilauktaung Range *mts* Myanmar/Thai.
   75 A2
Bilbao Spain **60** C1
Bilecik Turkey **65** C2
Biłgoraj Pol. **57** E2
Bilhorod-Dnistrovs'kyy Ukr. **44** D2
Bili Dem. Rep. Congo **105** C2
Bilibino Rus. Fed. **95** N2
Billings U.S.A. **132** E1
Bill of Portland *hd* U.K. **53** B4
Bilma Niger **101** D3
Biloela Austr. **115** E2
Bilohirs'k Ukr. **45** D2
Bilohir''ya Ukr. **44** C1
Bilopillya Ukr. **45** D1
Bilovods'k Ukr. **45** E2
Biloxi U.S.A. **138** C2
Bilpa Morea Claypan *salt flat* Austr.
   115 C2
Bilshausen Ger. **55** E2
Biltine Chad **101** E3
Bilyayivka Ukr. **44** D2
Bimini Islands Bahamas **139** E3

Bina-Etawa India **87** B2
Binaija, Gunung *mt.* Indon. **71** C3
Bindu Dem. Rep. Congo **104** B3
Bindura Zimbabwe **107** C1
Binefar Spain **61** D1
Bingara Austr. **117** E1
Bingen am Rhein Ger. **54** C3
Bingham U.S.A. **137** G1
Binghamton U.S.A. **137** E2
Bingöl Turkey **93** C2
Binjai Indon. **72** A1
Bintuhan Indon. **72** B2
Bintulu Malaysia **73** C1
Binzhou China **82** B2
Bioco *i.* Equat. Guinea **104** A2
Biograd na Moru Croatia **62** C2
Birao C.A.R. **104** C1
Biratnagar Nepal **87** C2
Birch Mountains Can. **126** C2
Birdsville Austr. **115** C2
Birecik Turkey **92** B2
Bireun Indon. **72** A1
Birganj Nepal **87** C2
Birhan *mt.* Eth. **103** B3
Birigüi Brazil **154** B2
Birjand Iran **88** C3
Birkenhead U.K. **52** B3
Birmingham U.K. **53** C3
Birmingham U.S.A. **138** C2
Bîr Mogreïn Maur. **100** A2
Birnin-Kebbi Nigeria **100** C3
Birnin Konni Niger **101** C3
Birobidzhan Rus. Fed. **81** E1
Birr Rep. of Ireland **51** C2
Birsay U.K. **50** C1
Bi'r Shalatayn Egypt **90** A2
Biržai Lith. **42** B1
Bisalpur India **87** B2
Bisbee U.S.A. **140** C2
Biscay, Bay of *sea* France/Spain **58** A2
Bischofshofen Austria **56** C3
Biscotasi Lake Can. **128** B2
Bishkek Kyrg. **89** E2
Bisho S. Africa **109** C3
Bishop U.S.A. **133** C3
Bishui China **81** E1
Bisinaca Col. **150** C2
Biskra Alg. **101** C1
Bismarck U.S.A. **134** C1
Bismarck Archipelago *is* P.N.G. **71** D3
Bismarck Sea P.N.G. **110**
Bissa, Djebel *mt.* Alg. **61** D2
Bissamcuttak India **85** C3
Bissau Guinea-Bissau **100** A3
Bissett Can. **127** F2
Bistcho Lake Can. **126** D2
Bistrița Romania **44** B2
Bistrița *r.* Romania **44** C2
Bitburg Ger. **54** C3
Bitche France **59** D2
Bitkine Chad **101** D3
Bitola Macedonia **65** B2
Bitonto Italy **63** C2
Bitterfontein S. Africa **108** A3
Bitterroot *r.* U.S.A. **132** D1
Bitterroot Range *mts* U.S.A. **132** C1
Bityug *r.* Rus. Fed. **43** E3
Biu Nigeria **101** D3
Biwa-ko *l.* Japan **79** C3
Biysk Rus. Fed. **89** F1
Bizerte Tunisia **101** C1
Bjargtangar *hd* Iceland **46** [inset]
Bjästa Sweden **46** D3
Bjerkvik Norway **46** D2
Bjørnøya *i.* Arctic Ocean **94** D2
Bla Mali **100** B3
Black *r.* U.S.A. **138** B1
Blackall Austr. **115** D2
Blackburn U.K. **52** B3
Blackfoot U.S.A. **132** D2

Black Forest *mts* Ger. **56** B3
Black Hills U.S.A. **134** C2
Black Isle *pen.* U.K. **50** B2
Black Lake Can. **127** E2
Black Lake *l.* Can. **127** E2
Black Mountains U.K. **53** B4
Blackpool U.K. **52** B3
Black River *r.* Vietnam **74** B1
Black River Falls U.S.A. **136** B2
Blacksburg U.S.A. **137** D3
Black Sea Asia/Europe **92** B1
Blacksod Bay Rep. of Ireland **51** A1
Blackstairs Mountains Rep. of Ireland **51** C2
Black Volta *r.* Africa **100** B4
Blackwater *r.* Rep. of Ireland **51** C2
Blackwater Lake Can. **126** C1
Blackwood *r.* Austr. **114** A3
Blagoevgrad Bulg. **64** B2
Blagoveshchensk Rus. Fed. **81** E1
Blaine Lake Can. **127** E2
Blair U.S.A. **135** D2
Blair Atholl U.K. **50** C2
Blairgowrie U.K. **50** C2
Blakely U.S.A. **139** D2
Blanc, Mont *mt.* France/Italy **59** D2
Blanca, Bahía *b.* Arg. **153** B4
Blanche, Lake *salt flat* Austr. **116** B1
Blanco *r.* Bol. **152** B2
Blanco, Cape U.S.A. **120**
Blanc-Sablon Can. **129** E1
Blanda *r.* Iceland **46** [inset]
Blandford Forum U.K. **53** B4
Blanding U.S.A. **133** E3
Blanes Spain **61** D1
Blangkejeren Indon. **72** A1
Blankenheim Ger. **54** C2
Blankenrath Ger. **54** C2
Blansko Czech Rep. **57** D3
Blantyre Malawi **107** C1
Blaydon U.K. **52** C2
Blayney Austr. **117** D2
Blenheim N.Z. **118** B3
Blida Alg. **100** C1
Blind River Can. **128** B2
Bloemfontein S. Africa **109** C2
Bloemhof S. Africa **109** C2
Bloemhof Dam S. Africa **109** C2
Blönduós Iceland **46** [inset]
Bloody Foreland *pt* Rep. of Ireland **51** B1
Bloomfield U.S.A. **140** C1
Bloomington *IL* U.S.A. **136** C2
Bloomington *IN* U.S.A. **136** C2
Blosseville Kyst *coastal area* Greenland **125** K2
Bluefield U.S.A. **136** D3
Bluefields Nic. **144** B3
Blue Mountains Austr. **117** D2
Blue Mountains U.S.A. **132** C1
Blue Nile *r.* Eth./Sudan **103** B3
Blue Ridge *mts* U.S.A. **139** D1
Blue Stack Mountains Rep. of Ireland **51** B1
Bluff N.Z. **118** A4
Bluff U.S.A. **133** E3
Blumenau Brazil **154** C3
Blyth Austr. **116** B2
Blyth U.K. **52** C2
Blythe U.S.A. **133** D4
Blytheville U.S.A. **138** C1
Bo Sierra Leone **100** A4
Boac Phil. **76** B2
Boa Esperança, Açude *resr* Brazil **151** E3
Boa Vista Brazil **150** C2
Bobadah Austr. **117** D2
Bobai China **83** B3

Bobaomby, Tanjona *c.* Madag. **107** [inset] D1
Bobo-Dioulasso Burkina **100** B3
Bobrov Rus. Fed. **43** F3
Bobrovytsya Ukr. **45** D1
Bobrynets' Ukr. **45** D2
Boby *mt.* Madag. **107** [inset] D2
Boca do Acre Brazil **150** C3
Bocaiúva Brazil **155** D1
Bocaranga C.A.R. **104** B2
Bochnia Pol. **57** E3
Bocholt Ger. **54** C2
Bochum Ger. **54** C2
Bochum S. Africa **109** C1
Bockenem Ger. **55** E1
Boda C.A.R. **104** B2
Bodaybo Rus. Fed. **95** J3
Bodélé *reg.* Chad **101** D3
Boden Sweden **46** E2
Bodmin U.K. **53** A4
Bodmin Moor *moorland* U.K. **53** A4
Bodø Norway **46** C2
Bodrum Turkey **65** C3
Boende Dem. Rep. Congo **104** C3
Bogalusa U.S.A. **138** C2
Bogandé Burkina **100** B3
Bogda Shan *mts* China **89** F2
Boggabilla Austr. **117** E1
Boggeragh Mountains Rep. of Ireland **51** B2
Bogny-sur-Meuse France **54** B3
Bog of Allen *reg.* Rep. of Ireland **51** C2
Bogong, Mount Austr. **117** D3
Bogor Indon. **72** B2
Bogoroditsk Rus. Fed. **43** E3
Bogotá Col. **150** B2
Bogotol Rus. Fed. **94** H3
Boguchany Rus. Fed. **95** I3
Boguchar Rus. Fed. **45** F2
Bo Hai *g.* China **82** B2
Bohain-en-Vermandois France **54** A3
Bohai Wan *b.* China **82** B2
Bohlokong S. Africa **109** C2
Böhmer Wald *mts* Ger. **55** F3
Bohodukhiv Ukr. **45** E1
Bohol *i.* Phil. **76** B3
Bohol Sea Phil. **76** B3
Bohu China **89** F2
Boi, Ponta do *pt* Brazil **155** D2
Bois *r.* Brazil **154** B1
Boise U.S.A. **132** C2
Boise City U.S.A. **141** D1
Boitumelong S. Africa **109** C2
Boizenburg Ger. **55** E1
Bojnūrd Iran **93** D2
Bokatola Dem. Rep. Congo **104** B3
Boké Guinea **100** A3
Bokele Dem. Rep. Congo **104** C3
Boknafjorden *sea chan.* Norway **47** B4
Bokoro Chad **101** D3
Bokovskaya Rus. Fed. **45** F2
Bokpyin Myanmar **75** A2
Boksitogorsk Rus. Fed. **43** D2
Bokspits S. Africa **108** C2
Bolama Guinea-Bissau **100** A3
Bolangir India **87** C2
Bolbec France **58** C2
Bole China **89** F2
Boleko Dem. Rep. Congo **104** B3
Bolgatanga Ghana **100** B3
Bolhrad Ukr. **44** C2
Boli China **78** B1
Bolintin-Vale Romania **44** C3
Bolivar U.S.A. **135** E3
Bolívar, Pico *mt.* Venez. **150** B2
Bolivia *country* S. America **152** B2
Bolkhov Rus. Fed. **43** E3
Bollène France **59** C3
Bollnäs Sweden **47** D3
Bollon Austr. **117** D1

Bollstedt Ger. **55** E2
Bolmen *l.* Sweden **47** C4
Bolobo Dem. Rep. Congo **104** B3
Bologna Italy **62** B2
Bologovo Rus. Fed. **43** D2
Bologoye Rus. Fed. **43** D2
Bolomba Dem. Rep. Congo **104** B2
Bolovens, Phouphieng *plat.* Laos **75** B2
Bol'shaya Martinovka Rus. Fed. **45** F
Bol'shevik, Ostrov *i.* Rus. Fed. **95** I1
Bol'shezemel'skaya Tundra *lowland* Rus. Fed. **40** E2
Bol'shoy Aluy *r.* Rus. Fed. **95** M2
Bol'shoy Kamen' Rus. Fed. **78** B2
Bol'shoy Kavkaz *mts* Asia/Europe *see* Caucasus
Bol'shoy Lyakhovskiy, Ostrov *i.* Rus. Fed. **95** L2
Bolsward Neth. **54** B1
Bolton U.K. **52** B3
Bolu Turkey **92** B1
Bolungarvík Iceland **46** [inset]
Bolzano Italy **62** B1
Boma Dem. Rep. Congo **104** B3
Bomaderry Austr. **117** E2
Bombala Austr. **117** D3
Bombay India *see* Mumbai
Bom Despacho Brazil **155** C1
Bomdila India **87** D2
Bom Jesus da Lapa Brazil **151** E4
Bom Jesus do Itabapoana Brazil **155** D2
Bømlo *i.* Norway **48** E2
Bon, Cap *c.* Tunisia **101** D1
Bonaire *i.* Neth. Antilles **145** D3
Bonaparte Archipelago *is* Austr. **114** B1
Bonavista Can. **129** E2
Bonavista Bay Can. **129** E2
Bondo Dem. Rep. Congo **104** C2
Bondoukou Côte d'Ivoire **100** B4
Bone, Teluk *b.* Indon. **73** D2
Bonerate, Kepulauan *is* Indon. **73** D2
Bonete, Cerro *mt.* Bol. **147**
Bonfinópolis de Minas Brazil **155** C1
Bonga Eth. **103** B4
Bongaigaon India **87** D2
Bongandanga Dem. Rep. Congo **104** C2
Bongo, Massif des *mts* C.A.R. **104** C
Bongor Chad **101** D3
Bongouanou Côte d'Ivoire **100** B4
Bông Sơn Vietnam **75** B2
Bonham U.S.A. **141** E2
Bonifacio France **59** D3
Bonifacio, Strait of France/Italy **62** A
Bonito Brazil **154** A2
Bonn Ger. **54** C2
Bonners Ferry U.S.A. **132** C1
Bonnie Rock Austr. **114** A3
Bonnyville Can. **127** C2
Bonorva Italy **62** A2
Bontang Indon. **73** C1
Bontoc Phil. **76** B2
Bontosunggu Indon. **73** C2
Bontrug S. Africa **109** C3
Booligal Austr. **117** D1
Boomi Austr. **117** D1
Boonah Austr. **117** E1
Boone *IA* U.S.A. **135** E2
Boone *NC* U.S.A. **136** D3
Booneville U.S.A. **138** C2
Boonville U.S.A. **135** E3
Boorowa Austr. **117** D2
Boothia, Gulf of Can. **125** G2
Boothia Peninsula Can. **124** F2
Boppard Ger. **54** C2
Boquilla, Presa de la *resr* Mex. **142**
Bor Serb. and Mont. **64** B2

Canoas Brazil **152** C3
Canoe Lake Can. **127** E2
Canoinhas Brazil **154** B3
Canon City U.S.A. **134** B3
Canora Can. **124** F3
Canowindra Austr. **117** D2
Cantábrica, Cordillera *mts* Spain **60** C1
Cantábrico, Mar *sea* Spain **60** B1
Canterbury U.K. **53** D4
Canterbury Bight *b.* N.Z. **118** B3
Canterbury Plains N.Z. **118** B3
Cân Thơ Vietnam **75** B2
Canto do Buriti Brazil **151** E3
Canton China *see* Guangzhou
Canton *MS* U.S.A. **138** C2
Canton *OH* U.S.A. **136** D2
Canyon U.S.A. **141** D1
Canyon Ferry Lake U.S.A. **132** D1
Cao Băng Vietnam **74** B1
Capão Bonito Brazil **154** C2
Caparaó, Serra do *mts* Brazil **155** D2
Cape Barren Island Austr. **115** D4
Cape Borda Austr. **116** B3
Cape Breton Island Can. **129** D2
Cape Coast Ghana **100** B4
Cape Cod Bay U.S.A. **137** F2
Cape Dorset Can. **125** G2
Cape Fear *r.* U.S.A. **139** E2
Cape Girardeau U.S.A. **135** F3
Capelinha Brazil **155** D1
Capelle aan de IJssel Neth. **54** B2
Capenda-Camulemba Angola **104** B3
Cape Town S. Africa **108** A3
Cape Verde *country* N. Atlantic Ocean **98**
Cape York Peninsula Austr. **115** D1
Cap-Haïtien Haiti **145** C3
Capitol Hill N. Mariana Is **71** E1
Čapljina Bos.-Herz. **63** C2
Capo d'Orlando Italy **62** B3
Capraia, Isola di *i.* Italy **62** A2
Caprara, Punta *pt* Italy **62** A2
Capri, Isola di *i.* Italy **62** B2
Caprivi Strip *reg.* Namibia **106** B1
Caquetá *r.* Col. **150** C3
Caracal Romania **44** B3
Caracas Venez. **150** C1
Caracol Brazil **151** E3
Caraguatatuba Brazil **155** C2
Carahue Chile **153** A4
Caraí Brazil **155** D1
Carangola Brazil **155** D2
Caransebeş Romania **44** B2
Caraquet Can. **129** D2
Caratasca, Laguna de *lag.* Hond. **144** B3
Caratinga Brazil **155** D1
Carauari Brazil **150** C3
Caravaca de la Cruz Spain **61** C2
Caravelas Brazil **155** E1
Carberry Can. **127** F3
Carbó Mex. **142** A2
Carbonara, Capo *c.* Italy **62** A3
Carbondale *CO* U.S.A. **134** B3
Carbondale *IL* U.S.A. **136** C3
Carbonear Can. **129** E2
Carbonita Brazil **155** D1
Carcaixent Spain **61** C2
Carcross Can. **126** B1
Cárdenas Mex. **143** C3
Cardiff U.K. **53** B4
Cardigan U.K. **53** A3
Cardigan Bay U.K. **53** A3
Cardston Can. **132** D1
Carei Romania **44** B2
Carentan France **58** B2

Carey, Lake *salt flat* Austr. **114** B2
Cargados Carajos Islands Mauritius **97**
Cariacica Brazil **155** D2
Caribbean Sea N. Atlantic Ocean **144** B3
Caribou U.S.A. **137** G1
Caribou Lake Can. **128** B1
Caribou Mountains Can. **126** D2
Carichic Mex. **142** B2
Carignan France **54** B3
Carinda Austr. **117** D2
Cariñena Spain **61** C1
Carleton Place Can. **128** C2
Carletonville S. Africa **109** C2
Carlingford Lough *inlet* Rep. of Ireland/U.K. **51** C1
Carlisle U.K. **52** B2
Carlisle U.S.A. **137** E2
Carlos Chagas Brazil **155** D1
Carlow Rep. of Ireland **51** C2
Carlsbad *CA* U.S.A. **133** C4
Carlsbad *NM* U.S.A. **140** D2
Carlyle Can. **134** C1
Carmacks Can. **126** B1
Carman Can. **127** F3
Carmarthen U.K. **53** A4
Carmarthen Bay U.K. **53** A4
Carmaux France **58** C3
Carmelita Guat. **143** C3
Carmen, Isla *i.* Mex. **142** A2
Carnac France **58** B2
Carnarvon S. Africa **108** B3
Carndonagh Rep. of Ireland **51** C1
Carnegie, Lake *salt flat* Austr. **114** B2
Carn Eighe *mt.* U.K. **50** B2
Car Nicobar *i.* India **75** A3
Carnot C.A.R. **104** B2
Carnot, Cape Austr. **116** B2
Carnsore Point *pt* Rep. of Ireland **51** C2
Carolina Brazil **151** E3
Caroline Island *atoll* Kiribati **111**
Caroline Islands N. Pacific Ocean **71** D2
Carpathian Mountains Europe **44** A2
Carpaţii Meridionali *mts* Romania *see* Transylvanian Alps
Carpentaria, Gulf of Austr. **115** C1
Carpentras France **59** D3
Carrantuohill *mt.* Rep. of Ireland **51** B3
Carrara Italy **59** E3
Carrickmacross Rep. of Ireland **51** C2
Carrick-on-Shannon Rep. of Ireland **51** B2
Carrick-on-Suir Rep. of Ireland **51** C2
Carrington U.S.A. **135** D1
Carrizo Springs U.S.A. **141** E3
Carrizozo U.S.A. **140** C2
Carroll U.S.A. **135** E2
Carrollton U.S.A. **139** C2
Carrot River Can. **127** E2
Carson City U.S.A. **133** C3
Cartagena Col. **150** B1
Cartagena Spain **61** C2
Cartago Costa Rica **144** B4
Carthage *MO* U.S.A. **135** E3
Carthage *TX* U.S.A. **141** F2
Cartwright Can. **129** E1
Caruarú Brazil **151** F3
Casablanca Morocco **100** B1
Casa Branca Brazil **154** C2
Casa de Janos Mex. **142** B1
Casa Grande U.S.A. **140** B2
Casale Monferrato Italy **62** A1
Casarano Italy **63** C2
Cascade U.S.A. **132** C2
Cascade Range *mts* Can./U.S.A. **132** B2
Cascais Port. **60** B2

Cascavel Brazil **154** B2
Caserta Italy **62** B2
Cashel Rep. of Ireland **51** C2
Casino Austr. **117** E1
Caspe Spain **61** C1
Casper U.S.A. **134** B2
Caspian Lowland Kazakh./Rus. Fed. **88** B2
Caspian Sea *l.* Asia/Europe **88** B2
Cassel France **54** A2
Cássia Brazil **154** C2
Cassiar Can. **126** C2
Cassiar Mountains Can. **126** B2
Cassilândia Brazil **154** B1
Cassino Italy **62** B2
Cassley *r.* U.K. **50** B2
Castanhal Brazil **151** E3
Castaño *r.* Arg. **152** B4
Castaños Mex. **142** B2
Casteljaloux France **58** C3
Castelló de la Plana Spain **61** C2
Castelo Branco Port. **60** B2
Castelvetrano Italy **62** B3
Casterton Austr. **116** C3
Castiglione della Pescaia Italy **62** B2
Castlebar Rep. of Ireland **51** B2
Castlebay U.K. **50** A2
Castleblayney Rep. of Ireland **51** C1
Castlederg U.K. **51** C1
Castle Douglas U.K. **50** C3
Castlegar Can. **126** D3
Castleisland Rep. of Ireland **51** B2
Castlemaine Austr. **116** C3
Castle Mountain Can. **126** B1
Castlerea Rep. of Ireland **51** B2
Castlereagh *r.* Austr. **117** D2
Castle Rock U.S.A. **134** C3
Castor Can. **127** D2
Castres France **58** C3
Castries St Lucia **145** D3
Castro Brazil **154** C2
Castro Chile **153** A5
Castro Verde Port. **60** B2
Castrovillari Italy **63** C3
Catacaos Peru **150** A3
Cataguases Brazil **155** D2
Catalão Brazil **154** C1
Cataluña *aut. comm.* Spain **61** D1
Catamarca Arg. **152** B3
Catanduanes *i.* Phil. **76** B2
Catanduva Brazil **154** C2
Catanduvas Brazil **154** B3
Catania Italy **62** C3
Catanzaro Italy **63** C3
Catarman Phil. **76** B2
Catbalogan Phil. **76** B2
Catemaco Mex. **143** C3
Catherine, Mount Egypt *see* Kātrīnā, Jabal
Cat Island Bahamas **145** C2
Cat Lake Can. **128** A1
Catoche, Cabo *c.* Mex. **143** D2
Catskill Mountains U.S.A. **137** F2
Cauayan Phil. **76** B3
Caubvick, Mount Can. **129** D1
Cauca *r.* Col. **150** B2
Caucaia Brazil **151** F3
Caucasus *mts* Asia/Europe **93** C1
Caudry France **54** A2
Caulonia Italy **63** C3
Causapscal Can. **129** D2
Cavaillon France **59** D3
Cavalcante Brazil **151** E4
Cavan Rep. of Ireland **51** C2
Cavernoso, Serra do *mts* Brazil **154** B3
Caxias Brazil **151** E3
Caxias do Sul Brazil **152** C3
Caxito Angola **104** B3

Chengdu China **82** A2
Chengmai China **83** B4
Chengxian China **82** A2
Chennai India **85** C3
Chenzhou China **83** B3
Chepstow U.K. **53** B4
Cherbourg France **58** B2
Cheremisinovo Rus. Fed. **43** E3
Cheremkhovo Rus. Fed. **80** C1
Cherepovets Rus. Fed. **43** E2
Cherkasy Ukr. **45** D2
Cherkessk Rus. Fed. **41** D4
Chernihiv Ukr. **45** D1
Cherninivka Ukr. **45** E2
Chernivtsi Ukr. **44** C1
Chernyakhiv Ukr. **44** C1
Chernyakhovsk Rus. Fed. **42** B3
Chernyanka Rus. Fed. **43** E3
Chernyshevskiy Rus. Fed. **95** J2
Chernyshkovskiy Rus. Fed. **45** F2
Cherokee U.S.A. **135** D2
Cherskogo, Khrebet *mts* Rus. Fed.
  95 L2
Chertkovo Rus. Fed. **45** F2
Chervonohrad Ukr. **44** B1
Chervyen' Belarus **42** C3
Cherykaw Belarus **43** D3
Chesapeake Bay U.S.A. **137** E3
Cheshskaya Guba *b.* Rus. Fed. **40** D2
Chester U.K. **52** B3
Chester *IL* U.S.A. **136** C3
Chester *SC* U.S.A. **139** D2
Chesterfield U.K. **52** C3
Chesterfield, Îles *is* New Caledonia
  115 E1
Chesterfield Inlet Can. **127** F1
Chesterfield Inlet *inlet* Can. **127** F1
Chesuncook Lake U.S.A. **137** G1
Chéticamp Can. **129** D2
Chetumal Mex. **143** D3
Chetwynd Can. **126** C2
Cheviot Hills U.K. **52** B2
Cheyenne U.S.A. **134** C2
Cheyenne *r.* U.S.A. **134** C2
Cheyenne Wells U.S.A. **134** C3
Chhapra India **87** C2
Chhatarpur India **87** B2
Chiai Taiwan **83** C3
Chiang Dao Thai. **74** A2
Chiang Mai Thai. **74** A2
Chiang Rai Thai. **74** A2
Chiavenno Italy **62** A1
Chibi China **83** B3
Chiboma Moz. **107** C2
Chibougamau Can. **128** C2
Chibuto Moz. **109** D1
Chicago U.S.A. **136** C2
Chichagof Island U.S.A. **126** B2
Chichester U.K. **53** C4
Chichester Range *mts* Austr. **114** A2
Chickasha U.S.A. **141** E1
Chiclayo Peru **150** B3
Chico *r.* Arg. **153** B5
Chico U.S.A. **133** B3
Chicoutimi Can. **129** C2
Chidley, Cape Can. **121**
Chieti Italy **62** B2
Chietla Mex. **143** C3
Chifeng China **82** B1
Chifre, Serra do *mts* Brazil **155** D1
Chiganak Kazakh. **89** E2
Chignahuapán Mex. **143** C3
Chigubo Moz. **107** C2
Chigu Co *l.* China **74** A1
Chihuahua Mex. **142** B2
Chikhachevo Rus. Fed. **42** C2
Chikuma-gawa *r.* Japan **79** C3
Chilanko *r.* Can. **126** C2
Chilas Jammu and Kashmir **86** B1
Childress U.S.A. **141** D2

Chile *country* S. America **152** A4
Chilecito Arg. **152** B3
Chilika Lake India **87** C3
Chililabombwe Zambia **106** B1
Chilko *r.* Can. **126** C2
Chilko Lake Can. **126** C2
Chillán Chile **153** A4
Chillicothe *MO* U.S.A. **135** E3
Chillicothe *OH* U.S.A. **136** D3
Chilliwack Can. **126** C2
Chiloé, Isla de *i.* Chile **153** A5
Chilpancingo Mex. **143** C3
Chiltern Austr. **117** D3
Chilung Taiwan **83** C3
Chimala Tanz. **105** D3
Chimbas Arg. **152** B4
Chimborazo *mt.* Ecuador **150** B3
Chimbote Peru **150** B3
Chimboy Uzbek. **88** C2
Chimoio Moz. **107** C1
Chimtargha, Qullai *mt.* Tajik. **89** D3
China *country* Asia **80** B2
China Mex. **143** C2
Chincha Alta Peru **150** B4
Chinchaga *r.* Can. **126** D2
Chinchorro, Banco *sea feature* Mex.
  143 D3
Chinde Moz. **107** C1
Chindo S. Korea **77** B3
Chin-do *i.* S. Korea **77** B3
Chindu China **80** C2
Chindwin *r.* Myanmar **74** A1
Chinghwa N. Korea **77** B2
Chingola Zambia **106** B1
Chinguar Angola **106** A1
Chinhae S. Korea **77** B2
Chinhoyi Zimbabwe **107** C1
Chiniot Pak. **86** B1
Chinipas Mex. **142** B2
Chinju S. Korea **77** B2
Chinko *r.* C.A.R. **104** C2
Chinle U.S.A. **140** C1
Chinmen Taiwan **83** B3
Chino Japan **79** C3
Chino Valley U.S.A. **140** B2
Chinon France **58** C2
Chinsali Zambia **105** D4
Chioggia Italy **62** B1
Chios Greece **65** C3
Chios *i.* Greece **65** C3
Chipata Zambia **107** C1
Chipindo Angola **106** A1
Chipinge Zimbabwe **107** C2
Chiplun India **85** B3
Chippenham U.K. **53** B4
Chipping Norton U.K. **53** C4
Chir *r.* Rus. Fed. **45** F2
Chirchiq Uzbek. **89** D2
Chiredzi Zimbabwe **107** C2
Chiricahua Peak U.S.A. **140** C2
Chiriquí, Golfo de *b.* Panama **144** B4
Chiri-san *mt.* S. Korea **77** B2
Chirripo *mt.* Costa Rica **144** B4
Chirundu Zimbabwe **107** B1
Chisasibi Can. **128** C2
Chisholm U.S.A. **135** E1
Chişinău Moldova **44** C2
Chistopol' Rus. Fed. **41** E3
Chita Rus. Fed. **81** D1
Chitado Angola **106** A1
Chitambo Zambia **107** C1
Chitato Angola **104** C3
Chitipa Malawi **105** D3
Chitradurga India **85** B3
Chitral Pak. **86** B1
Chitré Panama **144** B4
Chittagong Bangl. **87** D2
Chittaurgarh India **86** B2
Chitungwiza Zimbabwe **107** C1
Chiume Angola **106** B1

Chivhu Zimbabwe **107** C1
Chizhou China **83** B2
Chkalovsk Rus. Fed. **43** F2
Choele Choel Arg. **153** B4
Choiseul *i.* Solomon Is **110**
Choix Mex. **142** B2
Chojnice Pol. **57** D2
Ch'ok'ē Mountains Eth. **103** B3
Chokurdakh Rus. Fed. **95** L2
Chókwé Moz. **107** C2
Cholet France **58** B2
Chomutov Czech Rep. **56** C2
Chona *r.* Rus. Fed. **95** J2
Ch'ŏnan S. Korea **77** B2
Chone Ecuador **150** A3
Ch'ŏngjin N. Korea **77** B1
Chŏngju N. Korea **77** B2
Chŏngp'yŏng N. Korea **77** B2
Chongqing China **83** A3
Chongqing *mun.* China **82** A2
Chŏngŭp S. Korea **77** B2
Chongzuo China **83** A3
Chŏnju S. Korea **77** B2
Chonos, Archipiélago de los *is* Chile
  153 A5
Chopimzinho Brazil **154** B3
Chorley U.K. **52** B3
Chornomors'ke Ukr. **45** D2
Chortkiv Ukr. **44** C2
Ch'ŏrwŏn S. Korea **77** B2
Ch'osan N. Korea **77** B1
Chōshi Japan **79** D3
Choszczno Pol. **57** D2
Choûm Maur. **100** A2
Choybalsan Mongolia **81** D1
Choyr Mongolia **81** D1
Christchurch N.Z. **118** B3
Christchurch U.K. **53** C4
Christian, Cape Can. **125** H2
Christiana S. Africa **109** C2
Christina, Mount N.Z. **118** A3
Christmas Island *terr.* Indian Ocean
  70 B3
Chrysi *i.* Greece **65** C4
Chubut *r.* Arg. **153** B5
Chudniv Ukr. **44** C1
Chudovo Rus. Fed. **43** D2
Chugach Mountains U.S.A. **124** C2
Chūgoku-sanchi *mts* Japan **79** B4
Chuguyevka Rus. Fed. **78** B2
Chuhuyiv Ukr. **45** E2
Chukchi Sea Rus. Fed./U.S.A. **95** O2
Chukhloma Rus. Fed. **43** F2
Chukotskiy Poluostrov *pen.* Rus. Fed.
  95 O2
Chula Vista U.S.A. **133** C4
Chulym Rus. Fed. **94** H3
Chumbicha Arg. **152** B3
Chumikan Rus. Fed. **95** L3
Chumphon Thai. **75** A2
Ch'unch'ŏn S. Korea **77** B2
Chungking China *see* Chongqing
Chunya *r.* Rus. Fed. **95** I2
Chuquibamba Peru **150** B4
Chuquicamata Chile **152** B3
Chur Switz. **59** D2
Churachandpur India **74** A1
Churchill Can. **127** F2
Churchill *r. Man.* Can. **127** F2
Churchill *r. Nfld. and Lab.* Can. **129** D
Churchill, Cape Can. **127** F2
Churchill Falls Can. **129** D1
Churchill Lake Can. **127** E2
Churu India **86** B2
Chute-des-Passes Can. **129** C2
Chuuk *is* Micronesia **110**
Chuxiong China **74** B1
Ciadîr-Lunga Moldova **44** C2
Ciamis Indon. **72** B2
Cianjur Indon. **72** B2

Dargai Pak. **86** B1
Dargaville N.Z. **118** B2
Dargo Austr. **117** D3
Darhan Mongolia **80** D1
Darién, Golfo del *g.* Col. **150** B2
Darjiling India **87** C2
Darlag China **80** C2
Darling *r.* Austr. **116** C2
Darling Downs *hills* Austr. **117** D1
Darling Range *hills* Austr. **114** A3
Darlington U.K. **52** C2
Darlington Point Austr. **117** D2
Darłowo Pol. **57** D2
Darmstadt Ger. **55** D3
Darnah Libya **101** E1
Darnick Austr. **116** C2
Daroca Spain **61** C1
Dartford U.K. **53** D4
Dartmoor *hills* U.K. **53** A4
Dartmouth Can. **129** D2
Dartmouth U.K. **53** B4
Daru P.N.G. **71** D3
Darvaza Turkm. **88** C2
Darwin Austr. **114** C1
Dashoguz Turkm. **88** C2
Dasht *r.* Pak. **86** A2
Datadian Indon. **73** C1
Datça Turkey **65** C3
Datong China **82** B1
Datu Piang Phil. **76** B3
Daud Khel Pak. **86** B1
Daugava *r.* Latvia **42** B2
Daugavpils Latvia **42** C2
Daun Ger. **54** C2
Dauphin Can. **127** E2
Dauphin Lake Can. **127** F2
Davangere India **85** B3
Davao Phil. **76** B3
Davao Gulf Phil. **76** B3
Davenport U.S.A. **135** E2
Daventry U.K. **53** C3
Daveyton S. Africa **109** C2
David Panama **144** B4
Davidson Can. **127** E2
Davis U.S.A. **133** B3
Davis Inlet Can. **129** D1
Davis Sea Antarctica **119** F3
Davis Strait Can./Greenland **125** I2
Davos Switz. **59** D2
Dawqah Oman **91** C3
Dawson Can. **126** B1
Dawson U.S.A. **139** D2
Dawson Creek Can. **126** C2
Dawsons Landing Can. **126** C2
Dawu China **80** C2
Dax France **58** B3
Da Xueshan *mts* China **80** C2
Dayr az Zawr Syria **92** C2
Dayton U.S.A. **136** D3
Daytona Beach U.S.A. **139** D3
Da Yunhe *canal* China **82** B2
Dazhou China **82** A2
De Aar S. Africa **108** B3
Dead Sea *salt l.* Asia **92** B2
De'an China **83** B2
Deán Funes Arg. **152** B4
Dease Lake Can. **126** C2
Death Valley *depr.* U.S.A. **133** C3
Deauville France **58** C2
Debak Malaysia **73** C1
Debar Macedonia **65** B2
Debrecen Hungary **57** E3
Debre Markos Eth. **103** B3
Debre Tabor Eth. **103** B3
Debre Zeyit Eth. **103** B4
Decatur *AL* U.S.A. **138** C2
Decatur *IL* U.S.A. **136** C3
Deccan *plat.* India **85** B3
Děčín Czech Rep. **56** F2
Decorah U.S.A. **135** E2

Dedovichi Rus. Fed. **42** C2
Dedza Malawi **107** C1
Dee *r. England/Wales* U.K. **52** B3
Dee *r. Scotland* U.K. **50** C2
Deepwater Austr. **117** E1
Deer Lake Can. **129** E2
Deer Lodge U.S.A. **132** D1
Defiance U.S.A. **136** D2
Dêgê China **80** C2
Degeh Bur Eth. **103** C4
Deggendorf Ger. **56** C3
Degtevo Rus. Fed. **45** F2
Dehra Dun India **87** B1
Dehri India **87** C2
Dehui China **81** E2
Deinze Belgium **54** A2
Dej Romania **44** B2
De Kalb U.S.A. **136** C2
Dekemhare Eritrea **90** A3
Dekese Dem. Rep. Congo **104** C3
Delano U.S.A. **133** C3
Delano Peak U.S.A. **133** D3
Delap-Uliga-Djarrit Marshall Is **112**
Delārām Afgh. **86** A1
Delareyville S. Africa **109** C2
Delaronde Lake Can. **127** E2
Delaware U.S.A. **136** D2
Delaware *r.* U.S.A. **137** E3
Delaware *state* U.S.A. **137** E3
Delaware Bay U.S.A. **137** E3
Delegate Austr. **117** D3
Delémont Switz. **59** D2
Delft Neth. **54** B1
Delfzijl Neth. **54** C1
Delgado, Cabo *c.* Moz. **105** E4
Delhi India **86** B2
Deli *i.* Indon. **72** B2
Déline Can. **126** C1
Delitzsch Ger. **55** F2
Dellys Alg. **61** D2
Delmenhorst Ger. **55** D1
Delnice Croatia **62** B1
De-Longa, Ostrova *is* Rus. Fed.
   95 M1
Deloraine Can. **127** E3
Delphi *tourist site* Greece **65** B3
Del Rio U.S.A. **141** D3
Delta *CO* U.S.A. **134** B3
Delta *UT* U.S.A. **133** D3
Delta Junction U.S.A. **124** C2
Delvinë Albania **65** B3
Demanda, Sierra de la *mts* Spain
   60 C1
Demba Dem. Rep. Congo **104** C3
Dembī Dolo Eth. **103** B4
Demidov Rus. Fed. **43** D2
Deming U.S.A. **140** C2
Demirci Turkey **65** C3
Demirköy Turkey **64** C2
Demmin Ger. **56** C2
Demopolis U.S.A. **138** C2
Dempo, Gunung *vol.* Indon. **72** B2
Demyansk Rus. Fed. **43** D2
De Naawte S. Africa **108** B3
Denakil *reg.* Eritrea/Eth. **103** C3
Den Burg Neth. **54** B1
Dendermonde Belgium **54** B2
Dengkou China **82** A1
Dengzhou China **82** B2
Den Haag Neth. *see* The Hague
Denham Austr. **114** A2
Den Helder Neth. **54** B1
Deniliquin Austr. **116** C3
Denio U.S.A. **132** C2
Denison *IA* U.S.A. **135** D2
Denison *TX* U.S.A. **141** E2
Denizli Turkey **65** C3
Denman Austr. **117** E2
Denmark Austr. **114** A3
Denmark *country* Europe **47** C4

Denmark Strait Greenland/Iceland
   125 K2
Denpasar Indon. **73** C2
Denton U.S.A. **141** E2
D'Entrecasteaux, Point *pt* Austr.
   114 A3
Denver U.S.A. **134** B3
Deogarh *Orissa* India **87** C2
Deogarh *Rajasthan* India **86** B2
Deoghar India **87** C2
Deputatskiy Rus. Fed. **95** L2
Dêqên China **74** A1
Dera Bugti Pak. **86** A2
Dera Ghazi Khan Pak. **86** B1
Dera Ismail Khan Pak. **86** B1
Derbent Rus. Fed. **41** D4
Derby Austr. **114** B1
Derby U.K. **52** C3
Dereham U.K. **53** D3
Derg, Lough *l.* Rep. of Ireland **51** B2
Derhachi Ukr. **45** E1
De Ridder U.S.A. **138** B2
Derkul *r.* Rus. Fed./Ukr. **45** E2
Dêrub China **87** B1
Derudeb Sudan **102** B3
De Rust S. Africa **108** B3
Derventa Bos.-Herz. **63** C2
Derwent *r.* U.K. **52** C3
Derwent Water *l.* U.K. **52** B2
Derzhavinsk Kazakh. **89** D1
Desaguadero *r.* Bol. **152** B2
Désappointement, Îles du *is*
   Fr. Polynesia **111**
Deschambault Lake Can. **127** E2
Deschutes *r.* U.S.A. **132** B1
Desē Eth. **103** B3
Deseado Arg. **153** B5
Deseado *r.* Arg. **153** B5
Des Moines U.S.A. **135** E2
Des Moines *r.* U.S.A. **135** E2
Desna *r.* Rus. Fed./Ukr. **45** D1
Desnogorsk Rus. Fed. **43** D3
Dessau Ger. **55** F2
Destruction Bay Can. **126** B1
Desventurados, Islas de los *is*
   S. Pacific Ocean **149**
Detah Can. **126** C1
Detmold Ger. **55** D2
Detroit U.S.A. **136** D2
Detroit Lakes U.S.A. **135** D1
Deurne Neth. **54** B2
Deva Romania **44** B2
Deventer Neth. **54** C1
Deveron *r.* U.K. **50** C2
Devět Skal *h.* Czech Rep. **57** D3
Devil's Lake U.S.A. **135** D1
Devil's Paw *mt.* U.S.A. **126** B2
Devizes U.K. **53** C4
Devli India **86** B2
Devnya Bulg. **64** C2
Devon Can. **126** D2
Devon Island Can. **125** F1
Devonport Austr. **115** D4
Dewas India **86** B2
Dexter U.S.A. **135** F3
Deyang China **82** A2
Deyong, Tanjung *pt* Indon. **71** D3
Dezfūl Iran **93** C2
Dezhou China **82** B2
Dhahran Saudi Arabia **91** C2
Dhaka Bangl. **87** D2
Dhamār Yemen **90** B3
Dhamtari India **87** C2
Dhanbad India **87** C2
Dhankuta Nepal **87** C2
Dharmanagar India **74** A1
Dharmjaygarh India **87** C2
Dharwad India **85** B3
Dhasa India **86** B2

hubāb Yemen 90 B3
hule India 86 B2
iablo, Picacho del *mt.* Mex. 142 A1
iamantina *watercourse* Austr.
115 C2
iamantina Brazil 155 D1
iamantina, Chapada *plat.* Brazil
151 E4
iamantina Brazil 151 D4
ianbai China 83 B3
ianópolis Brazil 151 E4
ianra Côte d'Ivoire 100 B4
iapaga Burkina 100 C3
ibā al Ḥiṣn U.A.E. 91 C2
ibaya Dem. Rep. Congo 104 C3
ibrugarh India 84 D2
ickinson U.S.A. 134 C1
ickson U.S.A. 138 C1
icle *r.* Turkey *see* Tigris
ie France 59 D3
iefenbaker, Lake Can. 127 E2
iéma Mali 100 B3
iên Châu Vietnam 74 B2
iepholz Ger. 55 D1
ieppe France 58 C2
iffa Niger 101 D3
igby Can. 129 D2
igne-les-Bains France 59 D3
igoin France 59 C2
igos Phil. 76 B3
igul *r.* Indon. 71 D3
jlah, Nahr *r.* Iraq/Syria 66
jon France 59 D2
khil Djibouti 103 C3
kili Turkey 65 C3
ksmuide Belgium 54 A2
kwa Nigeria 101 D3
ila Eth. 103 B4
ili East Timor 71 C3
illenburg Ger. 55 D2
illon U.S.A. 132 D1
ilolo Dem. Rep. Congo 104 C4
imapur India 74 A1
imashq Syria *see* Damascus
imboola Austr. 116 C3
mitrovgrad Bulg. 64 C2
mitrovgrad Rus. Fed. 41 D3
inagat *i.* Phil. 76 B2
inan France 58 B2
inant Belgium 54 B2
inar Turkey 92 B2
inaric Alps *mts*
Bos.-Herz./Croatia 36
indigul India 85 B3
indiza Moz. 109 D1
ingelstädt Ger. 55 E2
ingle Rep. of Ireland 51 A2
ingle Bay Rep. of Ireland 51 A2
ingwall U.K. 50 B2
ingxi China 82 A2
inkelsbühl Ger. 55 E3
inngyê China 87 C2
onísio Cerqueira Brazil 154 B3
ourbel Senegal 100 A3
polog Phil. 76 B3
r Pak. 86 B1
rection, Cape Austr. 115 D1
rê Dawa Eth. 103 C4
rk Hartog Island Austr. 114 A2
rranbandi Austr. 117 D1
rs Saudi Arabia 90 B3
sappointment, Cape S. Georgia
153 E6
sappointment, Lake *salt flat* Austr.
14 B2
scovery Bay Austr. 116 C3
smal Swamp U.S.A. 137 E3
ss U.K. 53 D3

Dittaino *r.* Italy 62 C3
Diu India 86 B2
Divinópolis Brazil 155 D2
Divnoye Rus. Fed. 41 D4
Divo Côte d'Ivoire 100 B4
Diyriği Turkey 92 B2
Dixon U.S.A. 136 C2
Dixon Entrance *sea chan.* Can./U.S.A.
126 B2
Diyarbakır Turkey 92 C2
Diz Pak. 86 A2
Djado Niger 101 D2
Djado, Plateau du Niger 101 D2
Djambala Congo 104 B3
Djanet Alg. 101 C2
Djelfa Alg. 100 C1
Djéma C.A.R. 105 C2
Djenné Mali 100 B3
Djibo Burkina 100 B3
Djibouti *country* Africa 103 C3
Djibouti Djibouti 103 C3
Djougou Benin 100 C4
Djúpivogur Iceland 46 [inset]
Dmitriyevka Rus. Fed. 43 F3
Dmitriyev-L'govskiy Rus. Fed. 43 E3
Dmitrov Rus. Fed. 43 E2
Dnepr *r.* Rus. Fed. *see* Dnieper
Dnieper *r.* Rus. Fed. 43 D3
Dnieper *r.* Ukr. 45 D3
Dniester *r.* Ukr. 44 C2
Dnipro *r.* Ukr. *see* Dnieper
Dniprodzerzhyns'k Ukr. 45 D2
Dnipropetrovs'k Ukr. 45 E2
Dniprorudne Ukr. 45 D2
Dnister *r.* Ukr. *see* Dniester
Dno Rus. Fed. 42 C2
Doba Chad 101 D4
Dobele Latvia 42 B2
Döbeln Ger. 55 F2
Doberai, Jazirah *pen.* Indon. 71 C3
Dobo Indon. 71 C3
Doboj Bos.-Herz. 63 C2
Dobrich Bulg. 64 C2
Dobrinka Rus. Fed. 43 F3
Dobroye Rus. Fed. 43 E3
Dobrush Belarus 43 D3
Doce *r.* Brazil 155 E1
Doctor Arroyo Mex. 143 D3
Doctor Belisario Domínguez Mex.
142 B2
Dodecanese *is* Greece 65 C3
Dodekanisos *is* Greece *see*
Dodecanese
Dodge City U.S.A. 134 C3
Dodoma Tanz. 105 D3
Doetinchem Neth. 54 C2
Dofa Indon. 71 C3
Dogai Coring *salt l.* China 87 C1
Dog Creek Can. 126 C2
Dōgo *i.* Japan 79 B3
Dogondoutchi Niger 100 C3
Doğubeyazıt Turkey 93 C2
Doha Qatar 91 C2
Doi Saket Thai. 74 A2
Dokkum Neth. 54 B1
Dokshytsy Belarus 42 C3
Dokuchayevs'k Ukr. 45 E2
Dolak, Pulau *i.* Indon. 71 D3
Dolbeau Can. 129 C2
Dol-de-Bretagne France 58 B2
Dole France 59 D2
Dolgellau U.K. 53 D3
Dolgorukovo Rus. Fed. 43 E3
Dolgoye Rus. Fed. 43 E3
Dolinsk Rus. Fed. 81 F1
Dolisie Congo *see* Loubomo
Dolomites *mts* Italy 62 B1
Dolo Odo Eth. 103 D3
Dolyna Ukr. 44 B2
Domažlice Czech Rep. 56 C3

Dombås Norway 47 B3
Dombóvár Hungary 57 D3
Dome Creek Can. 126 C2
Dominica *country* West Indies 145 D3
Dominican Republic *country*
West Indies 145 C3
Domodedovo Rus. Fed. 43 E2
Domokos Greece 65 B3
Dompu Indon. 73 C2
Don *r.* Rus. Fed. 43 E3
Don *r.* U.K. 50 C2
Donaghadee U.K. 51 D1
Donald Austr. 116 C3
Donau *r.* Austria/Ger. *see* Danube
Donauwörth Ger. 55 D3
Don Benito Spain 60 B2
Doncaster U.K. 52 C3
Dondo Angola 104 B3
Dondo Moz. 107 C5
Dondra Head Sri Lanka 85 C4
Donegal Rep. of Ireland 51 B1
Donegal Bay Rep. of Ireland 51 B1
Donets'k Ukr. 45 E2
Donets'kyy Kryazh *hills* Rus. Fed./Ukr.
45 E2
Dongara Austr. 114 A2
Dongchuan China 83 A3
Dongfang China 83 A4
Dongfanghong China 78 B1
Donggala Indon. 73 C2
Donggang China 77 A2
Dongguan China 83 B3
Đông Ha Vietnam 74 B2
Đông Hôi Vietnam 74 B2
Dongou Congo 104 B2
Dongshan China 83 B3
Dongsheng China *see* Ordos
Dongtai China 82 C2
Dongting Hu *l.* China 83 B3
Dongying China 82 B2
Donnellys Crossing N.Z. 118 B2
Donostia - San Sebastián Spain 61 C1
Dooxo Nugaaleed *val.* Somalia 103 C4
Dorchester U.K. 53 B4
Dordabis Namibia 108 A1
Dordogne *r.* France 58 C2
Dordrecht Neth. 54 B2
Dordrecht S. Africa 109 C3
Doré Lake Can. 127 E2
Dorfmark Ger. 55 D1
Dori Burkina 100 B3
Doring *r.* S. Africa 108 A3
Dormans France 54 A3
Dornoch U.K. 50 B2
Dornoch Firth *est.* U.K. 50 B2
Dorogobuzh Rus. Fed. 43 D3
Dorohoi Romania 44 C1
Döröö Nuur *salt l.* Mongolia 80 C1
Dorotea Sweden 46 D3
Dorre Island Austr. 114 A2
Dorrigo Austr. 117 E2
Dorsale Camerounaise *slope*
Cameroon/Nigeria 104 B2
Dortmund Ger. 54 C2
Dortmund-Ems-Kanal *canal* Ger.
54 C2
Dos Bahías, Cabo *c.* Arg. 153 B5
Dosse *r.* Ger. 55 F1
Dosso Niger 100 C3
Dothan U.S.A. 139 C2
Dötlingen Ger. 55 D1
Douai France 58 C1
Douala Cameroon 104 A2
Douarnenez France 58 B2
Doubtful Sound N.Z. 118 A4
Douentza Mali 100 B3
Douglas Isle of Man 52 A2
Douglas S. Africa 108 B2
Douglas *AK* U.S.A. 126 B2
Douglas *AZ* U.S.A. 140 C2

Douglas *GA* U.S.A. **139** D2
Douglas *WY* U.S.A. **134** B2
Doullens France **58** C1
Dourada, Serra *hills* Brazil **154** B1
Dourados Brazil **154** B2
Dourados, Serra dos *hills* Brazil
  154 B2
Douro *r.* Port. **60** B1
Dover U.K. **53** D4
Dover U.S.A. **137** E3
Dover, Strait of France/U.K. **49** D3
Dover-Foxcroft U.S.A. **137** G1
Dowlatābād *Būshehr* Iran **91** C2
Dowlatābād *Kermān* Iran **91** C2
Downpatrick U.K. **51** D1
Dowshī Afgh. **86** A1
Dōzen *is* Japan **79** B3
Dozois, Réservoir *resr* Can. **128** C2
Dracena Brazil **154** B2
Drachten Neth. **54** C1
Drăgănești-Olt Romania **44** B3
Drăgășani Romania **44** B3
Drahichyn Belarus **42** C3
Drakensberg *mts* Lesotho/S. Africa
  109 C2
Drakensberg *mts* S. Africa **109** C2
Drake Passage S. Atlantic Ocean
  119 L4
Drama Greece **65** B2
Drammen Norway **47** C4
Drau *r.* Austria **62** B1
Drava *r.* Europe **63** C1
Drayton Valley Can. **126** D2
Dreieich Ger. **55** D2
Drepano, Akra *pt* Greece **65** B3
Dresden Ger. **55** F2
Dreux France **58** C2
Driemond Neth. **54** B1
Drina *r.* Bos.-Herz./Serb. and Mont.
  63 C2
Drniš Croatia **63** C2
Drobeta - Turnu Severin Romania
  44 B3
Drochtersen Ger. **55** D1
Drogheda Rep. of Ireland **51** C2
Drohobych Ukr. **44** B2
Dromore U.K. **51** C1
Drosh Pak. **86** B1
Drouin Austr. **117** D3
Drumheller Can. **127** D2
Drummond Island U.S.A. **136** D1
Drummondville Can. **129** C2
Druskininkai Lith. **42** B3
Druzhkivka Ukr. **45** E2
Druzhnaya Gorka Rus. Fed. **42** C2
Dryden Can. **128** C2
Drysdale *r.* Austr. **114** B1
Ḑubā Saudi Arabia **90** A2
Dubai U.A.E. **91** C2
Dubawnt Lake Can. **127** E1
Dubayy U.A.E. *see* Dubai
Dubbagh, Jabal ad *mt.* Saudi Arabia
  90 A2
Dubbo Austr. **117** D2
Dublin Rep. of Ireland **51** C2
Dublin U.S.A. **139** D2
Dubno Ukr. **44** C1
Du Bois U.S.A. **137** E2
Dubréka Guinea **100** A4
Dubrovnik Croatia **63** C2
Dubrovtsya Ukr. **44** C1
Dubrowna Belarus **43** D3
Dubuque U.S.A. **135** E2
Ducie Island *atoll* Pitcairn Is **111**
Duck Bay Can. **127** E2
Ðưc Trong Vietnam **75** B2
Duderstadt Ger. **55** E2
Dudinka Rus. Fed. **94** H2
Dudley U.K. **53** B3
Duero *r.* Spain **60** B1

Duffreboy, Lac *l.* Can. **129** C1
Dufftown U.K. **50** C2
Dugi Rat Croatia **63** C2
Duisburg Ger. **54** C2
Duiwelskloof S. Africa **109** D1
Dukathole S. Africa **109** C3
Dukhān Qatar **91** C2
Dukhovshchina Rus. Fed. **43** D2
Dūkštas Lith. **42** C2
Dulan China **80** C2
Dulce *r.* Arg. **152** B4
Dülmen Ger. **54** C2
Dulovo Bulg. **64** C2
Duluth U.S.A. **135** E1
Dumaguete Phil. **76** B3
Dumai Indon. **72** B1
Dumaran *i.* Phil. **76** B2
Dumas *AR* U.S.A. **138** B2
Dumas *TX* U.S.A. **141** D1
Dumbarton U.K. **50** B3
Dumayr Egypt **102** B1
Duna *r.* Hungary *see* Danube
Dunakeszi Hungary **57** D3
Dunărea *r.* Romania *see* Danube
Dunaújváros Hungary **57** D3
Dunayivtsi Ukr. **44** C2
Dunbar U.K. **50** C2
Dunbeath U.K. **50** C1
Duncan Can. **126** C3
Duncan U.S.A. **141** E2
Duncansby Head U.K. **50** C1
Dundalk Rep. of Ireland **51** C1
Dundalk Bay Rep. of Ireland **51** C2
Dundas Greenland **125** H1
Dundee S. Africa **109** D2
Dundee U.K. **50** C2
Dundrum Bay U.K. **51** D1
Dunedin N.Z. **118** B4
Dunfermline U.K. **50** C2
Dungannon U.K. **51** C1
Dungarpur India **86** B2
Dungarvan Rep. of Ireland **51** C2
Dungeness *hd* U.K. **53** D4
Dungiven U.K. **51** C1
Dungog Austr. **117** E2
Dungu Dem. Rep. Congo **105** C2
Dungun Malaysia **72** B1
Dungunab Sudan **102** B2
Dunhua China **77** B1
Dunhuang China **80** C2
Dunkerque France *see* Dunkirk
Dunkirk France **58** C1
Dunkirk U.S.A. **137** E2
Dún Laoghaire Rep. of Ireland **51** C2
Dunmurry U.K. **51** D1
Dunnet Head U.K. **50** C1
Duns U.K. **50** C3
Dunstable U.K. **53** C4
Dupnitsa Bulg. **64** B2
Dupree U.S.A. **134** C1
Durack *r.* Austr. **114** B1
Durango Mex. **142** B2
Durango Spain **60** C1
Durango U.S.A. **134** B3
Durant U.S.A. **141** E2
Durazno Uru. **153** C4
Durban S. Africa **109** D2
Durban-Corbières France **58** C3
Durbanville S. Africa **108** A3
Durbuy Belgium **54** B2
Düren Ger. **54** C2
Durg India **87** C2
Durham U.K. **52** C2
Durham U.S.A. **139** E1
Duri Indon. **72** B1
Durmitor *mt.* Serb. and Mont. **64** A2
Durness U.K. **50** B1
Durrës Albania **65** A2

Dursey Island Rep. of Ireland **51** A3
Dursunbey Turkey **65** C3
D'Urville, Tanjung *pt* Indon. **71** D3
D'Urville Island N.Z. **118** B3
Dushan China **83** A3
Dushanbe Tajik. **89** D3
Düsseldorf Ger. **54** C2
Duyun China **83** A3
Dvorichna Ukr. **45** E2
Dwarka India **86** A2
Dwarsberg S. Africa **109** C1
Dworshak Reservoir U.S.A. **132** C1
Dyat'kovo Rus. Fed. **43** D3
Dyce U.K. **50** C2
Dyer, Cape Can. **125** H2
Dyersburg U.S.A. **138** C1
Dyfrdwy *r.* England/Wales U.K. *see* Dee
Dyje *r.* Austria/Czech Rep. **57** D3
Dylewska Góra *h.* Pol. **57** D2
Dymytrov Ukr. **45** E2
Dyoki S. Africa **109** C3
Dyurtyuli Rus. Fed. **41** E3
Dzamīn Üüd Mongolia **81** D2
Dzaoudzi Mayotte **107** D1
Dzhanga Turkm. **93** D1
Dzhangala Kazakh. **88** C2
Dzhankoy Ukr. **45** D2
Dzhizak Uzbek. *see* Jizzax
Dzhubga Rus. Fed. **45** E3
Dzhugdzhur, Khrebet *mts* Rus. Fed.
  95 L3
Dzhungarskiy Alatau, Khrebet *mts*
  China/Kazakh. **89** E2
Dzhusaly Kazakh. **88** D2
Działdowo Pol. **57** E2
Dzuunmod Mongolia **80** D1
Dzyarzhynsk Belarus **42** C3
Dzyatlavichy Belarus **42** C3

E

Eagle *r.* Can. **129** E1
Eagle Cap *mt.* U.S.A. **132** C1
Eagle Lake Can. **128** A2
Eagle Lake U.S.A. **132** B2
Eagle Pass U.S.A. **141** D3
Eagle Plain Can. **124** C2
Ear Falls Can. **128** A1
East Antarctica *reg.* Antarctica **119** F1
Eastbourne U.K. **53** D4
East China Sea N. Pacific Ocean **81** E3
East Coast Bays N.Z. **118** B2
Eastend Can. **132** E1
Eastern Cape *prov.* S. Africa **109** C3
Eastern Desert Egypt **102** B2
Eastern Ghats *mts* India **85** B3
Easterville Can. **127** F2
East Falkland *i.* Falkland Is **153** C6
East Frisian Islands Ger. **54** C1
East Kilbride U.K. **50** B3
Eastleigh U.K. **53** C4
East Liverpool U.S.A. **137** D2
East London S. Africa **109** C3
Eastmain Can. **128** C1
Eastmain *r.* Can. **128** C1
Eastman U.S.A. **139** D2
East Sea N. Pacific Ocean *see*
  Japan, Sea of
East Siberian Sea Rus. Fed. **95** L2
East St Louis U.S.A. **136** B3
East Timor *country* Asia **69**
Eau Claire U.S.A. **136** B2
Eau Claire, Lac à l' *l.* Can. **128** C1
Eauripik *atoll* Micronesia **71** D2
Ebano Mex. **143** C2
Ebbw Vale U.K. **53** B4
Eberswalde-Finow Ger. **55** F1
Eboli Italy **62** C2

Ebolowa Cameroon 104 B2
Ebro r. Spain 61 D1
Ech Chélif Alg. 100 C1
Echeverria, Pico mt. Mex. 142 A2
Echoing r. Can. 127 F2
Echternach Lux. 54 C3
Echuca Austr. 116 C3
Écija Spain 60 B2
Eckernförde Ger. 56 B2
Ecuador country S. America 150 B3
Ed Eritrea 102 C3
Ed Da'ein Sudan 103 A3
Ed Damazin Sudan 103 B3
Ed Damer Sudan 102 B3
Ed Debba Sudan 102 B3
Ed Dueim Sudan 102 B3
Eddystone Point pt Austr. 115 D4
Ede Neth. 54 B1
Edéa Cameroon 104 B2
Edéia Brazil 154 C1
Eden Austr. 117 D3
Eden r. U.K. 52 B2
Edenburg S. Africa 109 C2
Edenderry Rep. of Ireland 51 C2
Edenhope Austr. 116 C3
Edessa Greece 65 B2
Edgeøya i. Svalbard 94 D1
Edinburg U.S.A. 141 E3
Edinburgh U.K. 50 C3
Edirne Turkey 64 C2
Edmonton Can. 126 D2
Edmundston Can. 137 G1
Edremit Turkey 65 C3
Edremit Körfezi b. Turkey 65 C3
Edson Can. 126 D2
Edward, Lake
   Dem. Rep. Congo/Uganda 105 C3
Edward's Creek Austr. 116 B3
Edwards Plateau U.S.A. 141 D2
Eenrum Neth. 54 C1
Éfaté i. Vanuatu 110
Effingham U.S.A. 136 C3
Egan Range mts U.S.A. 133 D3
Eger Hungary 57 E3
Egersund Norway 47 B4
Egilsstaðir Iceland 46 [inset]
Eğirdir Turkey 92 B2
Eğirdir Gölü l. Turkey 92 B2
Égletons France 58 C2
Egvekinot Rus. Fed. 95 O2
Egypt country Africa 102 A2
Ehen Hudag China 82 A2
Eibergen Neth. 54 C1
Eifel hills Ger. 54 C2
Eigg i. U.K. 50 A2
Eight Degree Channel India/Maldives
   85 B4
Eighty Mile Beach Austr. 114 B1
Eilat Israel 92 B3
Eilenburg Ger. 55 F2
Einbeck Ger. 55 D2
Eindhoven Neth. 54 B2
Eirunepé Brazil 150 C3
Eiseb watercourse Namibia 106 B1
Eisenach Ger. 55 E2
Eisenhüttenstadt Ger. 56 C2
Eisenstadt Austria 57 H3
Eisleben Lutherstadt Ger. 55 E2
Eivissa Spain 61 D2
Eivissa i. Spain see Ibiza
Ejea de los Caballeros Spain 61 C1
Ejeda Madag. 107 [inset] D2
Ekenäs Fin. 47 E4
Ekibastuz Kazakh. 89 E1
Ekostrovskaya Imandra, Ozero l.
   Rus. Fed. 46 G2
Eksjö Sweden 47 C4
Eksteenfontein S. Africa 108 A2
Ekwan r. Can. 128 B1
Ela Myanmar 74 A2

Elandsdoorn S. Africa 109 C2
Elassona Greece 65 B3
Elazığ Turkey 92 B2
Elba, Isola d' i. Italy 62 B2
El Banco Col. 150 B2
Elbasan Albania 65 B2
El Baúl Venez. 150 C2
El Bayadh Alg. 100 C1
Elbe r. Ger. 55 D1
Elbert, Mount U.S.A. 134 B3
Elberton U.S.A. 139 D2
Elbeuf France 58 C2
Elbistan Turkey 92 B2
Elbląg Pol. 57 D2
El'brus mt. Rus. Fed. 41 D4
Elburz Mountains Iran 93 C2
El Callao Venez. 150 C2
El Campo U.S.A. 141 E3
El Centro U.S.A. 133 C4
El Cerro Bol. 152 B2
Elche-Elx Spain 61 C2
Elda Spain 61 C2
Eldon U.S.A. 135 E3
Eldorado Arg. 154 B3
El Dorado AR U.S.A. 138 B2
El Dorado KS U.S.A. 135 D3
El Eglab plat. Alg. 100 B2
El Ejido Spain 60 C2
Elektrostal' Rus. Fed. 43 E2
El Encanto Col. 150 B3
El Eulma Alg. 61 E2
Eleuthera i. Bahamas 145 C2
El Fasher Sudan 103 A3
El Fuerte Mex. 142 B2
El Geneina Sudan 103 A3
El Geteina Sudan 102 B3
Elgin U.K. 50 C2
Elgin U.S.A. 136 C2
El Goléa Alg. 100 C1
El Golfo de Santa Clara Mex. 142 A1
Elgon, Mount Uganda 105 D2
El Ḥammâmi reg. Maur. 100 A2
El Hierro i. Canary Is 100 A3
El Higo Mex. 143 C2
El Homr Alg. 100 C2
Elim U.S.A. 124 B2
Elista Rus. Fed. 41 D4
Elizabeth U.S.A. 137 F2
Elizabeth City U.S.A. 139 E1
Elizabethtown U.S.A. 136 C3
El Jadida Morocco 100 B1
Ełk Pol. 57 E2
Elk City U.S.A. 141 E1
Elkford Can. 126 D2
Elkhart U.S.A. 136 C2
Elkhovo Bulg. 64 C2
Elkins U.S.A. 137 E3
Elko Can. 126 D3
Elko U.S.A. 132 C2
Elk Point Can. 127 D2
Ellef Ringnes Island Can. 124 F1
Ellendale U.S.A. 135 D1
Ellensburg U.S.A. 132 B1
Ellesmere, Lake N.Z. 118 B3
Ellesmere Island Can. 125 G1
Ellesmere Port U.K. 52 B3
Ellice r. Can. 124 F2
Elliotdale S. Africa 109 C3
Ellon U.K. 50 C2
Ellsworth U.S.A. 137 G2
Ellsworth Mountains Antarctica
   119 K2
Elmalı Turkey 65 C3
El Meghaïer Alg. 100 C1
El Milia Alg. 61 E2
Elmira U.S.A. 137 E2
El Moral Spain 61 C2
Elmshorn Ger. 55 D1
El Muglad Sudan 103 A3

El Nido Phil. 76 A2
El Obeid Sudan 103 B3
El Oro Mex. 142 B2
El Oued Alg. 101 C1
Eloy U.S.A. 140 B3
El Paso U.S.A. 140 C2
El Porvenir Mex. 142 B1
El Prat de Llobregat Spain 61 D1
El Progreso Hond. 143 D3
El Reno U.S.A. 141 E1
Elsa Can. 126 B1
El Salado Mex. 143 B2
El Salto Mex. 142 B2
El Salvador country Central America
   144 B3
El Salvador Mex. 143 B2
El Sauz Mex. 140 C3
El Socorro Mex. 142 A1
Elsterwerda Ger. 55 F2
El Temascal Mex. 143 C2
El Tigre Venez. 150 C2
El Tocuyo Venez. 145 D4
Elva Estonia 42 C2
Elvas Port. 60 B2
Elverum Norway 47 C3
El Wak Kenya 105 E2
Ely U.K. 53 D3
Ely MN U.S.A. 135 E1
Ely NV U.S.A. 133 D3
Emämrüd Iran 93 D2
Emån r. Sweden 47 D4
Emba Kazakh. 88 C2
Emba r. Kazakh. 88 C2
Embalenhle S. Africa 109 C2
Emborção, Represa de resr Brazil
   154 C1
Embu Kenya 105 D3
Emden Ger. 54 C1
Emerald Austr. 115 D3
Emerson Can. 127 F3
Emet Turkey 65 C3
eMgwenya S. Africa 109 D2
eMijindini S. Africa 109 D2
Emi Koussi mt. Chad 101 D3
Emine, Nos pt Bulg. 64 C2
Emirdağ Turkey 92 B2
Emmaste Estonia 42 B2
Emmeloord Neth. 54 B1
Emmelshausen Ger. 54 C2
Emmen Neth. 54 C1
Emory Peak U.S.A. 141 D3
Empalme Mex. 142 A2
Empangeni S. Africa 109 D2
Empoli Italy 62 B2
Emporia KS U.S.A. 135 D3
Emporia VA U.S.A. 137 E3
Ems r. Ger. 55 C1
Emsdetten Ger. 54 C1
Emzinoni S. Africa 109 C2
Enarotali Indon. 71 D3
Encarnación Mex. 142 B2
Encarnación Para. 152 C3
Encruzilhada Brazil 155 D1
Ende Indon. 73 D2
Endicott Mountains U.S.A. 124 C2
Enerhodar Ukr. 45 D2
Engel's Rus. Fed. 41 D3
Enggano i. Indon. 72 B2
England admin. div. U.K. 52 C3
English r. Can. 128 A1
English Channel France/U.K. 53 C5
Enid U.S.A. 141 E1
Enkhuizen Neth. 54 B1
Enköping Sweden 47 D4
Enna Italy 62 B3
Ennadai Lake Can. 127 E1
Ennedi, Massif mts Chad 101 E3
Enngonia Austr. 117 D1
Ennis Rep. of Ireland 51 B2

Ghazaouet Alg. **61** C2
Ghaziabad India **87** B2
Ghazipur India **87** C2
Ghazni Afgh. **86** A1
Ghent Belgium **54** A2
Gherla Romania **44** B2
Ghisonaccia France **59** D3
Ghotaru India **86** B2
Ghotki Pak. **86** A2
Giaginskaya Rus. Fed. **45** F3
Giant's Causeway *lava field* U.K. **51** C1
Gianyar Indon. **73** C2
Giarre Italy **62** C3
Giaveno Italy **62** A1
Gibeon Namibia **108** A2
Gibraltar Gibraltar **60** B2
Gibraltar, Strait of Morocco/Spain **60** B2
Gibson Desert Austr. **114** B2
Gichgeniyn Nuruu *mts* Mongolia **80** C1
Gidolē Eth. **103** B4
Gien France **58** C2
Gießen Ger. **55** D2
Gifhorn Ger. **55** E1
Gift Lake Can. **126** D2
Gifu Japan **79** C3
Gigha *i.* U.K. **50** B3
Gijón-Xixón Spain **60** B1
Gila *r.* U.S.A. **140** B2
Gila Bend U.S.A. **140** B2
Gilbert *r.* Austr. **115** D1
Gilbert Islands Kiribati **110**
Gildford U.S.A. **132** D1
Gilgandra Austr. **117** D2
Gilgit Jammu and Kashmir **86** B1
Gilgit *r.* Jammu and Kashmir **86** B1
Gilgunnia Austr. **117** D2
Gillam Can. **127** F2
Gillette U.S.A. **134** B2
Gillingham U.K. **53** D4
Gilmour Island Can. **128** C1
Gimli Can. **127** F2
Gīnīr Eth. **103** C4
Ginosa Italy **63** C2
Gippsland *reg.* Austr. **117** D3
Girdar Dhor *r.* Pak. **86** A2
Girdi Iran **91** D1
Giresun Turkey **92** B1
Girona Spain **61** D1
Girvan U.K. **50** B3
Gisborne N.Z. **118** C2
Gislaved Sweden **47** C4
Gitarama Rwanda **105** C3
Giulianova Italy **62** B2
Giurgiu Romania **44** C3
Giuvala, Pasul *pass* Romania **44** C2
Givors France **59** C2
Giyani S. Africa **109** D1
Giza Egypt **102** B2
Gjirokastër Albania **65** B2
Gjoa Haven Can. **124** F2
Gjøvik Norway **47** C3
Glace Bay Can. **129** E2
Glacier Peak *vol.* U.S.A. **132** B1
Gladstone Austr. **115** E2
Gláma *mts* Iceland **46** [inset]
Glamoč Bos.-Herz. **63** C2
Glan *r.* Ger. **54** C3
Glanaruddery Mountains
    Rep. of Ireland **51** B2
Glasgow U.K. **50** B3
Glasgow *KY* U.S.A. **136** C3
Glasgow *MT* U.S.A. **132** E1
Glastonbury U.K. **53** B4
Glauchau Ger. **55** F2
Glazov Rus. Fed. **40** F3
Glazunovka Rus. Fed. **43** E3
Glen Coe *val.* U.K. **50** B2
Glendale U.S.A. **140** B2

Glen Davis Austr. **117** E2
Glendive U.S.A. **134** C1
Glenelg *r.* Austr. **116** C3
Glen Innes Austr. **117** E1
Glenmorgan Austr. **117** D1
Glennallen U.S.A. **124** C2
Glenrothes U.K. **50** C2
Glens Falls U.S.A. **137** F2
Glen Shee *val.* U.K. **50** C2
Glenties Rep. of Ireland **51** B1
Glenwood U.S.A. **140** C2
Glenwood Springs U.S.A. **134** B3
Gliwice Pol. **57** D2
Globe U.S.A. **140** B2
Głogów Pol. **57** D2
Glomfjord Norway **46** C2
Glomma *r.* Norway **47** C4
Gloucester Austr. **117** E2
Gloucester U.K. **53** B4
Glöwen Ger. **55** F1
Glubokoye Kazakh. **89** F1
Glückstadt Ger. **55** D1
Gmünd Austria **56** C3
Gmunden Austria **56** C3
Gnarrenburg Ger. **55** D1
Gniezno Pol. **57** D2
Gnjilane Serb. and Mont. **64** B2
Goalpara India **87** D2
Goat Fell *h.* U.K. **50** B3
Goba Eth. **103** C4
Gobabis Namibia **108** A1
Gobernador Gregores Arg. **153** A5
Gobi *des.* China/Mongolia **82** A1
Goch Ger. **54** C2
Gochas Namibia **108** A1
Godavari *r.* India **85** C3
Goderich Can. **128** B2
Godhra India **86** B2
Gods *r.* Can. **127** F2
Gods Lake Can. **127** F2
Godthåb Greenland *see* Nuuk
Godwin Austen *mt.*
    China/Jammu and Kashmir *see* K2
Goéland, Lac au *l.* Can. **128** C2
Goélands, Lac aux *l.* Can. **129** D1
Goes Neth. **54** A2
Goiandira Brazil **154** C1
Goiânia Brazil **154** C1
Goiás Brazil **154** B1
Goio-Erê Brazil **154** B2
Gökçeada *i.* Turkey **65** C2
Gökçedağ Turkey **65** C3
Gokwe Zimbabwe **107** B1
Gol Norway **47** B3
Golaghat India **74** A1
Gol'chikha Rus. Fed. **40** H1
Gölcük Turkey **65** C2
Gołdap Pol. **57** E2
Goldberg Ger. **55** F1
Gold Coast Austr. **117** E1
Gold Coast *coastal area* Ghana **100** B4
Golden Can. **126** D2
Golden Bay N.Z. **118** B3
Golden Hinde *mt.* Can. **126** C3
Golden Vale *lowland* Rep. of Ireland **51** B2
Goldfield U.S.A. **133** C3
Gold River Can. **126** C3
Goldsboro U.S.A. **139** E1
Goleta U.S.A. **133** C4
Golmud China **80** C2
Golpāyegān Iran **93** D2
Golspie U.K. **50** C2
Goma Dem. Rep. Congo **105** C3
Gomati *r.* India **87** C2
Gombe Nigeria **101** D3
Gombi Nigeria **101** D3
Gómez Palacio Mex. **142** B2
Gonaïves Haiti **145** C3
Gonâve, Île de la *i.* Haiti **145** C3

Gonbad-e Kavus Iran **93** D2
Gonder Eth. **103** B3
Gondia India **87** C2
Gönen Turkey **65** C2
Gongola *r.* Nigeria **101** D4
Gongolgon Austr. **117** D2
Gongzhuling China **77** A1
Gonzáles Mex. **143** C2
Gonzales U.S.A. **141** E3
Good Hope, Cape of S. Africa **108** A3▮
Gooding U.S.A. **132** D2
Goodland U.S.A. **134** C3
Goodooga Austr. **117** D1
Goole U.K. **52** C3
Goolgowi Austr. **117** D2
Goolwa Austr. **116** B3
Goondiwindi Austr. **117** E1
Goose Lake U.S.A. **132** B2
Göppingen Ger. **56** B3
Gorakhpur India **87** C2
Goražde Bos.-Herz. **63** C2
Gördes Turkey **65** C3
Gordeyevka Rus. Fed. **43** D3
Goré Chad **101** D4
Gorē Eth. **103** B4
Gore N.Z. **118** A4
Gorey Rep. of Ireland **51** C2
Gorgān Iran **93** D2
Gori Georgia **93** C1
Gorizia Italy **62** B1
Gorlice Pol. **57** E3
Görlitz Ger. **56** C2
Gornji Milanovac Serb. and Mont. **64** B2
Gornji Vakuf Bos.-Herz. **63** C2
Gorno-Altaysk Rus. Fed. **89** F1
Gornotrakiyska Nizina *lowland* Bulg. **64** C2
Gornyak Rus. Fed. **89** F1
Goroka P.N.G. **71** D3
Gorokhovets Rus. Fed. **43** F2
Gorom Gorom Burkina **100** B3
Gorontalo Indon. **73** D1
Gorshechnoye Rus. Fed. **43** E3
Gorumna Island Rep. of Ireland **51** B2▮
Goryachiy Klyuch Rus. Fed. **45** E3
Gorzów Wielkopolski Pol. **56** D2
Gosford Austr. **117** E2
Goshogawara Japan **78** D2
Goslar Ger. **55** E2
Gospić Croatia **62** C2
Gostivar Macedonia **64** B2
Göteborg Sweden *see* Gothenburg
Gotha Ger. **55** E2
Gothenburg Sweden **47** C4
Gothenburg U.S.A. **134** C2
Gotland *i.* Sweden **47** D4
Gotse Delchev Bulg. **65** B2
Gotska Sandön *i.* Sweden **47** D4
Gōtsu Japan **79** B4
Göttingen Ger. **55** D2
Gouda Neth. **54** B1
Goudiri Senegal **100** A3
Goudoumaria Niger **101** D3
Gouin, Réservoir *resr* Can. **128** C2
Goulburn Austr. **117** D2
Goulburn *r.* N.S.W. Austr. **117** D2
Goulburn *r.* Vic. Austr. **117** C3
Goundam Mali **100** B3
Gouraya Alg. **61** D2
Gourdon France **58** C3
Gouré Niger **101** D3
Gourits *r.* S. Africa **108** B3
Gourma-Rharous Mali **100** B3
Gourock Range *mts* Austr. **117** D3
Governador Valadares Brazil **155** D1
Governor's Harbour Bahamas **139** E3▮
Govi Altayn Nuruu *mts* Mongolia **80** C▮

192

Guadalope r. Spain **61** C1
Guadalquivir r. Spain **60** B2
Guadalupe i. Mex. **130** B4
Guadalupe, Sierra de mts Spain **60** B2
Guadalupe Peak U.S.A. **140** D2
Guadalupe Victoria Mex. **142** B2
Guadalupe y Calvo Mex. **142** B2
Guadarrama, Sierra de mts Spain **60** C1
Guadeloupe terr. West Indies **145** D3
Guadiana r. Port./Spain **60** B2
Guadix Spain **60** C2
Guaíra Brazil **154** B2
Guajira, Península de la pen. Col. **145** C3
Gualaceo Ecuador **150** B3
Guam terr. N. Pacific Ocean **71** D2
Guamúchil Mex. **142** B2
Guanacevi Mex. **142** B2
Guanambi Brazil **151** E4
Guanare Venez. **150** C2
Guane Cuba **144** B2
Guang'an China **83** A2
Guangchang China **83** B3
Guangdong prov. China **83** B3
Guangxi Zhuangzu Zizhiqu aut. reg. China **83** A3
Guangyuan China **82** A2
Guangzhou China **83** B3
Guanhães Brazil **155** D1
Guanipa r. Venez. **145** D4
Guanling China **83** A3
Guanshui China **77** A1
Guantánamo Cuba **145** C2
Guaporé r. Bol./Brazil **152** B2
Guarapuava Brazil **154** B3
Guaraqueçaba Brazil **154** C3
Guaratinguetá Brazil **155** C2
Guarda Port. **60** B1
Guarda Mor Brazil **154** C1
Guardo Spain **60** C1
Guarujá Brazil **155** C2
Guasave Mex. **142** B2
Guatemala country Central America **144** A3
Guatemala City Guat. **144** A3
Guaviare r. Col. **150** C2
Guaxupé Brazil **155** C2
Guayaquil Ecuador **150** B3
Guayaquil, Golfo de g. Ecuador **146**
Guayaramerín Bol. **152** B2
Guaymas Mex. **142** A2
Guba Eth. **103** B3
Guba Dolgaya Rus. Fed. **40** E1
Gubbio Italy **59** E3
Gubkin Rus. Fed. **43** E3
Guelma Alg. **101** C1
Guelmine Morocco **100** A2
Guelph Can. **128** B2
Guémez Mex. **143** C2
Guénange France **54** C3
Guéret France **58** C2
Guernsey i. Channel Is **53** B5
Guerrero Negro Mex. **142** A2
Guers, Lac l. Can. **129** D1
Guiana Highlands mts Guyana/Venez. **150** C2
Guider Cameroon **104** B2
Guidonia-Montecelio Italy **62** B2
Guigang China **83** A3
Guignicourt France **54** A3
Guija Moz. **109** D1
Guildford U.K. **53** C4
Guilin China **83** B3
Guillaume-Delisle, Lac l. Can. **128** C1
Guimarães Port. **60** B1
Guinea country Africa **100** A3
Guinea, Gulf of Africa **100** C4
Guinea-Bissau country Africa **100** A3
Guingamp France **58** B2

Guipavas France **58** B2
Guiratinga Brazil **154** B1
Güiria Venez. **150** C1
Guise France **54** A3
Guiuan Phil. **76** B2
Guiyang China **83** A3
Guizhou prov. China **83** A3
Gujranwala Pak. **86** B1
Gujrat Pak. **86** B1
Gukovo Rus. Fed. **45** E2
Gulang China **82** A2
Gulbarga India **85** B3
Gulbene Latvia **42** C2
Gulfport U.S.A. **138** C2
Gulian China **81** E1
Guliston Uzbek. **89** D2
Gul'kevichi Rus. Fed. **45** F2
Gull Lake Can. **127** E2
Güllük Turkey **65** C3
Gulu Uganda **105** D2
Gumare Botswana **106** B1
Gumdag Turkm. **88** C3
Gumla India **87** C2
Gummersbach Ger. **54** C2
Guna India **86** B2
Gundagai Austr. **117** D3
Güney Turkey **65** C3
Gungu Dem. Rep. Congo **104** B3
Gunisao r. Can. **127** F2
Gunnedah Austr. **117** E2
Gunnison CO U.S.A. **134** B3
Gunnison UT U.S.A. **133** D3
Gunnison r. U.S.A. **134** B3
Guntakal India **85** B3
Gunungsitoli Indon. **72** A1
Gunungtua Indon. **72** A1
Günzburg Ger. **56** C3
Gunzenhausen Ger. **55** E3
Guojiaba China **82** B2
Gurgaon India **86** B2
Gurgueia r. Brazil **151** E3
Guri, Embalse de resr Venez. **150** C2
Gurinhatã Brazil **154** C1
Gurupi r. Brazil **151** E3
Guru Sikhar mt. India **86** B2
Gusau Nigeria **101** C3
Gushan China **77** A2
Gushgy Turkm. **86** A1
Gushi China **82** B2
Gusinoozersk Rus. Fed. **95** J3
Gus'-Khrustal'nyy Rus. Fed. **43** F2
Guspini Italy **62** A3
Gustavus U.S.A. **126** B2
Güstrow Ger. **55** F1
Gütersloh Ger. **55** D2
Gutu Zimbabwe **107** C1
Guwahati India **87** D2
Guyana country S. America **150** D2
Guymon U.S.A. **141** D1
Guyra Austr. **117** E2
Guyuan China **82** A2
Guzmán Mex. **142** B1
Guzmán, Lago de l. Mex. **142** B1
Gwadar Pak. **86** A2
Gwalior India **87** B2
Gwanda Zimbabwe **107** B2
Gwardafuy, Gees c. Somalia **103** D3
Gweebarra Bay Rep. of Ireland **51** B1
Gweedore Rep. of Ireland **51** B1
Gweru Zimbabwe **107** B1
Gwoza Nigeria **101** D3
Gwydir r. Austr. **117** E2
Gyangzê China **74** A1
Gyaring Co l. China **87** C1
Gyaring Hu l. China **80** C2
Gydan Peninsula Rus. Fed. **40** G1
Gydanskiy Poluostrov pen. Rus. Fed. see Gydan Peninsula
Gyigang China **74** A1

Gympie Austr. **115** E2
Gyöngyös Hungary **57** D3
Győr Hungary **57** D3
Gypsumville Can. **127** F2
Gyrfalcon Islands Can. **129** D1
Gyula Hungary **57** E3
Gyumri Armenia **93** C1
Gyzylarbat Turkm. **88** C3

H

Haapsalu Estonia **42** B2
Haarlem Neth. **54** B1
Haarstrang ridge Ger. **55** C2
Haast N.Z. **118** A3
Habbān Yemen **90** B3
Ḩabbānīyah, Hawr al l. Iraq **93** C2
Hachijō-jima i. Japan **79** C4
Hachinohe Japan **78** D2
Hacufera Moz. **107** C2
Ḩadd, Ra's al pt Oman **91** C2
Haddington U.K. **50** C3
Hadejia Nigeria **101** D3
Haderslev Denmark **47** B4
Hadyach Ukr. **45** D1
Haeju N. Korea **77** B2
Haeju-man b. N. Korea **77** B2
Haenam S. Korea **77** B3
Ḩafar al Bāṭin Saudi Arabia **90** B2
Haflong India **74** A1
Hafnarfjörður Iceland **46** [inset]
Hagar Nish Plateau Eritrea **90** A3
Hagåtña Guam **71** D2
Hagen Ger. **54** C2
Hagenow Ger. **55** E1
Hagensborg Can. **126** C2
Hagerstown U.S.A. **137** E3
Hagfors Sweden **47** C3
Hagi Japan **79** B4
Ha Giang Vietnam **74** B1
Hag's Head Rep. of Ireland **51** B2
Hague, Cap de la c. France **58** B2
Hai Tanz. **105** D3
Haicheng China **77** A1
Hai Dương Vietnam **74** B1
Haifa Israel **92** B2
Haifeng China **83** B3
Haikou China **83** B3
Ḩā'il Saudi Arabia **90** B2
Hailar China see Hulun Buir
Hailuoto i. Fin. **46** E2
Hainan i. China **81** D3
Hainan prov. China **83** A4
Haines U.S.A. **126** B2
Haines Junction Can. **126** B1
Hainich ridge Ger. **55** E2
Hainleite ridge Ger. **55** E2
Hai Phong Vietnam **74** B1
Haiti country West Indies **145** C3
Haiya Sudan **102** B3
Hajdúböszörmény Hungary **57** E3
Ḩajhir mt. Yemen **91** C3
Ḩajjah Yemen **90** B3
Ḩājjīābād Iran **93** D3
Hajma' Oman **91** C3
Haka Myanmar **74** A1
Hakkâri Turkey **93** C2
Hakodate Japan **78** D2
Ḩalab Syria see Aleppo
Ḩalabān Saudi Arabia **90** B2
Halabja Iraq **93** C2
Halaib Sudan **102** B2
Ḩalāniyāt, Juzur al is Oman **91** C3
Ḩālat 'Ammār Saudi Arabia **90** A2
Halban Mongolia **80** C1
Halberstadt Ger. **55** E2
Halcon, Mount Phil. **76** B2
Halden Norway **47** C4

Hegang China **81** E1
Heide Ger. **56** B2
Heide Namibia **108** A1
Heidelberg Ger. **55** D3
Heidelberg S. Africa **108** B3
Heilbronn Ger. **55** D3
Heilongjiang *prov.* China **78** B1
Heilong Jiang *r.* China **81** E1
Heinola Fin. **47** F3
Helagsfjället *mt.* Sweden **46** C3
Helena *AR* U.S.A. **138** B2
Helena *MT* U.S.A. **132** D1
Helensburgh U.K. **50** B2
Helgoland *i.* Ger. **56** B2
Helgoländer Bucht *g.* Ger. **56** B2
Hella Iceland **46** [inset]
Hellevoetsluis Neth. **54** B2
Hellín Spain **61** C2
Helmand *r.* Afgh. **86** A1
Helmbrechts Ger. **55** E2
Helmeringhausen Namibia **108** A2
Helmond Neth. **54** B2
Helmsdale U.K. **50** C1
Helmsdale *r.* U.K. **50** C1
Helmstedt Ger. **55** E1
Helong China **77** B1
Helsingborg Sweden **47** C4
Helsingfors Fin. *see* Helsinki
Helsingør Denmark **47** C4
Helsinki Fin. **47** E3
Helvick Head Rep. of Ireland **51** C2
Hemel Hempstead U.K. **53** C4
Hemmoor Ger. **55** D1
Hemnesberget Norway **46** C2
Henan *prov.* China **82** B2
Henderson *KY* U.S.A. **136** C3
Henderson *NC* U.S.A. **139** E1
Henderson *NV* U.S.A. **133** D3
Henderson *TX* U.S.A. **141** F2
Hendersonville U.S.A. **139** D1
Hendon U.K. **53** C4
Hengduan Shan *mts* China **74** A1
Hengelo Neth. **54** C1
Hengshui China **82** B2
Hengxian China **83** A3
Hengyang China **83** B3
Heniches'k Ukr. **45** D2
Hennef (Sieg) Ger. **54** C2
Henrietta Maria, Cape Can. **128** B1
Henryetta U.S.A. **141** E1
Henry Kater, Cape Can. **125** H2
Henstedt-Ulzburg Ger. **55** D1
Hentiesbaai Namibia **106** A2
Hepu China **83** A3
Herät Afgh. **86** A1
Herbert Can. **127** E2
Herbstein Ger. **55** D2
Hereford U.K. **53** B3
Hereford U.S.A. **141** D2
Herford Ger. **55** D1
Herkenbosch Neth. **54** C2
Herma Ness *hd* U.K. **50** [inset]
Hermanus S. Africa **108** A3
Hermidale Austr. **117** D2
Hermiston U.S.A. **132** C1
Hermit Islands P.N.G. **71** D3
Hermosillo Mex. **142** A2
Hernandarias Para. **154** B3
Herne Ger. **54** C2
Herning Denmark **47** B4
Herrieden Ger. **55** E3
Hertford U.K. **53** C4
Hertzogville S. Africa **109** C2
Hervey Bay Austr. **115** E2
Herzberg Ger. **55** F2
Herzogenaurach Ger. **55** E3
Heshan China **83** A3
Hess *r.* Can. **126** B1
Hesselberg *h.* Ger. **55** E3
Hessisch Lichtenau Ger. **55** D2

Hettinger U.S.A. **134** C1
Hettstedt Ger. **55** E2
Hexham U.K. **52** B2
Heyuan China **83** B3
Heywood Austr. **116** C3
Heze China **82** B2
Hezhou China **83** B3
Hiawatha U.S.A. **135** D3
Hibbing U.S.A. **135** E1
Hicks Bay N.Z. **118** C2
Hidaka-sanmyaku *mts* Japan **78** D2
Hidalgo Mex. **142** C2
Hidalgo del Parral Mex. **142** B2
Hidrolândia Brazil **154** C1
High Atlas *mts* Morocco *see* Haut Atlas
High Desert U.S.A. **132** B2
High Level Can. **126** D2
High Point U.S.A. **139** E1
High Prairie Can. **126** D2
High River Can. **126** D2
Highrock Lake Can. **127** E2
High Wycombe U.K. **53** C4
Hiiumaa *i.* Estonia **42** B2
Hijaz *reg.* Saudi Arabia **90** A2
Hikurangi *mt.* N.Z. **118** C2
Hildburghausen Ger. **55** E2
Hilders Ger. **55** E2
Hildesheim Ger. **55** D1
Hillah Iraq **93** C2
Hillesheim Ger. **54** C2
Hillsboro *OH* U.S.A. **136** D3
Hillsboro *TX* U.S.A. **141** E2
Hillston Austr. **117** D2
Hilton Head Island U.S.A. **139** D2
Hilversum Neth. **54** B1
Himalaya *mts* Asia **87** B1
Himeji Japan **79** B4
Himeville S. Africa **109** C2
Hinchinbrook Island Austr. **115** D1
Hindu Kush *mts* Afgh./Pak. **86** A1
Hinesville U.S.A. **139** D2
Hinganghat India **87** B2
Hınıs Turkey **93** C2
Hinnøya *i.* Norway **46** C2
Hinojosa del Duque Spain **60** B2
Hinthada Myanmar **74** A2
Hinton Can. **126** D2
Hirakud Reservoir India **87** C2
Hirosaki Japan **78** D2
Hiroshima Japan **79** B4
Hirschaid Ger. **55** E3
Hirschberg Ger. **55** E2
Hirson France **59** C2
Hirtshals Denmark **47** B4
Hisar India **86** B2
Hispaniola *i.* Caribbean Sea **145** C2
Hīt Iraq **93** C2
Hitachi Japan **79** D3
Hitachinaka Japan **79** D3
Hitra *i.* Norway **46** B3
Hiva Oa *i.* Fr. Polynesia **111**
Hjälmaren *l.* Sweden **47** D4
Hjalmar Lake Can. **127** E1
Hjørring Denmark **47** C4
Hlabisa S. Africa **109** D2
Hlið Iceland **46** [inset]
Hlobyne Ukr. **45** D2
Hlohlowane S. Africa **109** C2
Hlotse Lesotho **109** C2
Hlukhiv Ukr. **45** D1
Hlybokaye Belarus **42** C2
Ho Ghana **100** C4
Hoachanas Namibia **108** A1
Hobart Austr. **115** D4
Hobart U.S.A. **141** E1
Hobbs U.S.A. **141** D2
Hobro Denmark **47** B4
Hobyo Somalia **103** C4
Hoceima, Baie d'Al *b.* Morocco **60** C2
Hô Chi Minh City Vietnam **75** B2

Hôd *reg.* Maur. **100** B3
Hodeidah Yemen **90** B3
Hódmezővásárhely Hungary **57** E3
Hodna, Chott el *salt l.* Alg. **61** D2
Hoek van Holland Neth. *see*
    Hook of Holland
Hoeyang N. Korea **77** B2
Hof Ger. **55** E2
Hofheim in Unterfranken Ger. **55** E2
Höfn *Austurland* Iceland **46** [inset]
Höfn *Vestfirðir* Iceland **46** [inset]
Hofsjökull *ice cap* Iceland **46** [inset]
Höfu Japan **79** B4
Hoggar *plat.* Alg. **101** C2
Högsby Sweden **47** D4
Høgste Breakulen *mt.* Norway
    47 B3
Hohe Rhön *mts* Ger. **55** D2
Hohe Venn *moorland* Belgium **54** C2
Hohhot China **82** B1
Hoh Xil Shan *mts* China **87** C1
Hôi An Vietnam **75** B2
Hojai India **74** A1
Hokitika N.Z. **118** B3
Hokkaidō *i.* Japan **78** D2
Holberg Can. **126** C2
Holbrook U.S.A. **140** B2
Holdrege U.S.A. **135** D2
Holguín Cuba **145** C2
Hóll Iceland **46** [inset]
Holland U.S.A. **136** C2
Hollum Neth. **54** B1
Holly Springs U.S.A. **138** C2
Hollywood *CA* U.S.A. **133** C4
Hollywood *FL* U.S.A. **139** D3
Holm Norway **46** C2
Holman Can. **124** E2
Holmsund Sweden **46** E3
Holoog Namibia **108** A2
Holstebro Denmark **47** B4
Holston *r.* U.S.A. **139** D1
Holyhead U.K. **52** A3
Holy Island *England* U.K. **52** C2
Holy Island *Wales* U.K. **52** A3
Holyoke U.S.A. **134** C2
Holzminden Ger. **55** D2
Homalin Myanmar **74** A1
Homberg (Efze) Ger. **55** D2
Hombori Mali **100** B3
Homburg Ger. **54** C3
Home Bay Can. **125** H2
Homestead U.S.A. **139** D3
Hommelvik Norway **46** C3
Homs Syria **92** B2
Homyel' Belarus **43** D3
Hondeklipbaai S. Africa **108** A3
Hondo *r.* Belize/Mex. **143** D3
Hondo U.S.A. **141** E3
Honduras *country* Central America
    144 B3
Hønefoss Norway **47** C3
Honey Lake *salt l.* U.S.A. **132** B2
Honfleur France **58** C2
Hông Gai Vietnam **74** B1
Honghu China **83** B3
Hongjiang China **83** A3
Hong Kong China **83** B3
Hong Kong *aut. reg.* China **83** B3
Hongwŏn N. Korea **77** B1
Hongze Hu *l.* China **82** B2
Honiara Solomon Is **112**
Honjō Japan **78** D2
Honningsvåg Norway **46** F1
Honshū *i.* Japan **79** B3
Hood, Mount *vol.* U.S.A. **132** B1
Hood Point *pt* Austr. **114** A3
Hood River U.S.A. **132** B1
Hoogeveen Neth. **54** C1
Hoogezand-Sappemeer Neth. **54** C1
Hoog-Keppel Neth. **54** C2

Jartai China **82** A2
Jarú Brazil **150** C4
Jarud China *see* Lubei
Järvenpää Fin. **42** C1
Jarvis Island *terr.* S. Pacific Ocean
113
Jāsk Iran **91** C2
Jasło Pol. **57** E3
Jasper Can. **126** D2
Jasper *IN* U.S.A. **136** C3
Jasper *TX* U.S.A. **141** F2
Jastrzębie-Zdrój Pol. **57** D3
Jászberény Hungary **57** D3
Jataí Brazil **154** B1
Jati Pak. **86** A2
Jaú Brazil **154** C2
Jaú *r.* Brazil **150** C3
Jaumave Mex. **143** C2
Jaunpur India **87** C2
Jauru Brazil **154** B1
Java *i.* Indon. **72** B2
Javarthushuu Mongolia **81** D1
Java Sea Indon. *see* Jawa, Laut
Java Trench *sea feature* Indian Ocean
161 H6
Jawa *i.* Indon. *see* Java
Jawa, Laut *sea* Indon. **72** C2
Jawhar Somalia **103** C4
Jawor Pol. **57** D2
Jaworzno Pol. **57** D2
Jaya, Puncak *mt.* Indon. **71** D3
Jayapura Indon. **71** D3
Jean Marie River Can. **126** C1
Jeannin, Lac *l.* Can. **129** D1
Jebel, Bahr el *r.* Sudan/Uganda *see*
White Nile
Jebel Abyad Plateau Sudan **102** A3
Jedburgh U.K. **50** C3
Jeddah Saudi Arabia **90** A2
Jeetze *r.* Ger. **55** E1
Jefferson, Mount U.S.A. **133** C3
Jefferson City U.S.A. **135** E3
Jejuí Guazú *r.* Para. **154** B1
Jēkabpils Latvia **42** C2
Jelenia Góra Pol. **57** D2
Jelgava Latvia **42** B2
Jember Indon. **73** C2
Jena Ger. **55** E2
Jengish Chokusu *mt.* China/Kyrg. *see*
Pobeda Peak
Jenin West Bank **92** B2
Jennings U.S.A. **138** B2
Jequié Brazil **151** E4
Jequitaí Brazil **155** D1
Jequitinhonha Brazil **155** D1
Jequitinhonha *r.* Brazil **155** E1
Jérémie Haiti **145** C3
Jerez Mex. **142** B2
Jerez de la Frontera Spain **60** B2
Jergucat Albania **65** B3
Jerid, Chott el *salt l.* Tunisia **101** C1
Jerome U.S.A. **132** D2
Jersey *i.* Channel Is **53** B5
Jerumenha Brazil **151** E3
Jerusalem Israel/West Bank **92** B2
Jervis Bay Territory *admin. div.* Austr.
117 E3
Jesenice Slovenia **62** B1
Jesi Italy **62** B2
Jessen Ger. **55** F2
Jessore Bangl. **87** C2
Jesup U.S.A. **139** D2
Jesús Carranza Mex. **143** C3
Jhalawar India **86** B2
Jhang Pak. **86** B1
Jhansi India **87** B2
Jharsuguda India **87** C2
Jhelum Pak. **86** B1
Jiading China **82** C2
Jiamusi China **78** B1

Ji'an *Jiangxi* China **83** B3
Ji'an *Jilin* China **77** B1
Jianchuan China **74** A1
Jiangsu *prov.* China **82** B2
Jiangxi *prov.* China **83** B3
Jiangyou China **82** A2
Jianli China **83** B3
Jianqiao China **82** B2
Jianyang *Fujian* China **83** B3
Jianyang *Sichuan* China **83** A2
Jiaohe China **77** B1
Jiaozhou China **82** C2
Jiaozuo China **82** B2
Jiaxing China **82** C2
Jiayuguan China **80** C2
Jiddah Saudi Arabia *see* Jeddah
Jiehkkevárri *mt.* Norway **46** D2
Jiexiu China **82** B2
Jigzhi China **80** C2
Jihlava Czech Rep. **57** D3
Jijel Alg. **61** E2
Jijiga Eth. **103** C4
Jilf al Kabīr, Haḍabat al *plat.* Egypt
102 A2
Jilib Somalia **103** C4
Jilin China **77** B1
Jilin *prov.* China **82** C1
Jilin Hada Ling *mts* China **77** A1
Jīma Eth. **103** B4
Jiménez *Chihuahua* Mex. **142** B2
Jiménez *Tamaulipas* Mex. **143** C2
Jinan China **82** B2
Jinchang China **82** A2
Jincheng China **82** B2
Jindabyne Austr. **117** D3
Jindřichův Hradec Czech Rep. **56** D3
Jingdezhen China **83** B3
Jinggangshan China **83** B3
Jinghong China **74** B1
Jingmen China **82** B2
Jingning China **82** A2
Jingtai China **82** A2
Jingxi China **83** A3
Jingyu China **77** B1
Jingyuan China **82** A2
Jingzhou *Hubei* China **83** B2
Jingzhou *Hubei* China **83** B2
Jinhua China **83** B3
Jining *Nei Mongol* China **82** B1
Jining *Shandong* China **82** B2
Jinja Uganda **105** D2
Jinka Eth. **103** B4
Jinotepe Nic. **144** B3
Jinping China **83** A3
Jinsha Jiang *r.* China *see* Yangtze
Jinshi China **83** B3
Jinzhong China **82** B2
Jinzhou China **82** C1
Jiparaná *r.* Brazil **150** C3
Jirang China **87** C1
Jirkov Czech Rep. **55** F2
Jīroft Iran **91** C2
Jishou China **83** A3
Jiu *r.* Romania **44** B3
Jiuding Shan *mt.* China **82** A2
Jiujiang China **83** B3
Jiwani Pak. **91** D2
Jixi China **78** B1
Jīzān Saudi Arabia **90** B3
Jizzax Uzbek. **89** D2
Joaçaba Brazil **154** B3
João Pessoa Brazil **151** F3
João Pinheiro Brazil **155** C1
Jodhpur India **86** B2
Joensuu Fin. **46** F3
Jōetsu Japan **79** C3
Jofane Moz. **107** C2
Jõgeva Estonia **42** C2
Johannesburg S. Africa **109** C2
John Day U.S.A. **132** C2

John Day *r.* U.S.A. **132** B1
John d'Or Prairie Can. **126** D2
John H. Kerr Reservoir U.S.A. **137** E ?
John o'Groats U.K. **50** C1
Johnson City U.S.A. **139** D1
Johnson's Crossing Can. **126** B1
Johnstone U.K. **50** B3
Johnstown U.S.A. **137** E2
Johor Bahru Malaysia **72** B1
Jõhvi Estonia **42** C2
Joinville Brazil **154** C3
Joinville France **59** D2
Jokkmokk Sweden **46** D2
Jökulsá á Fjöllum *r.* Iceland **46** [inset]
Joliet U.S.A. **136** C2
Joliette Can. **128** C2
Jolo Phil. **76** B3
Jolo *i.* Phil. **76** B3
Jombang Indon. **73** C2
Jomsom Nepal **87** C2
Jonava Lith. **42** C2
Jonesboro *AR* U.S.A. **138** B1
Jonesboro *LA* U.S.A. **138** B2
Jones Sound *sea chan.* Can. **125** G1
Jönköping Sweden **47** C4
Jonquière Can. **129** C2
Jonuta Mex. **143** C3
Joplin U.S.A. **135** E3
Jordan *country* Asia **92** B2
Jordan *r.* Asia **92** B2
Jordan U.S.A. **132** E1
Jordan Valley U.S.A. **132** C2
Jorhat India **74** A1
Jørpeland Norway **47** B4
Jos Nigeria **101** C4
José Cardel Mex. **143** C3
Joseph, Lac *l.* Can. **129** D1
Joseph Bonaparte Gulf Austr. **114** B ?
Jos Plateau Nigeria **101** C4
Jotunheimen *mts* Norway **47** B3
Joubertina S. Africa **108** B3
Jouberton S. Africa **109** C2
Joutseno Fin. **47** F3
Juan de Fuca Strait Can./U.S.A.
132 B1
Juan Fernández, Archipiélago *is*
S. Pacific Ocean **149**
Juaréz Mex. **143** B2
Juàzeiro Brazil **151** E3
Juàzeiro do Norte Brazil **151** F3
Juba Sudan **103** B4
Jubba *r.* Somalia **103** C5
Jubbah Saudi Arabia **90** B2
Júcar *r.* Spain **61** C2
Juchitán Mex. **143** C3
Judenburg Austria **56** C3
Jühnde Ger. **55** D2
Juigalpa Nic. **144** B3
Juist *i.* Ger. **54** C1
Juiz de Fora Brazil **155** D2
Juliaca Peru **150** B4
Jumla Nepal **87** C2
Junagadh India **86** B2
Junction U.S.A. **141** E2
Junction City U.S.A. **135** D3
Jundiaí Brazil **154** C2
Juneau U.S.A. **126** B3
Junee Austr. **117** D2
Jungfrau *mt.* Switz. **59** D2
Juniata *r.* U.S.A. **137** E2
Junsele Sweden **46** D3
Juntura U.S.A. **132** C2
Juquiá Brazil **154** C2
Jur *r.* Sudan **103** A4
Jura *mts* France/Switz. **59** D2
Jura *i.* U.K. **50** B2
Jura, Sound of *sea chan.* U.K. **50** B3
Jurbarkas Lith. **42** B2
Jūrmala Latvia **42** B2
Juruá *r.* Brazil **150** C3

Kidderminster U.K. **53** B3
Kidira Senegal **100** A3
Kidnappers, Cape N.Z. **118** C2
Kiel Ger. **56** C2
Kielce Pol. **57** E2
Kielder Water *resr* U.K. **52** B2
Kieler Bucht *b.* Ger. **47** C5
Kiev Ukr. **44** D1
Kiffa Maur. **100** A3
Kigali Rwanda **105** D3
Kigoma Tanz. **105** C3
Kihnu *i.* Estonia **42** B2
Kiiminki Fin. **46** F2
Kii-suidō *sea chan.* Japan **79** B4
Kikinda Serb. and Mont. **64** B1
Kikondja Dem. Rep. Congo **105** C3
Kikori *r.* P.N.G. **71** D3
Kikwit Dem. Rep. Congo **104** B3
Kilchu N. Korea **77** B1
Kilembe Dem. Rep. Congo **104** B3
Kilgore U.S.A. **141** E2
Kilimanjaro *vol.* Tanz. **105** D3
Kilis Turkey **92** B2
Kiliya Ukr. **44** C2
Kilkee Rep. of Ireland **51** B2
Kilkeel U.K. **51** D1
Kilkenny Rep. of Ireland **51** C2
Kilkis Greece **65** B2
Killala Bay Rep. of Ireland **51** B1
Killaloe Rep. of Ireland **51** B2
Killam Can. **127** D2
Killarney Rep. of Ireland **51** B2
Killeen U.S.A. **141** E2
Killin U.K. **50** B2
Killybegs Rep. of Ireland **51** B1
Kilmarnock U.K. **50** B3
Kilmore Austr. **117** C3
Kilosa Tanz. **105** D3
Kilrush Rep. of Ireland **51** B2
Kilwa Dem. Rep. Congo **105** C3
Kilwa Masoko Tanz. **105** D3
Kimambi Tanz. **105** D3
Kimba Austr. **116** B2
Kimball U.S.A. **134** C2
Kimberley Can. **126** D3
Kimberley S. Africa **108** B2
Kimberley Plateau Austr. **114** B1
Kimch'aek N. Korea **77** B1
Kimch'ŏn S. Korea **77** B2
Kimmirut Can. **125** H2
Kimovsk Rus. Fed. **43** E3
Kimpese Dem. Rep. Congo **104** B3
Kimry Rus. Fed. **43** E2
Kinabalu, Gunung *mt.* Malaysia **73** C1
Kinbasket Lake Can. **126** D2
Kincardine Can. **128** B2
Kinchang Myanmar **74** A1
Kinda Dem. Rep. Congo **105** C3
Kinder Scout *h.* U.K. **52** C3
Kindersley Can. **124** E3
Kindia Guinea **100** A3
Kindu Dem. Rep. Congo **105** C3
Kineshma Rus. Fed. **43** F2
Kingaroy Austr. **115** E2
King City U.S.A. **133** B3
King George Islands Can. **128** C1
Kingisepp Rus. Fed. **42** C2
King Island Austr. **115** D3
King Leopold Ranges *hills* Austr. **114** B1
Kingman U.S.A. **140** B1
Kings *r.* U.S.A. **133** B3
Kingscote Austr. **116** B3
King's Lynn U.K. **53** D3
Kingsmill Group *is* Kiribati **110**
King Sound *b.* Austr. **114** B1
Kings Peak U.S.A. **132** B2
Kingsport U.S.A. **139** D1
Kingston Can. **128** C2
Kingston Jamaica **145** C3

Kingston U.S.A. **137** F2
Kingston South East Austr. **116** B3
Kingston upon Hull U.K. **52** C3
Kingstown St Vincent **145** D3
Kingsville U.S.A. **141** E3
Kingswood U.K. **53** B4
Kingussie U.K. **50** B2
King William Island Can. **124** F2
King William's Town S. Africa **109** C3
Kinka-san *i.* Japan **78** D3
Kinna Sweden **47** C4
Kinsale Rep. of Ireland **51** B3
Kinshasa Dem. Rep. Congo **104** B3
Kinston U.S.A. **139** E1
Kintai Lith. **42** B2
Kintampo Ghana **100** B4
Kintyre *pen.* U.K. **50** B3
Kipawa, Lac *l.* Can. **128** C2
Kirensk Rus. Fed. **95** J3
Kireyevsk Rus. Fed. **43** E3
Kiribati *country* Pacific Ocean **113**
Kırıkkale Turkey **92** B2
Kirillov Rus. Fed. **43** E2
Kirinyaga *mt.* Kenya *see* Kenya, Mount
Kirishi Rus. Fed. **43** D2
Kiritimati *atoll* Kiribati **111**
Kırkağaç Turkey **65** C3
Kirkcaldy U.K. **50** C2
Kirkcudbright U.K. **50** B3
Kirkenes Norway **46** G2
Kirkkonummi Fin. **42** B1
Kirkland Lake Can. **128** B2
Kirksville U.S.A. **135** E2
Kirkūk Iraq **93** C2
Kirkwall U.K. **50** C1
Kirov *Kaluzhskaya Oblast'* Rus. Fed. **43** D3
Kirov *Kirovskaya Oblast'* Rus. Fed. **40** D3
Kirovo-Chepetsk Rus. Fed. **40** E3
Kirovohrad Ukr. **45** D2
Kirovsk Rus. Fed. **46** G2
Kirovs'ke Ukr. **45** E2
Kirriemuir U.K. **50** C2
Kirs Rus. Fed. **40** E3
Kirsanov Rus. Fed. **45** F1
Kirthar Range *mts* Pak. **86** A2
Kiruna Sweden **46** E2
Kiryū Japan **79** C3
Kirzhach Rus. Fed. **43** E2
Kisangani Dem. Rep. Congo **105** C2
Kisantu Dem. Rep. Congo **104** B3
Kisaran Indon. **72** A1
Kiselevsk Rus. Fed. **94** H3
Kishanganj India **87** C2
Kishi Nigeria **100** C4
Kishinev Moldova *see* Chişinău
Kishkenekol' Kazakh. **89** E1
Kishorganj Bangl. **74** A1
Kishtwar Jammu and Kashmir **86** B1
Kisii Kenya **105** D3
Kiskunfélegyháza Hungary **57** D3
Kiskunhalas Hungary **57** D3
Kislovodsk Rus. Fed. **41** D4
Kismaayo Somalia **103** C5
Kisoro Uganda **105** C3
Kissidougou Guinea **100** A4
Kissimmee U.S.A. **139** D3
Kissimmee, Lake U.S.A. **139** D3
Kississing Lake Can. **127** E2
Kisumu Kenya **105** D3
Kita Mali **100** B3
Kitakami Japan **78** D3
Kitakami-gawa *r.* Japan **78** D3
Kita-Kyūshū Japan **79** B4
Kitale Kenya **105** D2
Kitami Japan **78** D4
Kitchener Can. **128** B2
Kitee Fin. **47** G3
Kitgum Uganda **105** D2

Kitimat Can. **126** C2
Kitona Dem. Rep. Congo **104** B3
Kitunda Tanz. **105** D3
Kitwanga Can. **126** C2
Kitwe Zambia **107** B1
Kitzingen Ger. **55** E3
Kiuruvesi Fin. **46** F3
Kivu, Lake Dem. Rep. Congo/Rwanda **105** C3
Kıyıköy Turkey **64** C2
Kizel Rus. Fed. **40** E3
Kızılca Dağ *mt.* Turkey **65** C3
Kizlyar Rus. Fed. **41** D4
Kjøllefjord Norway **46** F1
Kjøpsvik Norway **46** D2
Kladno Czech Rep. **56** C2
Klagenfurt Austria **56** C3
Klaipėda Lith. **42** B2
Klaksvík Faroe Is **48** B1
Klamath *r.* U.S.A. **132** B2
Klamath Falls U.S.A. **132** B2
Klamath Mountains U.S.A. **132** B2
Klang Malaysia **72** B1
Klatovy Czech Rep. **56** C2
Klawer S. Africa **108** A3
Klawock U.S.A. **126** B2
Kleena Kleene Can. **126** C2
Kleinbegin S. Africa **108** B2
Kleinsee S. Africa **108** A2
Klerksdorp S. Africa **109** C2
Kletnya Rus. Fed. **43** D3
Kleve Ger. **54** C2
Klimavichy Belarus **43** D3
Klimovo Rus. Fed. **43** D3
Klimovsk Rus. Fed. **43** E2
Klin Rus. Fed. **43** E2
Klínovec *mt.* Czech Rep. **55** F2
Klintehamn Sweden **47** D4
Klintsy Rus. Fed. **43** D3
Ključ Bos.-Herz. **63** C2
Kłodzko Pol. **57** D2
Kloosterhaar Neth. **54** C1
Klosterneuburg Austria **57** D3
Klötze (Altmark) Ger. **55** E1
Kluane Lake Can. **126** B1
Kluczbork Pol. **57** D2
Klukwan U.S.A. **126** B2
Klupro Pak. **86** A2
Klyaz'ma *r.* Rus. Fed. **43** F2
Klyetsk Belarus **42** C3
Knaresborough U.K. **52** C3
Knästen *h.* Sweden **47** C3
Knee Lake Can. **127** F2
Knesebeck Ger. **55** E1
Knetzgau Ger. **55** E2
Knin Croatia **63** C2
Knittelfeld Austria **56** C3
Knjaževac Serb. and Mont. **64** B2
Knokke-Heist Belgium **54** A2
Knoxville U.S.A. **139** D1
Knysna S. Africa **108** B3
Kōbe Japan **79** C4
København Denmark *see* Copenhagen
Koblenz Ger. **54** C2
Kobroör *i.* Indon. **71** C3
Kobryn Belarus **42** B3
Kočani Macedonia **64** B2
Kocasu *r.* Turkey **65** C2
Koch Bihar India **87** C2
Kōchi Japan **79** B4
Kochubey Rus. Fed. **41** D4
Kodarma India **87** C2
Kodiak Island U.S.A. **124** B3
Kodok Sudan **103** B4
Kodyma Ukr. **44** C2
Kodzhaele *mt.* Bulg./Greece **65** C2
Koës Namibia **108** A2
Koffiefontein S. Africa **108** C2
Koforidua Ghana **100** B4
Kōfu Japan **79** C3

Krasnohvardiys'ke Ukr. **45** D2
Krasnokamsk Rus. Fed. **40** E3
Krasnomayskiy Rus. Fed. **43** D2
Krasnoperekops'k Ukr. **45** D2
Krasnoslobodsk Rus. Fed. **41** D3
Krasnoufimsk Rus. Fed. **40** E3
Krasnoyarsk Rus. Fed. **95** I3
Krasnoye-na-Volge Rus. Fed. **43** F2
Krasnyy Rus. Fed. **43** D3
Krasnyy Kholm Rus. Fed. **43** E2
Krasnyy Luch Ukr. **41** C4
Krasnyy Sulin Rus. Fed. **45** F2
Krasyliv Ukr. **44** C2
Krefeld Ger. **54** C2
Kremenchuk Ukr. **45** D2
Kremenchuts'ka Vodoskhovyshche *resr* Ukr. **45** D2
Křemešník *h.* Czech Rep. **57** D3
Kreminna Ukr. **45** E2
Krems an der Donau Austria **57** D3
Kresttsy Rus. Fed. **43** D2
Kretinga Lith. **42** B2
Kreuzau Ger. **54** C2
Kreuztal Ger. **54** C2
Kribi Cameroon **104** A2
Krikellos Greece **65** B3
Kril'on, Mys *c.* Rus. Fed. **78** D1
Krishna *r.* India **85** C3
Krishnanagar India **87** C2
Kristiansand Norway **47** B4
Kristianstad Sweden **47** C4
Kristiansund Norway **46** B3
Kristinehamn Sweden **47** C4
Kriti *i.* Greece *see* Crete
Križevci Croatia **63** C1
Krk *i.* Croatia **62** B1
Krokom Sweden **46** C3
Krolevets' Ukr. **45** D1
Kronach Ger. **55** E2
Krŏng Kaôh Kŏng Cambodia **75** B2
Kronprins Frederik Bjerge *nunataks* Greenland **125** J2
Kroonstad S. Africa **109** C2
Kropotkin Rus. Fed. **45** F2
Krosno Pol. **57** E3
Krotoszyn Pol. **57** D2
Krui Indon. **72** B2
Krujë Albania **64** A2
Krumovgrad Bulg. **65** C2
Krung Thep Thai. *see* Bangkok
Krupki Belarus **42** C3
Kruševac Serb. and Mont. **64** B2
Krušné Hory *mts* Czech Rep. **55** F2
Kruzof Island U.S.A. **126** B3
Krychaw Belarus **43** D2
Krymsk Rus. Fed. **45** E3
Krytiko Pelagos *sea* Greece **65** C3
Kryvyy Rih Ukr. **45** D2
Ksabi Alg. **100** B2
Ksar Chellala Alg. **61** D2
Ksar el Boukhari Alg. **61** D2
Ksar el Kebir Morocco **100** B1
Kshenskiy Rus. Fed. **43** E3
Kŭ', Jabal al *h.* Saudi Arabia **90** B2
Kuala Belait Brunei **73** C1
Kuala Kerai Malaysia **72** B1
Kuala Lipis Malaysia **72** B1
Kuala Lumpur Malaysia **72** B1
Kualapembuang Indon. **73** C2
Kuala Terengganu Malaysia **72** B1
Kualatungal Indon. **72** B2
Kuamut Malaysia **73** C1
Kuandian China **77** A1
Kuantan Malaysia **72** B1
Kuban' *r.* Rus. Fed. **45** E2
Kubenskoye, Ozero *l.* Rus. Fed. **43** E2
Kubrat Bulg. **64** C2
Kubuang Indon. **73** C1
Kuching Malaysia **73** C1
Kuçovë Albania **65** A2

Kudat Malaysia **73** C1
Kudus Indon. **73** C2
Kufstein Austria **56** C3
Kugaaruk Can. **125** G2
Kugluktuk Can. **124** E2
Kuhmo Fin. **46** F3
Kūhrān, Kūh-e *mt.* Iran **91** C2
Kuiseb *watercourse* Namibia **108** A1
Kuito Angola **106** A1
Kuivaniemi Fin. **46** F2
Kuizing Rus. Fed. Korea **77** B2
Kukës Albania **64** B2
Kula Turkey **65** C3
Kula Kangri *mt.* Bhutan/China **87** D2
Kulandy Kazakh. **88** C2
Kuldīga Latvia **42** B2
Kule Botswana **108** B1
Kulebaki Rus. Fed. **43** F2
Kulmbach Ger. **55** E2
Kŭlob Tajik. **89** D3
Kul'sary Kazakh. **88** C2
Kulunda Rus. Fed. **89** E1
Kulundinskoye, Ozero *salt l.* Rus. Fed. **89** E1
Kulusuk Greenland **125** J2
Kumagaya Japan **79** C3
Kumamoto Japan **79** B4
Kumanovo Macedonia **64** B2
Kumasi Ghana **100** B4
Kumba Cameroon **104** A2
Kumdah Saudi Arabia **90** B2
Kumertau Rus. Fed. **41** E3
Kumi S. Korea **77** B2
Kumla Sweden **47** D4
Kumo Nigeria **101** D3
Kumon Range *mts* Myanmar **74** A1
Kumphawapi Thai. **74** B2
Kumylzhenskiy Rus. Fed. **45** F2
Kunashir, Ostrov *i.* Rus. Fed. **78** E2
Kunene *r.* Angola/Namibia **106** A1
Kungei Alatau *mts* Kazakh./Kyrg. **89** E2
Kungsbacka Sweden **47** C4
Kungu Dem. Rep. Congo **104** B2
Kungur Rus. Fed. **40** E3
Kunhing Myanmar **74** A1
Kunlun Shan *mts* China **87** B1
Kunming China **83** A3
Kunsan S. Korea **77** B2
Kununurra Austr. **114** B1
Künzelsau Ger. **55** D3
Kuopio Fin. **46** F3
Kupa *r.* Croatia/Slovenia **62** C1
Kupang Indon. **71** C3
Kupiškis Lith. **42** B2
Kupreanof Island U.S.A. **126** B2
Kup"yans'k Ukr. **45** E2
Kuqa China **89** F2
Kurashiki Japan **79** B4
Kurayoshi Japan **79** B3
Kurchatov Rus. Fed. **43** D3
Kürdzhali Bulg. **64** C2
Kure Japan **79** B4
Kuressaare Estonia **42** B2
Kurgan Rus. Fed. **41** F3
Kurganinsk Rus. Fed. **45** F3
Kurikka Fin. **47** E3
Kuril Islands Rus. Fed. **95** L3
Kuril'sk Rus. Fed. **95** L3
Kurkino Rus. Fed. **43** E3
Kurmuk Sudan **103** B3
Kurnool India **85** C3
Kuroiso Japan **79** D3
Kurri Kurri Austr. **117** E2
Kursk Rus. Fed. **43** E3
Kuruman S. Africa **108** B2
Kuruman *watercourse* S. Africa **108** B2
Kurume Japan **79** B4
Kurumkan Rus. Fed. **95** J3

Kurunegala Sri Lanka **85** C4
Kuşadası Turkey **65** C3
Kuşadası Körfezi *b.* Turkey **65** C3
Kuş Gölü *l.* Turkey **65** C2
Kushiro Japan **78** D2
Kushmurun Kazakh. **88** D1
Kushtia Bangl. **87** C2
Kuskokwim *r.* U.S.A. **95** P2
Kuskokwim Mountains U.S.A. **124** B2
Kussharo-ko *l.* Japan **78** D2
Kütahya Turkey **65** C3
K'ut'aisi Georgia **91** C1
Kutjevo Croatia **63** C1
Kutno Pol. **57** D2
Kutu Dem. Rep. Congo **104** B3
Kuujjua *r.* Can. **124** E2
Kuujjuaq Can. **129** D1
Kuujjuarapik Can. **128** C1
Kuusamo Fin. **46** F2
Kuvango Angola **106** A1
Kuvshinovo Rus. Fed. **43** D2
Kuwait *country* Asia **91** B2
Kuwait Kuwait **91** B2
Kuybyshev Ukr. **45** E2
Kuybyshevskoye Vodokhranilishche *resr* Rus. Fed. **41** D3
Kuytun China **89** F2
Kuyucak Turkey **65** C3
Kuznetsk Rus. Fed. **41** D3
Kuznetsovs'k Ukr. **44** C1
Kvalsund Norway **46** E1
Kwajalein *atoll* Marshall Is **110**
KwaMashu S. Africa **109** D2
Kwandang Indon. **73** C1
Kwangju S. Korea **77** B2
Kwanmo-bong *mt.* N. Korea **77** B1
Kwanobuhle S. Africa **109** C3
Kwanonzame S. Africa **108** B3
Kwatinidubu S. Africa **109** C3
KwaZamokhule S. Africa **109** C2
Kwazulu-Natal *prov.* S. Africa **109** D2
Kwekwe Zimbabwe **107** B1
Kwenge *r.* Dem. Rep. Congo **104** B3
Kwidzyn Pol. **57** D2
Kwilu *r.* Angola/Dem. Rep. Congo **104** B3
Kwoka *mt.* Indon. **71** C3
Kyabram Austr. **117** D3
Kyaikto Myanmar **74** A2
Kyakhta Rus. Fed. **80** D1
Kyancutta Austr. **116** B2
Kyaukpadaung Myanmar **74** A1
Kyaukpyu Myanmar **74** A2
Kybartai Lith. **42** B2
Kyebogyi Myanmar **74** A2
Kyeintali Myanmar **74** A2
Kyelang India **86** B1
Kyiv Ukr. *see* Kiev
Kyklades *is* Greece *see* Cyclades
Kyle Can. **127** E2
Kyle of Lochalsh U.K. **50** B2
Kyll *r.* Ger. **54** C2
Kyllini *mt.* Greece **65** B3
Kymi Greece **65** B3
Kyneton Austr. **116** C3
Kyoga, Lake Uganda **105** D2
Kyogle Austr. **117** E1
Kyŏnggi-man *b.* S. Korea **77** B2
Kyŏngju S. Korea **77** B2
Kyōto Japan **79** C4
Kyparissia Greece **65** B3
Kypshak, Ozero *salt l.* Kazakh. **89** D1
Kyra Panagia *i.* Greece **65** B3
Kyrenia Cyprus **92** B2
Kyrgyzstan *country* Asia **89** E2
Kyritz Ger. **55** F1
Kyrönjoki *r.* Fin. **46** E3
Kyrta Rus. Fed. **40** E2
Kyssa Rus. Fed. **40** D2

La Plata, Río de *sea chan.* Arg./Uru. **153** C4
La Potherie, Lac *l.* Can. **129** C1
Lappeenranta Fin. **47** F3
Lappersdorf Ger. **55** F3
Lappland *reg.* Europe **46** D2
Lâpseki Turkey **65** C2
Laptev Sea Rus. Fed. **95** K1
Laptevykh, More *sea* Rus. Fed. *see* Laptev Sea
Lapua Fin. **46** E3
La Quiaca Arg. **152** B3
Lâr Iran **91** C2
Larache Morocco **100** B1
Laramie U.S.A. **134** B2
Laramie Mountains U.S.A. **134** B2
Laranda Turkey *see* Karaman
Laranjeiras do Sul Brazil **154** B3
Larantuka Indon. **73** D2
Larat *i.* Indon. **71** C3
Larba Alg. **61** D2
Laredo Spain **60** C1
Laredo U.S.A. **141** E3
Largs U.K. **50** B3
La Rioja Arg. **152** B3
Larisa Greece **65** B3
Larkana Pak. **86** A2
Larnaca Cyprus **92** B2
Larne U.K. **51** D1
La Roche-en-Ardenne Belgium **54** B2
La Rochelle France **58** B2
La Roche-sur-Yon France **58** B2
La Roda Spain **61** C2
La Romana Dom. Rep. **145** D3
La Ronge Can. **124** E3
La Ronge, Lac *l.* Can. **124** F3
Larrimah Austr. **114** C1
Larsen Ice Shelf Antarctica **119** K3
Larvik Norway **47** C4
La Sarre Can. **128** C2
Las Cruces U.S.A. **140** C2
La Serena Chile **152** A3
Las Flores Arg. **153** C4
Las Heras Arg. **153** B4
Lashio Myanmar **74** A1
Lashkar Gãh Afgh. **86** A1
La Sila *reg.* Italy **63** C3
Las Lomitas Arg. **152** B3
Las Nieves Mex. **142** B2
Las Palmas de Gran Canaria Canary Is **100** A2
La Spezia Italy **62** B2
Las Plumas Arg. **153** B5
Last Mountain Lake Can. **127** E2
Las Tórtolas, Cerro *mt.* Chile **152** B3
Lastoursville Gabon **104** B3
Lastovo *i.* Croatia **62** B3
Las Tres Vírgenes, Volcán *vol.* Mex. **142** A2
Las Tunas Cuba **145** C2
Las Varas *Chihuahua* Mex. **142** B2
Las Varas *Nayarit* Mex. **142** B2
Las Vegas *NM* U.S.A. **140** C1
Las Vegas *NV* U.S.A. **133** C3
La Tabatière Can. **129** E1
Latakia Syria **92** B2
La Teste-de-Buch France **58** B3
Latina Italy **62** B2
La Tortuga, Isla *i.* Venez. **145** D3
La Trinidad Phil. **76** B2
Latskoye Rus. Fed. **43** E2
La Tuque Can. **129** C2
Latvia *country* Europe **42** B2
Lauchhammer Ger. **55** F2
Lauf an der Pegnitz Ger. **55** E3
Laufen Switz. **59** D2
Launceston Austr. **115** D4
Launceston U.K. **53** A4
Launggyaung Myanmar **74** A1
Laura Austr. **115** D1

Laurel *MS* U.S.A. **138** C2
Laurel *MT* U.S.A. **132** E1
Lauria Italy **63** C2
Laurinburg U.S.A. **139** E2
Lausanne Switz. **59** D2
Laut *i.* Indon. **73** C2
Lautersbach (Hessen) Ger. **55** D2
Laut Kecil, Kepulauan *is* Indon. **73** C2
Lauwersmeer *l.* Neth. **54** C1
Laval France **58** B2
Lavapié, Punta *pt* Chile **147**
Laverton Austr. **114** B2
Lavras Brazil **155** C2
Lavumisa Swaziland **109** D2
Lawas Malaysia **73** C1
Lawksawk Myanmar **74** A1
Lawra Ghana **100** B3
Lawrence U.S.A. **135** D3
Lawrenceburg U.S.A. **138** C1
Lawton U.S.A. **141** E2
Lawz, Jabal al *mt.* Saudi Arabia **90** A2
Laxá Sweden **47** C4
Lazarevac Serb. and Mont. **64** B2
Lázaro Cárdenas *Baja California* Mex. **142** A1
Lázaro Cárdenas *Michoacán* Mex. **142** B3
Lazdijai Lith. **42** B3
Lead U.S.A. **134** C2
Leader Can. **127** E2
Leadville U.S.A. **134** B3
Leaf Rapids Can. **127** E2
Leane, Lough *l.* Rep. of Ireland **51** B2
Leavenworth U.S.A. **135** E3
Lebach Ger. **54** C3
Lebanon *MO* U.S.A. **135** E3
Lebanon *NH* U.S.A. **137** F2
Lebanon *OR* U.S.A. **132** B2
Lebanon *PA* U.S.A. **137** E2
Lebanon *country* Asia **92** B2
Lebedyan' Rus. Fed. **43** E3
Lebedyn Ukr. **45** D1
Le Blanc France **58** C2
Lębork Pol. **57** D2
Lebowakgomo S. Africa **109** C1
Lebrija Spain **60** B2
Lebu Chile **153** A4
Le Bugue France **58** C3
Le Catelet France **54** A2
Lecce Italy **63** C2
Lecco Italy **62** A1
Lech *r.* Austria/Ger. **56** C3
Lechaina Greece **65** B3
Lechang China **83** B3
Leck Ger. **56** B2
Lectoure France **58** C3
Ledesma Spain **60** B1
Le Dorat France **58** C2
Leduc Can. **126** D2
Leech Lake U.S.A. **135** E1
Leeds U.K. **52** C3
Leek U.K. **52** C3
Leer (Ostfriesland) Ger. **54** C1
Leesburg U.S.A. **139** D3
Leesville U.S.A. **138** B2
Leeton Austr. **117** D2
Leeu-Gamka S. Africa **108** B3
Leeuwarden Neth. **54** B1
Leeuwin, Cape Austr. **114** A3
Leeward Islands Caribbean Sea **145** D3
Lefkada Greece **65** B3
Lefkada *i.* Greece **65** B3
Lefkosia Cyprus *see* Nicosia
Legaspi Phil. **76** B3
Legnago Italy **62** B1
Legnica Pol. **57** D2
Leh India **87** B1
Le Havre France **58** C2
Lehututu Botswana **108** B1

Leiah Pak. **86** B1
Leibnitz Austria **57** D3
Leicester U.K. **53** C3
Leichhardt *r.* Austr. **115** C1
Leiden Neth. **54** B1
Leie *r.* Belgium **54** A2
Leigh Creek Austr. **116** B2
Leikanger Norway **47** B3
Leimen Ger. **55** D3
Leine *r.* Ger. **55** D1
Leinster *reg.* Rep. of Ireland **51** C2
Leipzig Ger. **55** F2
Leiranger Norway **46** C2
Leiria Port. **60** B2
Leirvik Norway **47** B4
Leixlip Rep. of Ireland **51** C2
Leiyang China **83** B3
Leizhou China **83** B3
Leizhou Bandao *pen.* China **83** A3
Lékana Congo **104** B3
Lelystad Neth. **54** B1
Le Maire, Estrecho de *sea chan.* Arg. **153** B6
Léman, Lac *l.* France/Switz. *see* Geneva, Lake
Le Mans France **58** C2
Le Mars U.S.A. **135** D2
Leme Brazil **154** C2
Lemesos Cyprus *see* Limassol
Lemförde Ger. **55** D1
Lemieux Islands Can. **125** H2
Lemmon U.S.A. **134** C1
Lemoore U.S.A. **133** C3
Le Moyne, Lac *l.* Can. **129** D1
Lemro *r.* Myanmar **74** A1
Le Murge *hills* Italy **63** C2
Lena *r.* Rus. Fed. **95** K2
Lendery Rus. Fed. **46** G3
Lengerich Ger. **54** C1
Lengshuijiang China **83** B3
Lengshuitan China **83** B3
Lenine Ukr. **45** E2
Leningradskaya Rus. Fed. **45** E2
Lenin Peak Kyrg./Tajik. **89** E3
Leninskiy Rus. Fed. **43** E3
Lens Belgium **54** A2
Lens France **58** C1
Lensk Rus. Fed. **95** J2
Lenti Hungary **57** D3
Lentini Italy **62** C3
Léo Burkina **100** B3
Leoben Austria **56** D3
Leominster U.K. **53** B3
León Mex. **142** B2
León Nic. **144** B3
León Spain **60** B1
Leonardville Namibia **108** A1
Leonora Austr. **114** B2
Leopoldina Brazil **155** D2
Lephalale S. Africa **109** C1
Lephepe Botswana **109** C1
Lephoi S. Africa **109** C3
Leping China **83** B3
Le Puy-en-Velay France **59** C2
Lerala Botswana **109** C1
Lérida Col. **150** B3
Lerma Spain **60** C1
Leros *i.* Greece **65** C3
Le Roy, Lac *l.* Can. **128** C1
Lerum Sweden **47** C4
Lerwick U.K. **50** [inset]
Lesbos *i.* Greece **65** C3
Les Cayes Haiti **145** C3
Leshan China **80** C3
Leshukonskoye Rus. Fed. **40** D2
Leskovac Serb. and Mont. **64** B2
Lesneven France **58** B2
Lesnoye Rus. Fed. **43** E2
Lesosibirsk Rus. Fed. **95** I3
Lesotho *country* Africa **109** C2

Madison r. U.S.A. **132** D1
Madisonville U.S.A. **136** C3
Madiun Indon. **73** C2
Mado Gashi Kenya **105** D2
Madoi China **80** C2
Madrakah Saudi Arabia **90** A2
Madras India see Chennai
Madras U.S.A. **132** B2
Madre, Laguna lag. Mex. **143** C2
Madre de Dios r. Peru **150** C4
Madre del Sur, Sierra mts Mex.
　143 B3
Madre Occidental, Sierra mts Mex.
　142 B2
Madre Oriental, Sierra mts Mex.
　143 B2
Madrid Spain **60** C1
Madridejos Spain **60** C2
Madura i. Indon. **73** C2
Madura, Selat sea chan. Indon. **73** C2
Madurai India **85** B4
Maebashi Japan **79** C3
Mae Hong Son Thai. **74** A2
Mae Sai Thai. **74** A1
Mae Sariang Thai. **74** A2
Mae Suai Thai. **74** A2
Mafeteng Lesotho **109** C2
Mafia Island Tanz. **105** D3
Mafikeng S. Africa **109** C2
Mafinga Tanz. **105** D3
Mafra Brazil **154** C3
Magadan Rus. Fed. **95** M3
Magangue Col. **145** C4
Magdalena r. Col. **148**
Magdalena Mex. **142** A1
Magdalena U.S.A. **140** C2
Magdalena, Bahía b. Mex. **142** A2
Magdeburg Ger. **55** E1
Magellan, Strait of Chile **153** A6
Magherafelt U.K. **51** C1
Magnitogorsk Rus. Fed. **41** E3
Magnolia U.S.A. **138** B2
Magpie, Lac l. Can. **129** D1
Magṭaʻ Laḥjar Maur. **100** A3
Maguarinho, Cabo c. Brazil **151** E3
Magude Moz. **109** D2
Magwe Myanmar **74** A1
Mahābād Iran **93** C2
Mahajan India **86** B2
Mahakam r. Indon. **73** C2
Mahalapye Botswana **109** C1
Mahalevona Madag. **107** [inset] D1
Mahanadi r. India **87** C2
Mahanoro Madag. **107** [inset] D1
Maha Sarakham Thai. **75** B2
Mahavavy r. Madag. **107** [inset] D1
Mahbubnagar India **85** B3
Mahd adh Dhahab Saudi Arabia **90** B2
Mahdia Alg. **61** D2
Mahdia Guyana **150** D2
Mahesana India **86** B2
Mahi r. India **86** B2
Mahia Peninsula N.Z. **118** C2
Mahilyow Belarus **43** D3
Mahón Spain **61** D2
Mahony Lake Can. **126** C1
Mahuva India **86** B2
Mahya Daği mt. Turkey **64** C2
Maidstone Can. **127** E2
Maidstone U.K. **53** D4
Maiduguri Nigeria **101** D3
Mailani India **87** C2
Main r. Ger. **55** D2
Mai-Ndombe, Lac l. Dem. Rep. Congo
　104 C3
Main-Donau-Kanal canal Ger. **55** E3
Maine state U.S.A. **137** G1
Maingkwan Myanmar **74** A1

Mainland i. Scotland U.K. **50** C1
Mainland i. Scotland U.K. **50** [inset]
Maintirano Madag. **107** [inset] D1
Mainz Ger. **55** D2
Maiquetía Venez. **145** D3
Maitland N.S.W. Austr. **117** E2
Maitland S.A. Austr. **116** B2
Maíz, Islas del is Nic. **144** B3
Maizuru Japan **79** C3
Maja Jezercë mt. Albania **64** A2
Majene Indon. **73** C2
Majorca i. Spain **61** D2
Majuro atoll Marshall Is **110**
Majwemasweu S. Africa **109** C2
Makabana Congo **104** B3
Makale Indon. **73** C2
Makanchi Kazakh. **89** F2
Makarska Croatia **63** C2
Makassar Indon. **73** C2
Makassar, Selat str. Indon. **73** C2
Makat Kazakh. **88** C2
Makatini Flats lowland S. Africa
　109 D2
Makeni Sierra Leone **100** A4
Makgadikgadi salt pan Botswana
　106 B2
Makhachkala Rus. Fed. **41** D4
Makhado S. Africa **109** C1
Makhambet Rus. Fed. **43** E2
Makhazine, Barrage El dam Morocco
　60 B3
Makindu Kenya **105** D3
Makinsk Kazakh. **89** E1
Makiyivka Ukr. **45** E2
Makkah Saudi Arabia see Mecca
Makkovik Can. **129** E1
Makó Hungary **57** E2
Makokou Gabon **104** B2
Makongolosi Tanz. **105** D3
Makopong Botswana **108** B2
Makran reg. Iran/Pak. **91** D2
Makran Coast Range mts Pak. **86** A2
Maksatikha Rus. Fed. **43** E2
Mākū Iran **93** C2
Makum India **74** A1
Makurazaki Japan **79** B4
Makurdi Nigeria **101** C4
Malå Sweden **46** D3
Mala, Punta pt Panama **144** B4
Malabo Equat. Guinea **104** A2
Malacca, Strait of Indon./Malaysia
　72 A1
Malad City U.S.A. **132** D2
Maladzyechna Belarus **42** C3
Málaga Spain **60** C2
Malaita i. Solomon Is **110**
Malakal Sudan **103** B4
Malakula i. Vanuatu **110**
Malamala Indon. **73** D2
Malang Indon. **73** C2
Malanje Angola **104** B3
Mälaren l. Sweden **47** D4
Malargüe Arg. **153** B4
Malatya Turkey **92** B2
Malawi country Africa **107** C1
Malawi, Lake Africa see Nyasa, Lake
Malaya Vishera Rus. Fed. **43** D2
Malaybalay Phil. **76** B3
Malāyer Iran **93** C2
Malaysia country Asia **72** B1
Malazgirt Turkey **93** C2
Malbork Pol. **57** D2
Malchin Ger. **55** F1
Maldegem Belgium **54** A2
Malden Island Kiribati **111**
Maldives country Indian Ocean **85** B4
Male Maldives **85** B4
Maleas, Akra pt Greece **65** B3
Male Atoll Maldives **85** B4
Malé Karpaty hills Slovakia **57** D3

Malheur Lake U.S.A. **132** C2
Mali country Africa **100** B3
Mali Guinea **100** A3
Malili Indon. **73** D2
Malindi Kenya **105** E3
Malin Head Rep. of Ireland **51** C1
Malin More Rep. of Ireland **51** B1
Malkara Turkey **65** C2
Malʻkavichy Belarus **42** C3
Malko Tŭrnovo Bulg. **64** C2
Mallacoota Austr. **117** D3
Mallacoota Inlet b. Austr. **117** D3
Mallaig U.K. **50** B2
Mallery Lake Can. **127** F1
Mallorca i. Spain see Majorca
Mallow Rep. of Ireland **51** B2
Malmberget Sweden **46** E2
Malmédy Belgium **54** C2
Malmesbury S. Africa **108** A3
Malmö Sweden **47** C4
Malong China **83** A3
Malonga Dem. Rep. Congo **104** C4
Måløy Norway **47** B3
Maloyaroslavets Rus. Fed. **43** E2
Maloye Borisovo Rus. Fed. **43** E2
Malta country Europe **101** D1
Malta Latvia **42** C2
Malta i. Malta **36**
Malta U.S.A. **132** E1
Maltahöhe Namibia **108** A1
Malton U.K. **52** C2
Maluku is Indon. see Moluccas
Maluku, Laut sea Indon. **71** C3
Malung Sweden **47** C3
Maluti Mountains Lesotho **109** C2
Malvan India **85** B3
Malvern U.S.A. **138** B2
Malyn Ukr. **44** C1
Malyy Anyuy r. Rus. Fed. **95** M2
Malyy Lyakhovskiy, Ostrov i. Rus. Fed.
　95 L2
Mamafubedu S. Africa **109** C2
Mambasa Dem. Rep. Congo **105** C2
Mambéré r. C.A.R. **104** B2
Mamelodi S. Africa **109** C2
Mamoré r. Bol./Brazil **152** B2
Mamou Guinea **100** A3
Mamuju Indon. **73** C2
Man Côte d'Ivoire **100** B4
Man, Isle of i. Irish Sea **52** A2
Manacapuru Brazil **150** C3
Manacor Spain **61** D2
Manado Indon. **71** C2
Managua Nic. **144** B3
Manakara Madag. **107** [inset] D2
Manākhah Yemen **90** B3
Manama Bahrain **91** C2
Manam Island P.N.G. **71** D3
Mananara r. Madag. **107** [inset] D2
Mananara Avaratra Madag.
　107 [inset] D1
Mananjary Madag. **107** [inset] D2
Manantali, Lac de l. Mali **100** A3
Manas Hu l. China **89** F2
Manatuto East Timor **71** C3
Man-aung Kyun i. Myanmar **74** A2
Manaus Brazil **150** C3
Manavgat Turkey **92** B2
Manchester U.K. **52** B3
Manchester U.S.A. **137** F2
Mandabe Madag. **107** [inset] D2
Mandal Norway **47** B4
Mandala, Puncak mt. Indon. **71** D3
Mandalay Myanmar **74** A1
Mandalgovī Mongolia **80** D1
Mandan U.S.A. **134** C1
Mandara Mountains Cameroon/Nigeria
　104 B1
Mandas Italy **62** A3
Manderscheid Ger. **54** C2

Navolato Mex. **142** B2
Nawabshah Pak. **86** A2
Nawnghkio Myanmar **74** A1
Nawngleng Myanmar **74** A1
Naxçıvan Azer. **93** C2
Naxos *i.* Greece **65** C3
Nayar Mex. **142** B2
Nayoro Japan **78** D2
Nazareth Israel **92** B2
Nazas Mex. **142** B2
Nazas *r.* Mex. **142** B2
Nazca Peru **150** B4
Nazilli Turkey **65** C3
Nazrēt Eth. **103** B4
Nazwá Oman **91** C2
Nchelenge Zambia **105** C3
Ncojane Botswana **108** B1
N'dalatando Angola **104** B3
Ndélé C.A.R. **104** C2
Ndendé Gabon **104** B3
Ndjamena Chad **101** D3
Ndola Zambia **107** B1
Neagh, Lough *l.* U.K. **51** C1
Neale, Lake *salt flat* Austr. **114** C2
Nea Roda Greece **65** B2
Neath U.K. **53** B4
Nebine Creek *r.* Austr. **117** D1
Neblina, Pico da *mt.* Brazil **150** C2
Nebolchi Rus. Fed. **43** D2
Nebraska *state* U.S.A. **134** C2
Nebraska City U.S.A. **135** D2
Nebrodi, Monti *mts* Italy **62** B3
Necochea Arg. **153** C4
Nedlouc, Lac *l.* Can. **129** C1
Nédroma Alg. **61** C2
Needles U.S.A. **133** D4
Neemuch India **86** B2
Neepawa Can. **127** F2
Neftekamsk Rus. Fed. **41** E3
Nefteyugansk Rus. Fed. **40** G2
Negage Angola **104** B3
Negēlē Eth. **103** B4
Negra, Punta *pt* Peru **150** A3
Negrais, Cape Myanmar **75** A2
Negro *r.* Arg. **153** B5
Negro *r.* Brazil **154** A1
Negro *r.* S. America **150** D3
Negro *r.* Uru. **152** C4
Negro, Cabo *c.* Morocco **60** B2
Negros *i.* Phil. **76** B3
Nehbandān Iran **91** D1
Nehe China **81** E1
Neijiang China **83** A3
Neilburg Can. **127** E2
Nei Mongol Zizhiqu *aut. reg.* China **82** A1
Neiva Col. **150** B2
Nejanilini Lake Can. **127** F2
Nek'emtē Eth. **103** B4
Nekrasovskoye Rus. Fed. **43** F2
Nelidovo Rus. Fed. **43** D2
Nellore India **85** B3
Nelson Can. **126** D3
Nelson *r.* Can. **127** F2
Nelson N.Z. **118** B3
Nelson, Cape Austr. **116** C3
Nelson Bay Austr. **117** E2
Nelson House Can. **127** F2
Nelson Reservoir U.S.A. **132** E1
Nelspruit S. Africa **109** D2
Néma Maur. **100** B3
Neman Rus. Fed. **42** B2
Nemda *r.* Rus. Fed. **43** F2
Nemours France **58** C2
Nemuro Japan **78** E2
Nemyriv Ukr. **44** C2
Nenagh Rep. of Ireland **51** B2
Nene *r.* U.K. **53** D3
Nenjiang China **81** E1
Neosho U.S.A. **135** E3

Nepal *country* Asia **87** C2
Nepalganj Nepal **87** C2
Nephi U.S.A. **133** D3
Nephin *h.* Rep. of Ireland **51** B1
Nephin Beg Range *hills* Rep. of Ireland **51** B1
Nepisiguit *r.* Can. **129** D2
Nepoko *r.* Dem. Rep. Congo **105** C2
Nepomuk Czech Rep. **55** F3
Nérac France **58** C3
Nerang Austr. **117** E1
Nerchinsk Rus. Fed. **81** D1
Nerekhta Rus. Fed. **43** F2
Neretva *r.* Bos.-Herz./Croatia **63** C2
Neriquinha Angola **106** B1
Neris *r.* Lith. **42** B3
Nerl' *r.* Rus. Fed. **43** E2
Nerokhi Rus. Fed. **40** F2
Nerópolis Brazil **154** C1
Neryungri Rus. Fed. **95** K3
Neskaupstaður Iceland **46** [inset]
Ness, Loch *l.* U.K. **50** B2
Ness City U.S.A. **134** D3
Nestos *r.* Greece **65** B2
Netherlands *country* Europe **54** B1
Netherlands Antilles *terr.* West Indies **145** D3
Neubrandenburg Ger. **55** F1
Neuchâtel Switz. **59** D2
Neuenhagen Berlin Ger. **55** F1
Neuerburg Ger. **54** C2
Neufchâteau Belgium **54** B3
Neufchâteau France **59** D2
Neufchâtel-en-Bray France **58** C2
Neuhof Ger. **55** D2
Neu Lübbenau Ger. **55** F1
Neumarkt in der Oberpfalz Ger. **55** E3
Neumünster Ger. **56** B2
Neunkirchen Ger. **54** C3
Neuquén Arg. **153** B4
Neuquén *r.* Arg. **153** B4
Neuruppin Ger. **55** F1
Neuss Ger. **54** C2
Neustadt am Rübenberge Ger. **55** D1
Neustadt an der Aisch Ger. **55** E3
Neustadt an der Weinstraße Ger. **54** D3
Neustrelitz Ger. **55** F1
Neutraubling Ger. **55** F3
Neuwied Ger. **54** C2
Nevada U.S.A. **135** E3
Nevada *state* U.S.A. **133** C3
Nevada, Sierra *mts* Spain **60** C2
Nevada, Sierra *mts* U.S.A. **133** B2
Nevel' Rus. Fed. **42** C2
Nevers France **59** C2
Nevertire Austr. **117** D2
Nevesinje Bos.-Herz. **63** C2
Nevinnomyssk Rus. Fed. **41** D4
New Aiyansh Can. **126** C2
New Albany U.S.A. **136** C3
New Amsterdam Guyana **151** D2
Newark *NJ* U.S.A. **137** F2
Newark *OH* U.S.A. **136** D2
Newark-on-Trent U.K. **52** C3
New Bedford U.S.A. **137** F2
New Bern U.S.A. **139** E1
Newberry U.S.A. **139** D2
New Boston U.S.A. **141** F2
New Braunfels U.S.A. **141** E3
Newbridge Rep. of Ireland **51** C2
New Brunswick *prov.* Can. **129** D2
Newbury U.K. **53** C4
New Caledonia *terr.* S. Pacific Ocean **112**
Newcastle Austr. **117** E2
Newcastle S. Africa **109** C2
Newcastle U.K. **51** D1
New Castle U.S.A. **137** D2

Newcastle U.S.A. **134** C2
Newcastle-under-Lyme U.K. **52** B3
Newcastle upon Tyne U.K. **52** C2
Newcastle West Rep. of Ireland **51** B2
New Delhi India **86** B2
New Denver Can. **126** D3
New England Range *mts* Austr. **117** E
Newfoundland *i.* Can. **129** E2
Newfoundland and Labrador *prov.* Can. **129** E1
New Glasgow Can. **129** D2
New Guinea *i.* Indon./P.N.G. **71** D3
New Halfa Sudan **90** A3
New Hampshire *state* U.S.A. **137** F2
New Haven U.S.A. **137** F2
New Hazelton Can. **126** C2
New Iberia U.S.A. **138** B2
New Ireland *i.* P.N.G. **110**
New Jersey *state* U.S.A. **137** F3
New Liskeard Can. **128** C2
Newman Austr. **114** A2
New Mexico *state* U.S.A. **140** C2
New Orleans U.S.A. **138** B3
New Philadelphia U.S.A. **136** D2
New Plymouth N.Z. **118** B2
Newport *England* U.K. **53** C4
Newport *Wales* U.K. **53** B4
Newport *AR* U.S.A. **138** B1
Newport *OR* U.S.A. **132** B2
Newport *RI* U.S.A. **137** F2
Newport *VT* U.S.A. **137** F2
Newport *WA* U.S.A. **132** C1
Newport News U.S.A. **137** E3
New Providence *i.* Bahamas **139** E3
Newquay U.K. **53** A4
New Roads U.S.A. **138** B2
New Ross Rep. of Ireland **51** C2
Newry U.K. **51** C1
New Siberia Islands Rus. Fed. **95** L1
New South Wales *state* Austr. **117** D2
Newton *IA* U.S.A. **135** E2
Newton *KS* U.S.A. **135** D3
Newton Abbot U.K. **53** B4
Newton Stewart U.K. **50** B3
Newtown Rep. of Ireland **51** B2
Newtown U.K. **53** B3
New Town U.S.A. **134** C1
Newtownabbey U.K. **51** D1
Newtownards U.K. **51** D1
Newtown St Boswells U.K. **50** C3
Newtownstewart U.K. **51** C1
New Ulm U.S.A. **135** E2
New York U.S.A. **137** F2
New York *state* U.S.A. **137** E2
New Zealand *country* Oceania **118**
Neya Rus. Fed. **43** F2
Neya *r.* Rus. Fed. **43** F2
Neyriz Iran **93** D3
Neyshābūr Iran **88** C3
Nezahualcóyotl Mex. **143** C3
Nezahualcóyotl, Presa *resr* Mex. **143** C3
Ngabang Indon. **73** B1
Ngamring China **87** C2
Ngangla Ringco *salt l.* China **87** C1
Nganglong Kangri *mt.* China **87** C1
Nganglong Kangri *mts* China **87** C1
Ngangzê Co *salt l.* China **87** C1
Ngao Thai. **74** A2
Ngaoundéré Cameroon **104** B2
Ngaruawahia N.Z. **118** C2
Ngathainggyaung Myanmar **74** A2
Ngo Congo **104** B3
Ngoc Linh *mt.* Vietnam **75** B2
Ngol Bembo Nigeria **101** D4
Ngoring Hu *l.* China **80** C2
Ngourti Niger **101** D3
Nguigmi Niger **101** D3
Ngulu *atoll* Micronesia **71** D2
Nguru Nigeria **101** D3

Norwich *NY* U.S.A. **137** E2
Noshiro Japan **78** D2
Nosivka Ukr. **45** D1
Nosop *watercourse* Africa **108** B2
Nosovaya Rus. Fed. **40** E2
Noşratābād Iran **91** C2
Nossen Ger. **55** F2
Noteć *r.* Pol. **57** D2
Notodden Norway **47** B4
Noto-hantō *pen.* Japan **79** C3
Notre Dame, Monts *mts* Can. **129** D2
Notre Dame Bay Can. **129** E2
Nottaway *r.* Can. **128** C1
Nottingham U.K. **52** C3
Nouâdhibou Maur. **100** A2
Nouakchott Maur. **100** A3
Nouâmghâr Maur. **100** A3
Nouméa New Caledonia **112**
Nouna Burkina **100** B3
Nouvelle Calédonie *i.*
  S. Pacific Ocean **110**
Nova Esperança Brazil **154** B2
Nova Friburgo Brazil **155** D2
Nova Gradiška Croatia **63** C1
Nova Granada Brazil **154** C2
Nova Iguaçu Brazil **155** D2
Nova Kakhovka Ukr. **45** D2
Nova Lima Brazil **155** D1
Nova Londrina Brazil **154** B2
Nova Odesa Ukr. **45** D2
Nova Paraiso Brazil **150** C2
Nova Scotia *prov.* Can. **129** D2
Nova Venécia Brazil **155** D1
Novaya Sibir', Ostrov *i.* Rus. Fed.
  95 L1
Novaya Zemlya *is* Rus. Fed. **40** E1
Nové Zámky Slovakia **57** D3
Novhorod-Sivers'kyy Ukr. **45** D1
Novi Iskŭr Bulg. **64** B2
Novi Ligure Italy **62** A2
Novi Pazar Serb. and Mont. **64** B2
Novi Sad Serb. and Mont. **64** A1
Novoaleksandrovsk Rus. Fed. **45** F2
Novoanninskiy Rus. Fed. **45** F1
Novo Aripuanã Brazil **150** C3
Novoazovs'k Ukr. **45** E2
Novocherkassk Rus. Fed. **45** F2
Novodvinsk Rus. Fed. **40** D2
Novo Hamburgo Brazil **152** C3
Novo Horizonte Brazil **154** C2
Novohrad-Volyns'kyy Ukr. **44** C1
Novokhopersk Rus. Fed. **43** F3
Novokubansk Rus. Fed. **45** F2
Novokuznetsk Rus. Fed. **89** F1
Novo Mesto Slovenia **56** D1
Novomikhaylovskiy Rus. Fed. **45** E3
Novomoskovsk Rus. Fed. **43** E3
Novomoskovs'k Ukr. **45** E2
Novomyrhorod Ukr. **45** D2
Novonikolayevskiy Rus. Fed. **45** F1
Novooleksiyivka Ukr. **45** D2
Novopokrovskaya Rus. Fed. **45** F2
Novopskov Ukr. **45** E2
Novorossiysk Rus. Fed. **45** E3
Novorzhev Rus. Fed. **42** C2
Novosergiyevka Rus. Fed. **41** E3
Novoshakhtinsk Rus. Fed. **45** E2
Novosibirsk Rus. Fed. **94** H3
Novosibirskiye Ostrova *is* Rus. Fed.
  see New Siberia Islands
Novosil' Rus. Fed. **43** E3
Novosokol'niki Rus. Fed. **43** D2
Novotroyits'ke Ukr. **45** D2
Novoukrayinka Ukr. **45** D2
Novovolyns'k Ukr. **44** B1
Novozybkov Rus. Fed. **43** D3
Nový Jičín Czech Rep. **57** D3
Novyy Bor Rus. Fed. **40** E2
Novyy Oskol Rus. Fed. **45** E1
Novyy Port Rus. Fed. **40** G2

Novyy Urengoy Rus. Fed. **40** G2
Novyy Urgal Rus. Fed. **81** E1
Nowogard Pol. **56** D2
Nowra Austr. **117** E2
Now Shahr Iran **93** D2
Nowshera Pak. **86** B1
Nowy Sącz Pol. **57** E3
Nowy Targ Pol. **57** E3
Noyabr'sk Rus. Fed. **41** G2
Noyon France **58** C2
Nsanje Malawi **107** C1
Ntandembele Dem. Rep. Congo
  104 B3
Ntungamo Uganda **105** D3
Nu'aym *reg.* Oman **91** C2
Nubian Desert Sudan **102** B2
Nudo Coropuna *mt.* Peru **150** B4
Nueltin Lake Can. **127** F1
Nueva Lubecka Arg. **153** A5
Nueva Rosita Mex. **143** B2
Nuevo Casas Grandes Mex.
  142 B1
Nuevo Ideal Mex. **142** B2
Nuevo Laredo Mex. **143** C2
Nugaal *watercourse* Somalia **103** C4
Nuits-St-Georges France **59** C2
Nu Jiang *r.* China/Myanmar *see*
  Salween
Nuku'alofa Tonga **113**
Nuku Hiva *i.* Fr. Polynesia **111**
Nukulaelae *atoll* Tuvalu **111**
Nukunonu *atoll* Tokelau **111**
Nukus Uzbek. **88** C2
Nullagine Austr. **114** B2
Nullarbor Plain Austr. **114** B3
Numan Nigeria **101** D4
Numazu Japan **79** C3
Numedal *val.* Norway **47** B3
Numfoor *i.* Indon. **71** C3
Numurkah Austr. **117** D3
Nunap Nua *c.* Greenland *see*
  Farewell, Cape
Nunavik *reg.* Can. **125** H3
Nunavut *admin. div.* Can. **124** G2
Nuneaton U.K. **53** C3
Nunivak Island U.S.A. **95** O3
Nuñomoral Spain **60** B1
Nuoro Italy **62** A2
Nuqrah Saudi Arabia **90** B2
Nuremberg Ger. **55** E3
Nuriootpa Austr. **116** B2
Nurmes Fin. **46** F3
Nürnberg Ger. *see* Nuremberg
Nu Shan *mts* China **74** A1
Nushki Pak. **86** A2
Nuuk Greenland **125** I2
Nuussuaq Greenland **125** I2
Nuussuaq *pen.* Greenland **125** I2
Nuwaybi' al Muzayyinah Egypt **92** B3
Nuweveldberge *mts* S. Africa **108** B3
Nyagan' Rus. Fed. **40** G2
Nyainqêntanglha Feng *mt.* China
  87 D1
Nyainqêntanglha Shan *mts* China
  87 D2
Nyala Sudan **103** A3
Nyandoma Rus. Fed. **40** D2
Nyanga *r.* Gabon **104** B3
Nyanga Zimbabwe **107** C1
Nyasa, Lake Africa **107** C1
Nyborg Denmark **47** C4
Nyborg Norway **46** F1
Nybro Sweden **47** D4
Nyeri Kenya **105** D3
Nyima China **87** C1
Nyingchi China **80** C3
Nyíregyháza Hungary **57** E3
Nykøbing Denmark **47** C5
Nyköping Sweden **47** D4
Nymagee Austr. **117** D2

Nynäshamn Sweden **47** D4
Nyngan Austr. **117** D2
Nyoman *r.* Belarus/Lith. **42** B3
Nyons France **59** D3
Nýřany Czech Rep. **55** F3
Nyrob Rus. Fed. **40** E2
Nyssa U.S.A. **132** C2
Nyunzu Dem. Rep. Congo **105** C3
Nyzhn'ohirs'kyy Ukr. **45** D2
Nzega Tanz. **105** D3
Nzérékoré Guinea **100** B4
N'zeto Angola **104** B3

O

Oahe, Lake U.S.A. **134** C2
Oahu *i.* U.S.A. **120**
Oakbank Austr. **116** C2
Oakdale U.S.A. **138** B2
Oakey Austr. **117** E1
Oak Harbor U.S.A. **132** B1
Oak Hill U.S.A. **136** D3
Oakland U.S.A. **133** B3
Oakover *r.* Austr. **114** B2
Oakridge U.S.A. **132** B2
Oak Ridge U.S.A. **139** D1
Oamaru N.Z. **118** B4
Oas Phil. **76** B2
Oaxaca Mex. **143** C3
Ob' *r.* Rus. Fed. **40** F2
Obala Cameroon **104** B2
Oban U.K. **50** B2
O Barco Spain **60** B1
Oberá Arg. **154** A3
Oberon Austr. **117** D2
Oberpfälzer Wald *mts* Ger. **55** F3
Oberviechtach Ger. **55** F3
Obi *i.* Indon. **71** C3
Óbidos Brazil **151** D3
Obihiro Japan **78** D2
Obluch'ye Rus. Fed. **81** E1
Obninsk Rus. Fed. **43** E2
Obo C.A.R. **105** C2
Obock Djibouti **103** C3
Obouya Congo **104** B3
Oboyan' Rus. Fed. **43** E3
Obregón, Presa *resr* Mex. **142** B2
Obrenovac Serb. and Mont. **64** B2
Obshchiy Syrt *hills* Rus. Fed. **41** E3
Obskaya Guba *sea chan.* Rus. Fed.
  40 G2
Obuasi Ghana **100** B4
Obukhiv Ukr. **44** D1
Ob"yachevo Rus. Fed. **40** D2
Ocala U.S.A. **139** D3
Ocampo Mex. **142** B2
Ocaña Spain **60** C2
Occidental, Cordillera *mts* Col.
  150 B2
Occidental, Cordillera *mts* Peru
  150 B4
Ocean City U.S.A. **137** E3
Ocean Falls Can. **126** C2
Oceanside U.S.A. **133** C4
Ochakiv Ukr. **45** D2
Ocher Rus. Fed. **40** E3
Ochsenfurt Ger. **55** E3
Oconee *r.* U.S.A. **139** D2
Ocosingo Mex. **143** C3
Ocussi *enclave* East Timor **71** C3
Oda, Jebel *mt.* Sudan **102** B2
Ōdate Japan **78** D2
Odawara Japan **79** C3
Odda Norway **47** B3
Odemira Port. **60** B2
Ödemiş Turkey **65** C3
Odense Denmark **47** C4
Odenwald *reg.* Ger. **55** D3

Polacca U.S.A. **140** B1
Pola de Lena Spain **60** B1
Poland *country* Europe **57** D2
Polatsk Belarus **42** C2
Pol-e Khomrī Afgh. **86** A1
Polewali Indon. **73** C2
Poli Cameroon **104** B2
Police Pol. **56** F2
Policoro Italy **63** C2
Poligny France **59** D2
Polillo Islands Phil. **76** B2
Polis'ke Ukr. **44** C1
Polkowice Pol. **57** D2
Pollino, Monte *mt.* Italy **63** C3
Polohy Ukr. **45** E2
Polokwane S. Africa **109** C1
Polonne Ukr. **44** C1
Polson U.S.A. **132** D1
Poltava Ukr. **45** D2
Poltava Rus. Fed. **78** B2
Poltavskaya Rus. Fed. **45** E2
Pôlva Estonia **42** C2
Polyarnyy Rus. Fed. **46** G2
Polyarnyye Zori Rus. Fed. **46** G2
Polygyros Greece **65** B2
Polykastro Greece **92** A1
Polynesia *is* Pacific Ocean **158** E5
Pombal Port. **60** B2
Pomezia Italy **62** B2
Pomokaira *reg.* Fin. **46** F2
Pomorie Bulg. **64** C2
Pomorska, Zatoka *b.* Pol. **56** C2
Pompéu Brazil **155** D1
Ponca City U.S.A. **141** E1
Ponce Puerto Rico **145** D3
Pondicherry India **85** B3
Pond Inlet Can. **125** G2
Ponferrada Spain **60** B1
Pongo *watercourse* Sudan **103** A4
Pongola *r.* S. Africa **109** D2
Ponoka Can. **126** D2
Ponta Grossa Brazil **154** B3
Pontalina Brazil **154** C1
Pont-à-Mousson France **59** D2
Ponta Porã Brazil **154** A2
Pontarlier France **59** D2
Pontcharra France **56** B3
Pontchartrain, Lake U.S.A. **138** B2
Ponte de Sor Port. **60** B2
Ponteix Can. **127** E3
Pontes-e-Lacerda Brazil **150** D4
Pontevedra Spain **60** B1
Pontiac *IL* U.S.A. **136** C2
Pontiac *MI* U.S.A. **136** D2
Pontianak Indon. **72** B2
Pontivy France **58** B2
Pontoetoe Suriname **151** D2
Pontoise France **49** D4
Ponton Can. **127** F2
Pontypool U.K. **53** B4
Ponziane, Isole *is* Italy **62** B2
Poochera Austr. **116** A2
Poole U.K. **53** C4
Poona India *see* Pune
Pooncarie Austr. **116** C2
Poopó, Lago de *l.* Bol. **152** B2
Popayán Col. **150** B2
Popigay *r.* Rus. Fed. **95** J2
Popiltah Austr. **116** C2
Poplar *r.* Can. **127** F2
Poplar Bluff U.S.A. **135** E3
Popocatépetl, Volcán *vol.* Mex. **121**
Popokabaka Dem. Rep. Congo
    104 B3
Popovo Bulg. **64** C2
Poprad Slovakia **57** E3
Porangatu Brazil **151** E4
Porbandar India **86** A2
Porcupine *r.* Can./U.S.A. **124** C2
Poreč Croatia **62** B1

Pori Fin. **47** E3
Porirua N.Z. **118** B3
Porkhov Rus. Fed. **42** C2
Pornic France **58** B2
Poronaysk Rus. Fed. **81** F1
Poros Greece **65** B3
Porsgrunn Norway **47** B4
Portadown U.K. **51** C1
Portaferry U.K. **51** D1
Portage U.S.A. **136** C2
Portage la Prairie Can. **127** F3
Port Alberni Can. **126** C3
Portalegre Port. **60** B2
Portales U.S.A. **141** D2
Port Alexander U.S.A. **126** B2
Port Alice Can. **126** C2
Port Angeles U.S.A. **132** B1
Port Arthur Austr. **115** D4
Port Arthur U.S.A. **141** F3
Port Askaig U.K. **50** A3
Port Augusta Austr. **116** B2
Port-au-Prince Haiti **145** C3
Port aux Choix Can. **129** E1
Port Blair India **75** A2
Port Campbell Austr. **116** C3
Port Chalmers N.Z. **118** B4
Port Charlotte U.S.A. **139** D3
Port-de-Paix Haiti **145** C3
Port Edward Can. **126** B2
Porteirinha Brazil **155** D1
Portel Brazil **151** D3
Port Elgin Can. **128** B2
Port Elizabeth S. Africa **109** C3
Port Ellen U.K. **50** A3
Port Erin Isle of Man **52** A2
Porterville S. Africa **108** A3
Porterville U.S.A. **133** C3
Port Fairy Austr. **116** C3
Port Fitzroy N.Z. **118** C2
Port-Gentil Gabon **104** A3
Port Harcourt Nigeria **101** C4
Port Hardy Can. **126** C2
Port Hawkesbury Can. **129** D2
Port Hedland Austr. **114** A2
Porthmadog U.K. **52** A3
Port Hope Simpson Can. **129** E1
Port Huron U.S.A. **136** D2
Portimão Port. **60** B2
Portland *N.S.W.* Austr. **117** D2
Portland *Vic.* Austr. **116** C3
Portland *ME* U.S.A. **137** F2
Portland *OR* U.S.A. **132** B1
Portland Canal *inlet* Can. **126** B2
Portlaoise Rep. of Ireland **51** C2
Port Lavaca U.S.A. **141** E3
Port Lincoln Austr. **116** B2
Port Loko Sierra Leone **100** A4
Port Louis Mauritius **99**
Port Macquarie Austr. **117** E2
Port McNeill Can. **126** C2
Port-Menier Can. **129** D2
Port Moresby P.N.G. **71** D3
Port Ness U.K. **50** A1
Port Nolloth S. Africa **108** A2
Porto Port. *see* Oporto
Porto Acre Brazil **150** C3
Porto Alegre Brazil **152** C4
Porto Artur Brazil **151** D4
Porto dos Gaúchos Óbidos Brazil
    151 D4
Porto Esperidião Brazil **150** D4
Portoferraio Italy **62** B2
Porto Franco Brazil **151** E3
Port of Spain Trin. and Tob. **145** D3
Portogruaro Italy **62** B1
Portomaggiore Italy **62** B2
Porto Mendes Brazil **154** B2
Porto Murtinho Brazil **152** C3
Porto Nacional Brazil **151** E4
Porto-Novo Benin **100** C4

Porto Primavera, Represa *resr* Brazil
    154 B2
Porto Santana Brazil **151** D3
Porto Seguro Brazil **155** E1
Porto Tolle Italy **62** B2
Porto Torres Italy **62** A2
Porto-Vecchio France **59** D3
Porto Velho Brazil **150** C3
Portoviejo Ecuador **150** A3
Port Phillip Bay Austr. **116** C3
Port Pirie Austr. **116** B2
Portree U.K. **50** A2
Port Renfrew Can. **126** C3
Portrush U.K. **51** C1
Port Said Egypt **102** B1
Port Shepstone S. Africa **109** D3
Portsmouth U.K. **53** C4
Portsmouth *NH* U.S.A. **137** F2
Portsmouth *OH* U.S.A. **136** D3
Portsmouth *VA* U.S.A. **137** E3
Portstewart U.K. **51** C1
Port St Joe U.S.A. **139** C3
Port St Johns S. Africa **109** C3
Port Sudan Sudan **102** B3
Port Sulphur U.S.A. **138** C3
Port Talbot U.K. **53** B4
Portugal *country* Europe **60** B2
Portumna Rep. of Ireland **51** B2
Port-Vendres France **59** C3
Port Vila Vanuatu **112**
Porvoo Fin. **47** F3
Poryŏng S. Korea **77** B2
Posadas Arg. **152** C3
Poshekhon'ye Rus. Fed. **43** E2
Posio Fin. **46** F2
Poso Indon. **73** D2
Posse Brazil **151** E4
Pößneck Ger. **55** E2
Post U.S.A. **141** D2
Poste-de-la-Baleine Can. *see*
    Kuujjuarapik
Postmasburg S. Africa **108** B2
Posušje Bos.-Herz. **63** C2
Poteau U.S.A. **141** F1
Potenza Italy **63** C2
Poti *r.* Brazil **151** E3
P'ot'i Georgia **93** C1
Potiskum Nigeria **101** D3
Potomac, South Branch *r.* U.S.A.
    137 E3
Potosí Bol. **152** B2
Pototan Phil. **76** B2
Potrero del Llano Mex. **140** D3
Potsdam Ger. **55** F1
Potsdam U.S.A. **137** F2
Pottstown U.S.A. **137** E2
Pottsville U.S.A. **137** E2
Pouch Cove Can. **129** E2
Poughkeepsie U.S.A. **137** F2
Poulton-le-Fylde U.K. **52** B3
Pouso Alegre Brazil **155** C2
Poŭthĭsăt Cambodia **75** B2
Považská Bystrica Slovakia **57** D3
Povlen *mt.* Serb. and Mont. **64** A2
Póvoa de Varzim Port. **60** B1
Povorino Rus. Fed. **45** F1
Powell U.S.A. **134** B2
Powell, Lake *resr* U.S.A. **133** D3
Powell River Can. **126** C3
Poxoréu Brazil **154** B1
Poyang Hu *l.* China **83** B3
Požarevac Serb. and Mont. **64** B2
Poza Rica Mex. **143** C2
Požega Croatia **63** C1
Požega Serb. and Mont. **64** B2
Pozm Tīāb Iran **91** D2
Poznań Pol. **57** D2
Pozoblanco Spain **60** C2
Pozzuoli Italy **62** B2
Prabumulih Indon. **72** B2

P'yŏngsan N. Korea **77** B2
P'yŏngyang N. Korea **77** B2
Pyramid Lake U.S.A. **132** C2
Pyramids of Giza *tourist site* Egypt
  92 B3
Pyrenees *mts* Europe **61** D1
Pyrgos Greece **65** B3
Pyryatyn Ukr. **45** D1
Pyrzyce Pol. **56** C2
Pytalovo Rus. Fed. **42** C2
Pyxaria *mt.* Greece **65** B3

Q

Qaanaaq Greenland *see* Thule
Qacha's Nek Lesotho **109** C3
Qādub Yemen **91** C3
Qagan Nur China **82** B1
Qaidam Pendi *basin* China **80** C2
Qalansïyah Yemen **91** C3
Qal'at Bīshah Saudi Arabia **90** B2
Qamanirjuaq Lake Can. **127** F1
Qamar, Ghubbat al *b.* Yemen **91** C3
Qam Hadīl Saudi Arabia **90** B3
Qarshi Uzbek. **89** D3
Qaryat al Ulyā Saudi Arabia **91** B2
Qasigiannguit Greenland **125** I2
Qaşr-e Qand Iran **91** D2
Qaşr-e Shīrīn Iran **93** C2
Qassimiut Greenland **125** I2
Qa'tabah Yemen **90** B3
Qatar *country* Asia **91** C2
Qattara Depression Egypt **102** A2
Qausuittuq Can. *see* Resolute
Qazax Azer. **93** C1
Qazımämmäd Azer. **93** C1
Qazvīn Iran **93** C2
Qeqertarsuaq *i.* Greenland **125** I2
Qeqertarsuatsiaat Greenland **125** I2
Qeqertarsuup Tunua *b.* Greenland
  125 I2
Qeshm Iran **91** C2
Qianjiang *Chongqing* China **83** A3
Qianjiang *Hubei* China **83** B2
Qian Shan *mts* China **77** A1
Qidong China **82** C2
Qiemo China **89** F3
Qijiang China **83** A3
Qijiaojing China **80** C2
Qikiqtarjuaq Can. **125** H2
Qila Ladgasht Pak. **86** A2
Qilian Shan *mts* China **80** C2
Qillak *i.* Greenland **125** J2
Qimen China **83** B3
Qimusseriarsuaq *b.* Greenland **125** H1
Qinā Egypt **102** B2
Qingdao China **82** C2
Qinghai *prov.* China **87** D1
Qinghai Hu *salt l.* China **80** C2
Qinghai Nanshan *mts* China **80** C2
Qingyuan *Guangdong* China **83** B3
Qingyuan *Liaoning* China **77** A1
Qingzang Gaoyuan *plat.* China *see*
  Tibet, Plateau of
Qingzhou China **82** B2
Qinhuangdao China **82** B2
Qin Ling *mts* China **82** A2
Qinyang China **82** B2
Qinzhou China **83** A3
Qionghai China **83** B4
Qionglai Shan *mts* China **82** A2
Qiongshan China **83** B4
Qiqihar China **81** E1
Qīr Iran **93** D3
Qitaihe China **78** B1
Qixian China **82** B2
Qogir Feng *mt.*
  China/Jammu and Kashmir *see* K2

Qom Iran **93** D2
Qomolangma Feng *mt.* China/Nepal *see*
  Everest, Mount
Qo'ng'irot Uzbek. **88** C2
Qo'qon Uzbek. **89** E2
Qoraqalpog'iston Uzbek. **88** C2
Quakenbrück Ger. **54** C1
Quang Ngai Vietnam **75** B2
Quang Tri Vietnam **74** B2
Quanzhou *Fujian* China **83** B3
Quanzhou *Guangxi* China **83** B3
Quartu Sant'Elena Italy **62** A3
Quartzsite U.S.A. **140** B2
Quba Azer. **93** C1
Queanbeyan Austr. **117** D3
Québec Can. **129** C2
Québec *prov.* Can. **128** C1
Quedlinburg Ger. **55** E2
Queen Charlotte Can. **126** B2
Queen Charlotte Islands Can. **126** B2
Queen Charlotte Sound *sea chan.* Can.
  126 C2
Queen Charlotte Strait Can. **126** C2
Queen Elizabeth Islands Can. **124** E1
Queen Maud Gulf Can. **124** F2
Queen Maud Land *reg.* Antarctica
  119 C2
Queen Maud Mountains Antarctica
  119 I1
Queensland *state* Austr. **115** D2
Queenstown Austr. **115** D4
Queenstown N.Z. **118** A4
Queenstown S. Africa **109** C3
Quelimane Moz. **107** C1
Quemado U.S.A. **140** C2
Queréncia do Norte Brazil **154** B2
Querétaro Mex. **143** B2
Querfurt Ger. **55** E2
Quesnel Can. **126** C2
Quesnel Lake Can. **126** C2
Quetta Pak. **86** A1
Quezaltenango Guat. **143** C3
Quezon Phil. **76** A3
Quezon City Phil. **76** B2
Quibala Angola **106** A1
Quibdó Col. **150** B2
Quiberon France **58** B2
Quillan France **58** C3
Quilmes Arg. **153** C4
Quilon India **85** B4
Quilpie Austr. **115** D2
Quilpué Chile **153** A4
Quimbele Angola **104** B3
Quimilí Arg. **152** B3
Quimper France **58** B2
Quimperlé France **58** B2
Quincy *IL* U.S.A. **136** B3
Quincy *MA* U.S.A. **137** F2
Qui Nhon Vietnam **75** B2
Quinto Spain **61** C1
Quionga Moz. **105** E4
Quirindi Austr. **117** E2
Quissico Moz. **107** C2
Quitapa Angola **104** B4
Quito Ecuador **150** B3
Quixadá Brazil **151** F3
Qujing China **83** A3
Qumar He *r.* China **87** D1
Quoich *r.* Can. **127** F1
Quorn Austr. **116** B2
Qurayat Oman **91** C2
Qūrghonteppa Tajik. **89** D3
Quzhou China **83** B3

R

Raab *r.* Austria **57** D3
Raahe Fin. **46** E3

Raalte Neth. **54** C1
Raas *i.* Indon. **73** C2
Raba Indon. **73** C2
Rabat Morocco **100** B1
Rābigh Saudi Arabia **90** A2
Race, Cape Can. **129** E2
Raceland U.S.A. **138** B3
Rach Gia Vietnam **75** B3
Racine U.S.A. **136** C2
Radā' Yemen **90** B3
Rădăuți Romania **44** C2
Radcliff U.S.A. **136** C3
Radebeul Ger. **55** F2
Radhanpur India **86** B2
Radisson Can. **128** C1
Radom Pol. **57** E2
Radomsko Pol. **57** D2
Radomyshl' Ukr. **44** C1
Radoviš Macedonia **63** D2
Radviliškis Lith. **42** B2
Raḍwá, Jabal *mt.* Saudi Arabia **90** A2
Radyvyliv Ukr. **44** C1
Rae Bareli India **87** C2
Rae-Edzo Can. **126** D1
Rae Lakes Can. **126** D1
Raeren Belgium **54** C2
Raetihi N.Z. **118** C2
Rafaela Arg. **152** B4
Rafaï C.A.R. **104** C2
Rafḥā' Saudi Arabia **90** B2
Rafsanjān Iran **93** D2
Ragang, Mount *vol.* Phil. **76** B3
Ragusa Italy **62** B3
Raha Indon. **73** D2
Rahachow Belarus **42** D3
Rahimyar Khan Pak. **86** B2
Raichur India **85** B3
Raigarh India **87** C2
Rainbow Lake Can. **126** D2
Rainier, Mount *vol.* U.S.A. **132** B1
Rainy Lake Can./U.S.A. **127** F3
Rainy River Can. **127** F3
Raipur India **87** C2
Raisio Fin. **47** E3
Rajahmundry India **85** C3
Rajang *r.* Malaysia **73** C1
Rajanpur Pak. **86** B2
Rajapalaiyam India **85** B4
Rajasthan Canal India **86** B2
Rajgarh India **86** B2
Rajkot India **86** B2
Rajpur India **86** B2
Rajshahi Bangl. **87** C2
Rakaia *r.* N.Z. **118** B3
Rakhiv Ukr. **44** B2
Rakitnoye Rus. Fed. **45** E1
Rakke Estonia **42** C2
Rakvere Estonia **42** C2
Raleigh U.S.A. **139** E1
Ralik Chain *is* Marshall Is **110**
Rambutyo Island P.N.G. **71** D3
Ramgarh India **86** B2
Rāmhormoz Iran **93** C2
Râmnicu Sărat Romania **44** C2
Râmnicu Vâlcea Romania **44** B2
Ramon' Rus. Fed. **43** E3
Ramotswa Botswana **109** C1
Rampur India **87** B2
Ramree Island Myanmar **74** A2
Ramsey Isle of Man **52** A2
Ramsgate U.K. **53** D4
Ramsing India **74** A1
Ranaghat India **87** C2
Ranau Malaysia **73** C1
Rancagua Chile **153** A4
Ranchi India **87** C2
Randers Denmark **47** C4
Rangiora N.Z. **118** B3
Rangitaiki *r.* N.Z. **118** C2

Riihimäki Fin. **47** E3
Rijeka Croatia **62** B1
Riley U.S.A. **132** C2
Rimah, Wādī al *watercourse*
  Saudi Arabia **90** B2
Rimavská Sobota Slovakia **57** E3
Rimini Italy **62** B2
Rimouski Can. **129** D2
Ringebu Norway **47** C3
Ringkøbing Denmark **47** B4
Ringvassøya *i.* Norway **46** D2
Rinteln Ger. **55** D1
Riobamba Ecuador **150** B3
Rio Branco Brazil **150** C4
Rio Branco do Sul Brazil **154** C3
Rio Brilhante Brazil **154** B2
Rio Claro Brazil **154** C2
Río Colorado Arg. **153** B4
Río Cuarto Arg. **153** B4
Rio de Janeiro Brazil **155** D2
Rio do Sul Brazil **154** C3
Río Gallegos Arg. **153** B6
Río Grande Arg. **153** B6
Rio Grande Brazil **152** C4
Río Grande Mex. **142** B2
Rio Grande *r.* Mex./U.S.A. **142** C2
Rio Grande City U.S.A. **141** E3
Ríohacha Col. **150** B1
Rioja Peru **150** B3
Río Lagartos Mex. **143** D2
Riom France **59** C2
Río Mulatos Bol. **152** B2
Rio Negro Brazil **154** C3
Rio Pardo de Minas Brazil **155** D1
Río Rancho U.S.A. **140** C1
Río Tigre Ecuador **150** B3
Rio Verde Brazil **154** B1
Río Verde Mex. **143** C2
Rio Verde de Mato Grosso Brazil
  154 B1
Ripky Ukr. **44** D1
Ripley U.K. **52** C3
Ripoll Spain **61** D1
Ripon U.K. **52** C2
Rishiri-tō *i.* Japan **78** D1
Risør Norway **47** B4
Ritchie S. Africa **108** B2
Ritchie's Archipelago *is* India **75** A2
Ritzville U.S.A. **132** C1
Rivadavia Arg. **152** B3
Riva del Garda Italy **62** B1
Rivas Nic. **144** B3
Rivera Uru. **152** C4
Riverhurst Can. **127** E2
Riverdale S. Africa **108** B3
Riverside U.S.A. **133** C4
Riverton U.S.A. **134** B2
Riverview Can. **129** D2
Rivesaltes France **58** C3
Rivière-du-Loup Can. **129** D2
Rivne Ukr. **44** C1
Riwaka N.Z. **118** B3
Riyadh Saudi Arabia **90** B2
Rize Turkey **93** C1
Rizhao China **82** B2
Roanne France **59** C2
Roanoke U.S.A. **137** E3
Roanoke *r.* U.S.A. **139** E1
Roanoke Rapids U.S.A. **139** E1
Robe Austr. **116** B3
Röbel Ger. **55** F1
Robertsfors Sweden **46** E3
Robertson S. Africa **108** A3
Robertsport Liberia **100** A4
Roberval Can. **129** C2
Robinson Range *hills* Austr. **114** A2
Robinvale Austr. **116** C2
Roblin Can. **127** E2
Robson, Mount Can. **126** D2

Rocca Busambra *mt.* Italy **62** B3
Rocha Uru. **153** C4
Rochdale U.K. **52** B3
Rochedo Brazil **154** B1
Rochefort Belgium **54** B2
Rochefort France **58** B2
Rochester *MN* U.S.A. **135** E2
Rochester *NH* U.S.A. **137** F2
Rochester *NY* U.S.A. **137** E2
Rockford U.S.A. **136** C2
Rockhampton Austr. **115** E2
Rock Hill U.S.A. **139** D2
Rockingham Austr. **114** A3
Rock Island U.S.A. **136** B2
Rock Springs *MT* U.S.A. **134** B1
Rocksprings U.S.A. **141** D3
Rock Springs *WY* U.S.A. **134** B2
Rocky Ford U.S.A. **134** C3
Rocky Mount U.S.A. **139** E1
Rocky Mountains Can./U.S.A. **130** C2
Rocourt-St-Martin France **54** A3
Rocroi France **54** B3
Rødbyhavn Denmark **56** C2
Roddickton Can. **129** E1
Rodez France **58** C3
Roding Ger. **55** F3
Rodniki Rus. Fed. **43** F2
Rodos Greece *see* Rhodes
Rodos *i.* Greece *see* Rhodes
Roebourne Austr. **114** A2
Roebuck Bay Austr. **114** B1
Roedtan S. Africa **109** C1
Roermond Neth. **54** B2
Roeselare Belgium **54** A2
Rogers U.S.A. **138** B1
Roggeveldberge *esc.* S. Africa **108** B3
Rognan Norway **46** D2
Rogue *r.* U.S.A. **132** B2
Roja Latvia **42** B2
Rokan *r.* Indon. **72** B1
Rokiškis Lith. **42** C1
Rokycany Czech Rep. **55** F3
Rokytne Ukr. **44** C1
Rolândia Brazil **154** B2
Rolla U.S.A. **135** E3
Roma Austr. **115** D2
Roma *i.* Indon. **71** C3
Roma Italy *see* Rome
Roma Lesotho **109** C2
Roma U.S.A. **141** E3
Romain, Cape U.S.A. **139** E2
Roman Romania **44** C2
Romania *country* Europe **44** B2
Roman-Kosh *mt.* Ukr. **45** D3
Romanovka *Respublika Buryatiya*
  Rus. Fed. **81** D1
Romanovka *Saratovskaya Oblast'*
  Rus. Fed. **45** F1
Rombas France **59** D2
Romblon Phil. **76** B2
Rome Italy **62** B2
Rome *GA* U.S.A. **139** C2
Rome *NY* U.S.A. **137** E2
Romford U.K. **53** D4
Romilly-sur-Seine France **59** C2
Romny Ukr. **45** D2
Romorantin-Lanthenay France **58** C2
Romsey U.K. **53** C4
Roncador, Serra do *hills* Brazil **151** D4
Ronda Spain **60** B2
Rondon Brazil **154** B2
Rondonópolis Brazil **154** B1
Rondu Jammu and Kashmir **86** B1
Rong'an China **83** A3
Rongjiang China **83** A3
Rongklang Range *mts* Myanmar **74** A1
Rønne Denmark **47** C4
Ronne Ice Shelf Antarctica **119** K2
Ronnenberg Ger. **55** D1
Ronse Belgium **54** A2

Roorkee India **87** B2
Roosendaal Neth. **54** B2
Roosevelt U.S.A. **132** E2
Roosevelt, Mount Can. **126** C2
Roosevelt Island Antarctica **119** I2
Roquefort France **58** B3
Roraima, Mount Guyana **150** C2
Røros Norway **47** C3
Rosario Arg. **153** B4
Rosario *Baja California* Mex. **142** A1
Rosario *Sinaloa* Mex. **142** B2
Rosario *Sonora* Mex. **142** B2
Rosário Oeste Brazil **151** D4
Rosarito Mex. **142** A2
Rosarno Italy **63** C3
Roscoff France **58** B2
Roscommon Rep. of Ireland **51** B2
Roscrea Rep. of Ireland **51** C2
Roseau Dominica **145** D3
Roseau U.S.A. **135** D1
Roseburg U.S.A. **132** B2
Rosenberg U.S.A. **141** E3
Rosendal Norway **48** E2
Rosengarten Ger. **55** D1
Rosenheim Ger. **56** D1
Rosetown Can. **127** E2
Roshchino Rus. Fed. **42** C1
Rosh Pinah Namibia **108** A2
Roşiori de Vede Romania **44** C3
Roskilde Denmark **47** C4
Roslavl' Rus. Fed. **43** D3
Rossano Italy **63** C3
Rossan Point *pt* Rep. of Ireland **51** B1
Ross Ice Shelf Antarctica **119** H1
Rossignol, Lake Can. **129** D2
Rossland Can. **126** D3
Rosslare Rep. of Ireland **51** C2
Rosso Maur. **100** A3
Rosso, Capo *c.* France **59** D3
Ross-on-Wye U.K. **53** B4
Rossosh' Rus. Fed. **45** E1
Ross River Can. **126** B1
Røssvatnet *l.* Norway **46** C2
Rostāq Iran **93** D3
Rosthern Can. **124** E3
Rostock Ger. **56** C2
Rostov Rus. Fed. **43** E2
Rostov-na-Donu Rus. Fed. **45** E2
Rosvik Sweden **46** E2
Roswell U.S.A. **140** D2
Rota *i.* N. Mariana Is **71** D2
Rot am See Ger. **55** E3
Rote *i.* Indon. **71** C3
Rotenburg (Wümme) Ger. **55** D1
Roth Ger. **55** E3
Rothbury U.K. **52** C2
Rothenburg ob der Tauber Ger. **55**
Rotherham U.K. **52** C3
Rothesay U.K. **50** B3
Roto Austr. **117** D2
Rotondo, Monte *mt.* France **59** D3
Rotorua N.Z. **118** C2
Rotorua, Lake N.Z. **118** C2
Rottenbach Ger. **55** E2
Rottenmann Austria **56** C3
Rotterdam Neth. **54** B2
Rottweil Ger. **56** B3
Rotuma *i.* Fiji **110**
Roubaix France **59** C1
Rouen France **58** C2
Round Mountain Austr. **117** E2
Round Pond *l.* Can. **129** E2
Round Rock U.S.A. **141** E3
Roundup U.S.A. **132** E1
Rousay *i.* U.K. **50** C1
Rouyn-Noranda Can. **128** C2
Rovaniemi Fin. **46** F2
Roven'ki Rus. Fed. **45** E2
Roven'ky Ukr. **45** E2
Rovereto Italy **62** B1

Shaowu China **83** B3
Shaoxing China **83** C2
Shaoyang China **83** B3
Shaqrā' Saudi Arabia **102** C2
Sharhorod Ukr. **44** C2
Sharjah U.A.E. **91** C2
Sharkawshchyna Belarus **42** C2
Shark Bay Austr. **114** A2
Sharm ash Shaykh Egypt **90** A2
Sharon U.S.A. **137** D2
Shar'ya Rus. Fed. **40** D3
Shashe *r.* Botswana/Zimbabwe **107** B2
Shashemenē Eth. **103** B4
Shasta, Mount *vol.* U.S.A. **132** B2
Shasta Lake U.S.A. **132** B2
Shatsk Rus. Fed. **43** F3
Shatura Rus. Fed. **43** E2
Shaunavon Can. **127** E3
Shawano U.S.A. **136** C2
Shawinigan Can. **129** C2
Shawnee U.S.A. **141** E1
Shay Gap Austr. **114** B2
Shchekino Rus. Fed. **43** E3
Shchelkovo Rus. Fed. **43** E2
Shchigry Rus. Fed. **43** E3
Shchors Ukr. **45** D1
Shchuchyn Belarus **42** B3
Shebekino Rus. Fed. **45** E1
Sheberghān Afgh. **86** A1
Sheboygan U.S.A. **136** C2
Shebsh *r.* Rus. Fed. **45** E3
Sheelin, Lough *l.* Rep. of Ireland **51** C2
Sheffield U.K. **52** C3
Sheksna Rus. Fed. **43** E2
Sheksninskoye Vodokhranilishche
   resr Rus. Fed. **43** E2
Shelagskiy, Mys *pt* Rus. Fed. **95** N2
Shelburne Can. **129** D2
Shelby U.S.A. **132** D1
Shelbyville *IN* U.S.A. **136** C3
Shelbyville *TN* U.S.A. **139** C1
Shelikhova, Zaliv *g.* Rus. Fed. **95** M2
Shellbrook Can. **127** E2
Shelton U.S.A. **132** B1
Shenandoah U.S.A. **135** D2
Shenandoah *r.* U.S.A. **137** E3
Shendam Nigeria **104** A2
Shendi Sudan **90** A3
Shenkursk Rus. Fed. **40** D2
Shenyang China **82** C1
Shenzhen China **83** B3
Shepetivka Ukr. **44** C1
Shepparton Austr. **117** D3
Sheppey, Isle of *i.* U.K. **53** D4
Sherbrooke *N.S.* Can. **129** D2
Sherbrooke *Que.* Can. **129** C2
Shereiq Sudan **102** B3
Sheridan U.S.A. **134** B2
Sherman U.S.A. **141** E2
's-Hertogenbosch Neth. **54** B2
Shetland Islands *Scotland* U.K.
   50 [inset]
Shetpe Kazakh. **88** C2
Sheyenne *r.* U.S.A. **135** D1
Shibām Yemen **91** B3
Shibetsu Japan **78** E2
Shicheng China **83** B3
Shiel, Loch *l.* U.K. **50** B2
Shihezi China **89** F2
Shijiazhuang China **82** B2
Shikarpur Pak. **86** A2
Shikoku *i.* Japan **79** B4
Shikotsu-ko *l.* Japan **78** D2
Shilega Rus. Fed. **40** D2
Shiliguri India **87** C2
Shillong India **87** D2
Shilovo Rus. Fed. **43** F3
Shimbiris *mt.* Somalia **103** C3
Shimizu Japan **79** C3
Shimla India **87** B1

Shimoga India **85** B3
Shimonoseki Japan **79** B4
Shin, Loch *l.* U.K. **50** B1
Shīndand Afgh. **86** A1
Shingū Japan **79** C4
Shingwedzi S. Africa **109** D1
Shingwedzi *r.* S. Africa **109** D1
Shinyanga Tanz. **105** D3
Shiono-misaki *c.* Japan **79** C4
Shiprock U.S.A. **140** C1
Shiqian China **83** A3
Shiquan China **82** A2
Shirane-san *mt.* Japan **79** C3
Shīrāz Iran **93** D3
Shiretoko-misaki *c.* Japan **78** E2
Shiriya-zaki *c.* Japan **78** D2
Shiv India **86** B2
Shivpuri India **87** B2
Shiyan China **82** B2
Shizuishan China **82** A2
Shizuoka Japan **79** C4
Shklow Belarus **43** D3
Shkodër Albania **63** C2
Shmidta, Ostrov *i.* Rus. Fed. **95** I1
Shor Barsa-Kel'mes *salt marsh* Uzbek.
   93 D1
Shoshone U.S.A. **133** C3
Shoshone Mountains U.S.A. **133** C3
Shoshong Botswana **109** C1
Shostka Ukr. **45** D1
Shouxian China **82** B2
Showak Sudan **90** A3
Show Low U.S.A. **140** B2
Shpola Ukr. **45** D2
Shreveport U.S.A. **138** B2
Shrewsbury U.K. **53** B3
Shu'ab, Ra's *pt* Yemen **91** C3
Shuangjiang China **74** A1
Shuangliao China **77** A1
Shuangyang China **77** B1
Shuangyashan China **78** B1
Shubarkuduk Kazakh. **88** C2
Shubrā al Khaymah Egypt **102** B1
Shugozero Rus. Fed. **43** D2
Shumba Zimbabwe **106** B1
Shumen Bulg. **64** C2
Shumilina Belarus **42** C2
Shumyachi Rus. Fed. **43** D3
Shungnak U.S.A. **124** B2
Shuqrah Yemen **90** B3
Shushkodom Rus. Fed. **43** F2
Shushtar Iran **93** C2
Shuswap Lake Can. **126** D2
Shuya Rus. Fed. **43** F2
Shuyskoye Rus. Fed. **43** F2
Shwebo Myanmar **74** A1
Shwedwin Myanmar **74** A1
Shwegyin Myanmar **74** A2
Shymkent Kazakh. **89** D2
Shyroke Ukr. **45** D2
Sia Indon. **71** C3
Siahan Range *mts* Pak. **86** A2
Sialkot Pak. **86** B1
Siargao *i.* Phil. **76** B3
Šiauliai Lith. **42** B2
Šibenik Croatia **63** C2
Siberia *reg.* Rus. Fed. **95** J2
Siberut *i.* Indon. **72** A2
Sibi Pak. **86** A2
Sibiu Romania **44** B2
Sibolga Indon. **72** A1
Sibsagar India **74** A1
Sibu Malaysia **73** C1
Sibut C.A.R. **104** B2
Sibuyan *i.* Phil. **76** B2
Sibuyan Sea Phil. **76** B2
Sicamous Can. **126** D2
Sichon Thai. **75** A3
Sichuan *prov.* China **82** A2
Sichuan Pendi *basin* China **83** A3

Sicié, Cap *c.* France **59** D3
Sicilia *i.* Italy *see* Sicily
Sicilian Channel Italy/Tunisia **62** B3
Sicily *i.* Italy **62** B3
Sicuani Peru **150** B4
Siddhapur India **86** B2
Sideros, Akra *pt* Greece **65** C3
Sidi Aïssa Alg. **61** D2
Sidi Ali Alg. **61** D2
Sidi Bel Abbès Alg. **100** B1
Sidi Ifni Morocco **100** A2
Sidikalang Indon. **72** A1
Sidi Okba Alg. **61** E3
Sidlaw Hills U.K. **50** C1
Sidmouth U.K. **53** B4
Sidney *MT* U.S.A. **134** C1
Sidney *NE* U.S.A. **134** C2
Sidney *OH* U.S.A. **136** D2
Sidney Lanier, Lake U.S.A. **139** C2
Sidoan Indon. **73** D1
Sidon Lebanon **92** B2
Sidrolândia Brazil **154** B2
Siedlce Pol. **57** E2
Sieg *r.* Ger. **54** C2
Siegen Ger. **54** D2
Siĕmréab Cambodia **75** B2
Siena Italy **62** B2
Sieradz Pol. **57** D2
Sierra Grande Arg. **153** B5
Sierra Leone *country* Africa **100** A4
Sierra Mojada Mex. **142** B2
Sierra Vista U.S.A. **140** B2
Sierre Switz. **59** D2
Sifnos *i.* Greece **65** B3
Sig Alg. **61** C2
Sigguup Nunaa *pen.* Greenland **125** I2
Sighetu Marmaţiei Romania **44** B2
Sighişoara Romania **44** B2
Sigli Indon. **72** A1
Siglufjörður Iceland **46** [inset]
Sigmaringen Ger. **56** B3
Signy-l'Abbaye France **54** B3
Sigüenza Spain **60** C1
Siguiri Guinea **100** B3
Sigulda Latvia **42** C2
Sihanoukville Cambodia **75** B2
Siilinjärvi Fin. **46** F3
Siirt Turkey **93** C2
Sijunjung Indon. **72** B2
Sikar India **86** B2
Sikasso Mali **100** B3
Sikeston U.S.A. **135** F3
Sikhote-Alin' *mts* Rus. Fed. **78** B2
Sikinos *i.* Greece **65** C3
Silao Mex. **142** B2
Silchar India **74** A1
Siletiteniz, Ozero *salt l.* Kazakh. **89** E1
Silgarhi Nepal **87** C2
Silifke Turkey **92** B2
Siling Co *salt l.* China **87** C1
Silistra Bulg. **64** C2
Silivri Turkey **92** A1
Siljan *l.* Sweden **47** C3
Silkeborg Denmark **47** B4
Sillamäe Estonia **42** C2
Siloam Springs U.S.A. **138** B1
Silobela S. Africa **109** C2
Šilutė Lith. **42** B2
Silvan Turkey **93** C2
Silver City U.S.A. **140** C2
Silverton U.S.A. **134** B3
Simao China **74** B1
Simàrd, Lac *l.* Can. **128** C2
Simav Turkey **65** C3
Simav Dağları *mts* Turkey **65** C3
Simba Dem. Rep. Congo **104** C2
Simcoe, Lake Can. **137** C2
Simeulue *i.* Indon. **72** A1
Simferopol' Ukr. **45** D3

Sulu Sea N. Pacific Ocean **76** A3
Sulzbach-Rosenberg Ger. **55** E3
Sumāil Oman **91** C2
Sumatera *i.* Indon. *see* Sumatra
Sumatra *i.* Indon. **72** A1
Šumava *mts* Czech Rep. **55** F3
Sumba *i.* Indon. **73** D2
Sumba, Selat *sea chan.* Indon. **73** C2
Sumbawa *i.* Indon. **73** C2
Sumbawabesar Indon. **73** C2
Sumbawanga Tanz. **105** D3
Sumbe Angola **106** A1
Sumburgh U.K. **50** [inset]
Sumburgh Head U.K. **50** [inset]
Sumenep Indon. **73** C2
Sumisu-jima *i.* Japan **79** D4
Summerside Can. **129** D2
Summersville U.S.A. **136** D3
Summit Lake Can. **126** C2
Šumperk Czech Rep. **57** D3
Sumqayıt Azer. **93** C1
Sumter U.S.A. **139** D2
Sumy Ukr. **45** D1
Sunamganj Bangl. **87** D2
Sunan N. Korea **77** B2
Şunaynah Oman **91** C2
Sunbury Austr. **116** C3
Sunbury U.S.A. **137** E2
Sunch'ŏn N. Korea **77** B2
Sunch'ŏn S. Korea **77** B3
Sun City S. Africa **109** C2
Sunda, Selat *str.* Indon. **72** B2
Sundance U.S.A. **134** C2
Sundarbans *coastal area* Bangl./India **87** C2
Sunderland U.K. **52** C2
Sundre Can. **126** D2
Sundsvall Sweden **47** D3
Sundumbili S. Africa **109** D2
Sungailiat Indon. **72** B2
Sungaipenuh Indon. **72** B2
Sungai Petani Malaysia **72** B1
Sungurlu Turkey **92** B1
Sunndal Norway **48** E1
Sunndalsøra Norway **46** B3
Sunnyside U.S.A. **132** C1
Sunnyvale U.S.A. **133** B3
Suntar Rus. Fed. **95** J2
Suntsar Pak. **86** A2
Sunyani Ghana **100** B4
Suoyarvi Rus. Fed. **94** E2
Superior *AZ* U.S.A. **140** B2
Superior *NE* U.S.A. **135** D2
Superior *WI* U.S.A. **134** B1
Superior, Lake Can./U.S.A. **136** C1
Suponevo Rus. Fed. **43** D3
Süq ash Shuyūkh Iraq **93** C2
Suqian China **82** B2
Sūq Suwayq Saudi Arabia **90** A2
Suquţrā *i.* Yemen *see* Socotra
Şūr Oman **91** C2
Sur, Punta *pt* Arg. **147**
Surab Pak. **86** A2
Surabaya Indon. **73** C2
Surakarta Indon. **73** C2
Surat India **86** B2
Suratgarh India **86** B2
Surat Thani Thai. **75** A3
Surazh Rus. Fed. **43** D3
Surdulica Serb. and Mont. **64** B2
Surendranagar India **86** B2
Surgut Rus. Fed. **40** G2
Surigao Phil. **76** B3
Surin Thai. **75** B2
Suriname *country* S. America **151** D2
Surulangun Indon. **72** B2
Susanino Rus. Fed. **43** F2
Susanville U.S.A. **132** B2
Suşehri Turkey **92** B1
Sušice Czech Rep. **55** F3

Sussex Can. **129** D2
Süstedt Ger. **55** D1
Sustrum Ger. **54** C1
Susuman Rus. Fed. **95** L2
Susurluk Turkey **65** C3
Sutak Jammu and Kashmir **87** B1
Sutherland S. Africa **108** B3
Sutton Coldfield U.K. **53** C3
Suttsu Japan **78** D2
Suva Fiji **112**
Suvorov Rus. Fed. **43** E3
Suwałki Pol. **57** E2
Suwannaphum Thai. **75** B2
Suwannee *r.* U.S.A. **139** D3
Suwarrow *atoll* Cook Is **111**
Suways, Qanāt as *canal* Egypt *see* Suez Canal
Suwŏn S. Korea **77** B2
Sūzā Iran **91** C2
Suzdal' Rus. Fed. **43** F2
Suzhou *Anhui* China **82** B2
Suzhou *Jiangsu* China **82** C2
Suzu Japan **79** C3
Suzu-misaki *pt* Japan **79** C3
Svalbard *terr.* Arctic Ocean **94** C1
Svatove Ukr. **45** E2
Svay Riĕng Cambodia **75** B2
Sveg Sweden **47** C3
Svelgen Norway **48** E1
Švenčionys Lith. **42** C2
Svendborg Denmark **47** C4
Sverdlovsk Rus. Fed. *see* Yekaterinburg
Sveti Nikole Macedonia **64** B2
Svetlaya Rus. Fed. **78** C1
Svetlogorsk Rus. Fed. **42** B3
Svetlyy Rus. Fed. **42** B3
Svetogorsk Rus. Fed. **47** F3
Svilengrad Bulg. **64** C2
Svinecea Mare, Vârful *mt.* Romania **44** B3
Svir' *r.* Rus. Fed. **43** E1
Svishtov Bulg. **64** C2
Svitavy Czech Rep. **57** D3
Svitlovods'k Ukr. **45** D2
Svobodnyy Rus. Fed. **81** E1
Svolvær Norway **46** C2
Svyetlahorsk Belarus **42** C3
Swainsboro U.S.A. **139** D2
Swakop *watercourse* Namibia **108** A1
Swakopmund Namibia **106** A2
Swan Hill Austr. **116** C3
Swan Hills Can. **126** D2
Swan Lake Can. **127** E2
Swan River Can. **127** E2
Swansea Austr. **117** E2
Swansea U.K. **53** B4
Swartruggens S. Africa **109** C2
Swatow China *see* Shantou
Swaziland *country* Africa **109** D2
Sweden *country* Europe **47** D3
Sweetwater U.S.A. **141** D2
Sweetwater *r.* U.S.A. **134** B2
Swellendam S. Africa **108** B3
Świdnica Pol. **57** D2
Świdwin Pol. **57** D2
Świebodzin Pol. **57** D2
Świecie Pol. **57** D2
Swift Current Can. **124** E3
Swilly, Lough *inlet* Rep. of Ireland **51** C1
Swindon U.K. **53** C4
Świnoujście Pol. **56** C2
Switzerland *country* Europe **59** D2
Swords Rep. of Ireland **51** C2
Syanno Belarus **42** C3
Sychevka Rus. Fed. **43** D2
Sydney Austr. **117** E2
Sydney Can. **129** D2
Sydney Mines Can. **129** D2
Syeverodonets'k Ukr. **45** E2

Syktyvkar Rus. Fed. **40** E2
Sylacauga U.S.A. **139** C2
Sylhet Bangl. **87** D2
Sylt *i.* Ger. **56** B2
Symi *i.* Greece **65** C3
Synel'nykove Ukr. **45** D2
Syracuse Italy **62** C3
Syracuse *KS* U.S.A. **134** C3
Syracuse *NY* U.S.A. **137** E2
Syrdar'ya *r.* Asia **89** D2
Syria *country* Asia **92** B2
Syrian Desert Asia **92** B2
Syros *i.* Greece **65** B3
Syzran' Rus. Fed. **41** D3
Szczecin Pol. **56** C2
Szczecinek Pol. **57** D2
Szczytno Pol. **57** E2
Szeged Hungary **57** E3
Székesfehérvár Hungary **57** D3
Szekszárd Hungary **57** D3
Szentes Hungary **57** E3
Szentgotthárd Hungary **57** D3
Szigetvár Hungary **57** D3
Szolnok Hungary **57** E3
Szombathely Hungary **57** D3

T

Ţābah Saudi Arabia **90** B2
Ţabas Iran **93** D2
Ţābask, Kūh-e *mt.* Iran **93** D3
Tabatinga Brazil **150** C3
Tabelbala Alg. **100** B2
Taber Can. **127** D3
Tábor Czech Rep. **56** C3
Tabora Tanz. **105** D3
Tabou Côte d'Ivoire **100** B4
Tabrīz Iran **93** C2
Tabūk Saudi Arabia **90** A2
Täby Sweden **42** A2
Tacheng China **89** F2
Tachov Czech Rep. **56** C3
Tacloban Phil. **76** B2
Tacna Peru **150** B4
Tacoma U.S.A. **132** B1
Tacuarembó Uru. **152** C4
Tacupeto Mex. **140** C3
Tadjoura Djibouti **103** C3
Tadmur Syria **92** B2
Tadoule Lake Can. **127** F2
Taegu S. Korea **77** B2
Taejŏn S. Korea **77** B2
Taejŏng S. Korea **77** B3
T'aepaek S. Korea **77** B2
Ta'erqi China **81** E1
Tafalla Spain **61** C1
Tafi Viejo Arg. **152** B3
Taftān, Kūh-e *mt.* Iran **91** D2
Taganrog Rus. Fed. **45** E2
Taganrog, Gulf of Rus. Fed./Ukr. **45** E2
Tagaung Myanmar **74** A1
Tagaytay City Phil. **76** B2
Tagbilaran Phil. **76** B3
Tagudin Phil. **76** B2
Tagum Phil. **76** B3
Tagus *r.* Port. **60** B2
Tagus *r.* Spain **60** B2
Tahan, Gunung *mt.* Malaysia **72** B1
Tahat, Mont *mt.* Alg. **101** C2
Tahe China **81** E1
Tahiti *i.* Fr. Polynesia **111**
Tahlequah U.S.A. **141** F1
Tahoe, Lake U.S.A. **133** B3
Tahoe City U.S.A. **133** B3
Tahoua Niger **101** C3
Tahrūd Iran **91** C2
Tahsis Can. **126** C3
Tai'an China **82** B2

aichung Taiwan **83** C3
ihape N.Z. **118** C2
i Hu *l.* China **82** C2
ilem Bend Austr. **116** B3
ainan Taiwan **83** C3
iobeiras Brazil **155** D1
aipei Taiwan **83** C3
iping Malaysia **72** B1
ishan China **83** B3
itao, Península de *pen.* Chile
 153 A5
aitung Taiwan **83** C3
ivalkoski Fin. **46** F2
ivaskero *h.* Fin. **46** E2
iwan *country* Asia **83** C3
iwan Strait China/Taiwan **83** B3
aiyuan China **82** B2
izhou *Jiangsu* China **82** B2
izhou *Zhejiang* China **83** C3
'izz Yemen **90** B3
jamulco, Volcán de *vol.* Guat.
 143 C3
ajikistan *country* Asia **89** E3
aj Mahal *tourist site* India **87** B2
ajo *r.* Spain *see* Tagus
ak Thai. **74** A2
ikaka N.Z. **118** B3
kamatsu Japan **79** B4
kaoka Japan **79** C3
kapuna N.Z. **118** B2
kasaki Japan **79** C3
katokwane Botswana **108** B1
katshwaane *Ghanzi* Botswana
 108 B1
kayama Japan **79** C3
kefu Japan **79** C3
kengon Indon. **72** A1
kêv Cambodia **75** B2
khemaret Alg. **61** D2
Khmau Cambodia **75** B2
kikawa Japan **78** D2
kla Lake Can. **126** C2
kla Landing Can. **126** C2
klimakan Desert China **89** F3
klimakan Shamo *des.* China *see*
 Taklimakan Desert
ku *r.* Can./U.S.A. **126** B2
kua Pa Thai. **75** A3
kum Nigeria **101** C4
lachyn Belarus **42** C3
lagang Pak. **86** B1
lara Peru **150** A3
laud, Kepulauan *is* Indon. **71** C2
lavera de la Reina Spain **60** C2
lca Chile **153** A4
lcahuano Chile **153** A4
ldom Rus. Fed. **43** E2
ldykorgan Kazakh. **89** E2
lia Austr. **116** A2
liabu *i.* Indon. **71** C3
lisay Phil. **76** B2
liwang Indon. **73** C2
ll 'Afar Iraq **93** C2
llahassee U.S.A. **139** D2
llinn Estonia **42** B2
llulah U.S.A. **138** B2
lmont-St-Hilaire France **58** B2
l'ne Ukr. **44** D2
lodi Sudan **103** B3
loqân Afgh. **86** A1
lovaya Rus. Fed. **43** F3
loyoak Can. **124** F2
lsi Latvia **42** B2
ltal Chile **152** A3
ltson *r.* Can. **127** D1
lu Indon. **72** A1
lwood Austr. **117** D1
lmala Rus. Fed. **45** F1
lmale Ghana **100** B4
lmanrasset Alg. **101** C2

Tamar *r.* U.K. **53** A4
Tamazunchale Mex. **143** C2
Tambacounda Senegal **100** A3
Tambelan, Kepulauan *is* Indon. **72** B1
Tambey Rus. Fed. **40** G1
Tambov Rus. Fed. **43** F3
Tamiahua, Laguna de *lag.* Mex.
 143 C2
Tampa U.S.A. **139** D3
Tampa Bay U.S.A. **139** D3
Tampere Fin. **47** E3
Tampico Mex. **143** C2
Tamsagbulag Mongolia **81** D1
Tamsweg Austria **56** C3
Tamworth Austr. **117** E2
Tamworth U.K. **53** C3
Tana *r.* Kenya **105** E3
Tanabe Japan **79** C4
Tana Bru Norway **46** F1
Tanahgrogot Indon. **73** C2
Tanahjampea *i.* Indon. **73** D2
Tanami Desert Austr. **114** C1
Tanana U.S.A. **124** B2
Tanaro *r.* Italy **62** A1
Tanch'ŏn N. Korea **77** B1
Tandag Phil. **76** B3
Tăndărei Romania **44** C3
Tandil Arg. **153** C4
Tando Adam Pak. **86** A2
Tando Muhammmad Khan Pak. **86** A2
Tanezrouft *reg.* Alg./Mali **100** B2
Tanga Tanz. **105** D3
Tanganyika, Lake Africa **105** C3
Tanger Morocco *see* Tangier
Tangermünde Ger. **55** E1
Tanggula Shan *mt.* China **87** D1
Tanggula Shan *mts* China **87** C1
Tangier Morocco **100** B1
Tangra Yumco *salt l.* China **87** C1
Tangshan China **82** B2
Taniantaweng Shan *mts* China **80** C2
Tanimbar, Kepulauan *is* Indon. **71** C3
Tanjay Phil. **76** B3
Tanjungbalai Indon. **72** A1
Tanjungpandan Indon. **72** B2
Tanjungpinang Indon. **72** B1
Tanjungredeb Indon. **73** C2
Tanjungselor Indon. **73** C1
Tank Pak. **86** B1
Tanna *i.* Vanuatu **110**
Tanout Niger **101** C3
Tansen Nepal **87** C2
Tanță Egypt **102** B1
Tanzania *country* Africa **105** D3
Taonan China **81** E1
Taos U.S.A. **140** C1
Taoudenni Mali **100** B2
Tapa Estonia **42** C2
Tapachula Mex. **143** C3
Tapajós *r.* Brazil **151** D3
Tapaktuan Indon. **72** A1
Tapanatepec Mex. **143** C3
Tapauá Brazil **150** C3
Tapeta Liberia **100** B4
Tapi *r.* India **86** B2
Tappahannock U.S.A. **137** E3
Tapurucuara Brazil **150** C3
Taquari *r.* Brazil **154** A1
Taquarí, Pantanal do *marsh* Brazil
 154 A1
Taquarí, Serra do *hills* Brazil
 154 B1
Taquaritinga Brazil **154** C2
Taraba *r.* Nigeria **101** D4
Țarăbulus Libya *see* Tripoli
Tarakan Indon. **73** C1
Taran, Mys *pt* Rus. Fed. **42** A3
Taranaki, Mount *vol.* N.Z. **118** B2
Tarancón Spain **60** C1

Taranto Italy **63** C2
Taranto, Golfo di *g.* Italy **63** C2
Tarapoto Peru **150** B3
Tarasovskiy Rus. Fed. **45** F2
Tarauacá Brazil **150** B3
Tarauacá *r.* Brazil **150** C3
Tarawa *atoll* Kiribati **110**
Taraz Kazakh. **89** E2
Tarazona Spain **61** C1
Tarbagatay, Khrebet *mts* Kazakh.
 89 F2
Tarbert *Scotland* U.K. **50** B3
Tarbert *Scotland* U.K. **50** A2
Tarbes France **58** C3
Tarbet U.K. **50** B2
Tarcoola Austr. **116** A2
Taree Austr. **117** E2
Târgoviște Romania **44** C3
Targuist Morocco **60** C3
Târgu Jiu Romania **44** B2
Târgu Mureș Romania **44** B2
Târgu Neamț Romania **44** C2
Tarif U.A.E. **91** C2
Tarija Bol. **152** B3
Tarim Yemen **91** B3
Tarim Basin China **89** F3
Tarim He *r.* China **89** F2
Tarim Pendi *basin* China *see*
 Tarim Basin
Taritatu *r.* Indon. **71** D3
Tarko-Sale Rus. Fed. **40** G2
Tarkwa Ghana **100** B4
Tarlac Phil. **76** B2
Tärnaby Sweden **46** D2
Tarnak *r.* Afgh. **86** A1
Târnăveni Romania **44** B2
Tarnobrzeg Pol. **57** E2
Tarnów Pol. **57** E2
Taroudannt Morocco **100** B1
Tarquinia Italy **62** B2
Tarragona Spain **61** D1
Tàrrega Spain **61** D1
Tarsus Turkey **92** B1
Tartagal Arg. **152** B3
Tartas France **58** B3
Tartu Estonia **42** C2
Țarțūs Syria **92** B2
Tarumirim Brazil **155** D1
Tarusa Rus. Fed. **43** E3
Tarvisio Italy **62** B2
Tashk, Daryācheh-ye *l.* Iran **93** D3
Tashkent Uzbek. **89** E2
Tasialujjuaq, Lac *l.* Can. **129** C1
Tasiat, Lac *l.* Can. **128** C1
Tasiujaq Can. **129** D1
Taskesken Kazakh. **89** F2
Tasman Bay N.Z. **118** B3
Tasmania *i.* Austr. **110**
Tasmania *state* Austr. **115** D4
Tasman Mountains N.Z. **118** B3
Tasman Sea S. Pacific Ocean **115** E3
Tassili du Hoggar *plat.* Alg. **101** C2
Tassili n'Ajjer *plat.* Alg. **101** C2
Tataba Indon. **73** D2
Tatabánya Hungary **57** D3
Tatarbunary Ukr. **44** C2
Tatarskiy Proliv *str.* Rus. Fed. **81** F1
Tateyama Japan **79** C4
Tathlina Lake Can. **126** D1
Tathlīth Saudi Arabia **90** B3
Tathlīth, Wādī *watercourse*
 Saudi Arabia **90** B2
Tathra Austr. **117** D3
Tatkon Myanmar **74** A1
Tatla Lake Can. **126** C3
Tatra Mountains Pol. **57** D3
Tatsinskiy Rus. Fed. **45** F2
Tatta Pak. **86** A2
Tatuí Brazil **154** C2
Tatum U.S.A. **141** D2

Tatvan Turkey **93** C2
Taua Brazil **151** E3
Taubaté Brazil **155** C2
Tauberbischofsheim Ger. **55** D3
Taumarunui N.Z. **118** C2
Taunggyi Myanmar **74** A1
Taung-ngu Myanmar **74** A2
Taungup Myanmar **74** A2
Taunton U.K. **53** B4
Taunus *hills* Ger. **54** C2
Taupo N.Z. **118** C2
Taupo, Lake N.Z. **118** C2
Tauragė Lith. **42** B2
Tauranga N.Z. **118** C2
Taurus Mountains Turkey **92** B2
Tavas Turkey **65** C3
Tavda Rus. Fed. **40** F3
Tavira Port. **60** B2
Tavistock U.K. **53** A4
Tavoy Myanmar **75** A2
Tavşanlı Turkey **65** C3
Taw *r.* U.K. **53** A4
Tawas City U.S.A. **136** D2
Tawau Malaysia **73** C1
Tawitawi *i.* Phil. **76** A3
Taxco Mex. **143** C3
Taxiatosh Uzbek. **88** C2
Taxkorgan China **89** E3
Tay *r.* U.K. **50** C2
Tay, Firth of *est.* U.K. **50** C2
Tay, Loch *l.* U.K. **50** B2
Taylor Can. **126** C2
Taylor U.S.A. **141** E2
Taylorville U.S.A. **136** C3
Taymā' Saudi Arabia **90** A2
Taymura *r.* Rus. Fed. **95** I2
Taymyr, Ozero *l.* Rus. Fed. **95** I2
Taymyr, Poluostrov *pen.* Rus. Fed. *see*
  Taymyr Peninsula
Taymyr Peninsula Rus. Fed. **95** H2
Tây Ninh Vietnam **75** B2
Taytay Phil. **76** A2
Taz *r.* Rus. Fed. **40** G2
Taza Morocco **100** B1
Tazin Lake Can. **127** E2
Tazoult Lambèse Alg. **61** E2
Tazovskaya Guba *sea chan.* Rus. Fed.
  40 G2
T'bilisi Georgia **93** C1
Tbilisskaya Rus. Fed. **45** F2
Tchibanga Gabon **104** B3
Tcholliré Cameroon **104** B2
Tczew Pol. **57** D2
Teacapán Mex. **142** B2
Te Anau N.Z. **118** A4
Te Anau, Lake N.Z. **118** A4
Teapa Mex. **143** C3
Te Awamutu N.Z. **118** C2
Tébessa Alg. **101** C1
Tebingtinggi *Sumatera Selatan* Indon.
  72 B2
Tebingtinggi *Sumatera Utara* Indon.
  72 A1
Techiman Ghana **100** B4
Tecomán Mex. **142** B3
Tecoripa Mex. **142** B2
Técpan Mex. **143** B3
Tecuala Mex. **142** B2
Tecuci Romania **44** C2
Tedzhen Turkm. **88** D3
Tedzhen *r.* Turkm. **88** D3
Teeli Rus. Fed. **89** G1
Tees *r.* U.K. **52** C2
Tefenni Turkey **65** C3
Tegal Indon. **72** B2
Tegucigalpa Hond. **144** B3
Teguidda-n-Tessoumt Niger **101** C3
Tehek Lake Can. **127** F1
Téhini Côte d'Ivoire **100** B4
Tehrān Iran **93** D2

Tehuacán Mex. **143** C3
Tehuantepec, Golfo de *g.* Mex.
  143 C3
Tehuantepec, Istmo de *isth.* Mex.
  143 C3
Teifi *r.* U.K. **53** A3
Tejo *r.* Port. *see* Tagus
Tejupilco Mex. **143** B3
Tekapo, Lake N.Z. **118** B3
Tekax Mex. **143** D2
Tekezē Wenz *r.* Eritrea/Eth. **102** B3
Tekirdağ Turkey **65** C2
Te Kuiti N.Z. **118** C2
Tel *r.* India **87** C2
T'elavi Georgia **93** C1
Tel Aviv-Yafo Israel **92** B2
Telchac Puerto Mex. **143** D2
Telegraph Creek Can. **126** B2
Telêmaco Borba Brazil **154** B2
Telford U.K. **53** B3
Telo Indon. **72** A2
Tel'pos-Iz, Gora *mt.* Rus. Fed. **40** E2
Telšiai Lith. **42** B2
Telukbatang Indon. **73** B2
Telukdalam Indon. **72** A1
Teluk Intan Malaysia **72** B1
Temagami Lake Can. **128** C2
Temanggung Indon. **73** C2
Temba S. Africa **109** C2
Tembilahan Indon. **72** B2
Tembo Aluma Angola **104** B3
Teme *r.* U.K. **53** B3
Temerluh Malaysia **72** B1
Temirtau Kazakh. **89** E1
Temora Austr. **117** D2
Temple U.S.A. **141** E2
Templemore Rep. of Ireland **51** C2
Templin Ger. **55** F1
Tempoal Mex. **143** C2
Temryuk Rus. Fed. **45** E2
Temuco Chile **153** A4
Temuka N.Z. **118** B3
Tenabo Mex. **143** C2
Tenali India **85** C3
Tenasserim Myanmar **75** A2
Tenby U.K. **53** A4
Tendaho Eth. **103** C3
Tende France **59** D3
Tende, Col de *pass* France/Italy **59** D3
Ten Degree Channel India **75** A3
Tendō Japan **78** D3
Ténenkou Mali **100** B3
Ténéré, Erg du *des.* Niger **101** D3
Ténéré du Tafassâsset *des.* Niger
  101 D2
Tenerife *i.* Canary Is **100** A2
Ténès Alg. **61** D2
Tengah, Kepulauan *is* Indon. **73** C2
Tengchong China **74** A1
Tenggarong Indon. **73** C2
Tengger Shamo *des.* China **82** A2
Tengxian China **83** B3
Tenke Dem. Rep. Congo **105** C4
Tenkodogo Burkina **100** B3
Tennant Creek Austr. **114** C1
Tennessee *r.* U.S.A. **138** C1
Tennessee *state* U.S.A. **138** C1
Tenosique Mex. **143** C3
Tenteno Indon. **73** D2
Tenterfield Austr. **117** E1
Teodoro Sampaio Brazil **154** B2
Teófilo Otôni Brazil **155** D1
Teopisca Mex. **143** C3
Tepache Mex. **142** B2
Te Paki N.Z. **118** B1
Tepalcatepec Mex. **142** B3
Tepatitlán Mex. **142** B2
Tepehuanes Mex. **142** B2
Tepelenë Albania **65** B2
Tepic Mex. **142** B2

Teplice Czech Rep. **56** C2
Teploye Rus. Fed. **43** E3
Tequila Mex. **142** B2
Teramo Italy **62** B2
Terbuny Rus. Fed. **43** E3
Terebovlya Ukr. **44** C2
Terek *r.* Rus. Fed. **41** D4
Teresina Brazil **151** E3
Teresópolis Brazil **155** D2
Teressa Island India **75** A3
Tergnier France **54** A3
Terme Turkey **92** B1
Termini Imerese Italy **62** B3
Términos, Laguna de *lag.* Mex.
  143 C3
Termiz Uzbek. **89** D3
Termoli Italy **62** B2
Ternate Indon. **71** C2
Terneuzen Neth. **54** A2
Terni Italy **62** B2
Ternopil' Ukr. **44** C2
Terpeniya, Mys *c.* Rus. Fed. **81** F1
Terpeniya, Zaliv *g.* Rus. Fed. **81** F1
Terrace Can. **126** B2
Terrace Bay Can. **128** B2
Terra Firma S. Africa **108** B2
Terre Haute U.S.A. **136** B3
Terrenceville Can. **129** E2
Terschelling *i.* Neth. **54** B1
Tertenia Italy **62** A3
Teruel Spain **61** C1
Tervola Fin. **46** E2
Tešanj Bos.-Herz. **63** C2
Teseney Eritrea **102** B3
Teshio-gawa *r.* Japan **78** D2
Teslin Can. **126** B1
Teslin Lake Can. **126** B1
Tesouro Brazil **154** B1
Tessaoua Niger **101** C3
Tetas, Punta *pt* Chile **147**
Tete Moz. **107** C1
Teteriv *r.* Ukr. **44** D1
Teterow Ger. **55** F1
Tetiyiv Ukr. **44** C2
Tétouan Morocco **100** B1
Tetovo Macedonia **64** B2
Teuco *r.* Arg. **152** B3
Teul de González Ortega Mex. **142** B
Teutoburger Wald *hills* Ger. **55** D1
Tevere *r.* Italy *see* Tiber
Teviot N.Z. **118** A4
Tewantin Austr. **115** E2
Te Wharau N.Z. **118** C3
Texarkana U.S.A. **141** F2
Texas Austr. **117** E1
Texas *state* U.S.A. **141** E2
Texas City U.S.A. **141** F3
Texel *i.* Neth. **54** B1
Texoma, Lake U.S.A. **141** E2
Teyateyaneng Lesotho **109** C2
Teykovo Rus. Fed. **43** F2
Teza *r.* Rus. Fed. **43** F2
Tezpur India **87** D2
Tezu India **74** A1
Tha-anne *r.* Can. **127** F1
Thabana-Ntlenyana *mt.* Lesotho
  109 C2
Thaba Putsoa *mt.* Lesotho **109** C2
Thabazimbi S. Africa **109** C1
Thabong S. Africa **109** C2
Thagyettaw Myanmar **75** A2
Thai Binh Vietnam **74** B1
Thailand *country* Asia **75** B2
Thailand, Gulf of Asia **75** B2
Thai Nguyên Vietnam **74** B1
Thakèk Laos **74** B2
Thalang Thai. **75** A3
Thal Desert Pak. **86** B1
Thale (Harz) Ger. **55** E2
Tha Li Thai. **74** B2

Tokar Sudan **102** B3
Tokara-rettō *is* Japan **81** E3
Tokarevka Rus. Fed. **43** F3
Tokelau *terr.* S. Pacific Ocean **113**
Tokelau *is* Tokelau **111**
Tokmak Ukr. **45** E2
Tokmok Kyrg. **89** E2
Tokoroa N.Z. **118** C2
Toksun China **89** F2
Tokushima Japan **79** B4
Tōkyō Japan **79** C3
Tôlañaro Madag. **107** [inset] D2
Toledo Brazil **154** B2
Toledo Spain **60** C2
Toledo U.S.A. **136** D2
Toledo, Montes de *mts* Spain **60** C2
Toledo Bend Reservoir U.S.A. **138** B2
Toliara Madag. **107** [inset] D2
Tolitoli Indon. **73** D1
Tolmezzo Italy **62** B1
Tolosa Spain **58** B3
Toluca Mex. **143** C3
Tol'yatti Rus. Fed. **41** D3
Tomah U.S.A. **136** B2
Tomakomai Japan **78** D2
Tomar Port. **60** B2
Tomaszów Lubelski Pol. **57** E2
Tomaszów Mazowiecki Pol. **57** E2
Tomatlán Mex. **142** B3
Tombigbee *r.* U.S.A. **138** C2
Tombos Brazil **155** D2
Tombouctou Mali *see* Timbuktu
Tombua Angola **106** A1
Tom Burke S. Africa **109** C1
Tomingley Austr. **117** D2
Tomini, Teluk *g.* Indon. **73** D2
Tomislavgrad Bos.-Herz. **63** C2
Tom Price Austr. **114** A2
Tomsk Rus. Fed. **94** H3
Tomtabacken *h.* Sweden **47** C4
Tonalá Mex. **143** C3
Tonantins Brazil **150** C3
Tønder Denmark **56** B2
Tonga *country* S. Pacific Ocean **113**
Tongatapu Group *is* Tonga **111**
Tongcheng China **83** B3
Tongchuan China **82** A2
Tongdao China **83** A3
Tongduch'ŏn S. Korea **77** B2
Tongeren Belgium **54** B2
Tonghae S. Korea **77** B2
Tonghai China **83** A3
Tonghua China **77** B1
Tongjosŏn-man *b.* N. Korea **77** B2
Tongking, Gulf of China/Vietnam **83** A3
Tongliao China **82** C1
Tongling China **82** B2
Tongo Austr. **116** C2
Tongren China **83** A3
Tongshan China **82** B2
Tongshi China *see* Wuzhishan
Tongtian He *r.* China *see* Yangtze
Tongue U.K. **50** B1
T'ongyŏng S. Korea **77** B3
Tongyu China **81** E2
Tongyuanpu China **77** A1
Tonk India **86** B2
Tonle Sap *l.* Cambodia **75** B2
Tonopah U.S.A. **133** C3
Tønsberg Norway **47** C4
Tooele U.S.A. **132** D2
Tooleybuc Austr. **116** C3
Toowoomba Austr. **117** E1
Topeka U.S.A. **135** D3
Topia Mex. **142** B2
Topolobampo Mex. **142** B2
Topozero, Ozero *l.* Rus. Fed. **46** G2
Toppenish U.S.A. **132** B1

Torbalı Turkey **65** C3
Torbat-e Heydarīyeh Iran **88** C3
Torbat-e Jām Iran **88** D3
Tordesillas Spain **60** C1
Tordesilos Spain **61** C1
Torelló Spain **61** D1
Torgau Ger. **55** F2
Torgelow Ger. **55** G1
Torhout Belgium **54** A2
Torino Italy *see* Turin
Tori-shima *i.* Japan **79** D4
Torixoréu Brazil **154** B1
Tor'kovskoye Vodokhranilishche *resr* Rus. Fed. **43** F2
Tormes *r.* Spain **60** B1
Torneälven *r.* Sweden **46** E2
Torngat Mountains Can. **129** D1
Tornio Fin. **46** E2
Toro Spain **60** B1
Toronto Can. **128** C2
Tororo Uganda **105** D2
Toros Dağları *mts* Turkey *see* Taurus Mountains
Torquay U.K. **53** B4
Torrão Port. **60** B2
Torre *mt.* Port. **60** B1
Torreblanca Spain **61** D1
Torrecerredo *mt.* Spain **60** C1
Torre de Moncorvo Port. **60** B1
Torrelavega Spain **60** C1
Torremolinos Spain **60** C2
Torrens, Lake *salt flat* Austr. **116** B2
Torrent Spain **61** C2
Torreón Mex. **142** B2
Torres Novas Port. **60** B2
Torres Strait Austr. **110**
Torres Vedras Port. **60** B2
Torrevieja Spain **61** C2
Torridon U.K. **50** B2
Torrijos Spain **60** C2
Torrington *CT* U.S.A. **137** F2
Torrington *WY* U.S.A. **134** C2
Torroella de Montgrí Spain **61** D1
Tórshavn Faroe Is **48** B1
Tortolì Italy **62** A3
Tortosa Spain **61** D1
Toruń Pol. **57** D2
Tory Island Rep. of Ireland **51** B1
Torzhok Rus. Fed. **43** D2
Tosca S. Africa **108** B2
Toscano, Arcipelago *is* Italy **62** A2
Tosno Rus. Fed. **43** D2
Tostado Arg. **152** B3
Tostedt Ger. **55** D1
Tosya Turkey **92** B1
Tot'ma Rus. Fed. **43** F2
Tottori Japan **79** B3
Touba Côte d'Ivoire **100** B4
Toubkal, Jbel *mt.* Morocco **100** B1
Tougan Burkina **100** B3
Touggourt Alg. **101** C1
Toul France **59** D2
Touliu Taiwan **83** C3
Toulon France **59** D3
Toulouse France **58** C3
Tourcoing France **54** A2
Tournai Belgium **54** A2
Tournus France **59** C2
Touros Brazil **151** F3
Tours France **58** C2
Tousside, Pic *mt.* Chad **101** D2
Touwsrivier S. Africa **108** B3
Towada Japan **78** D2
Townsend U.S.A. **132** D1
Townsville Austr. **115** D1
Towori, Teluk *b.* Indon. **73** D2
Toxkan He *r.* China **89** F2
Tōya-ko *l.* Japan **78** D2
Toyama Japan **79** C3
Toyota Japan **79** C3

Tozeur Tunisia **101** C1
Tqvarch'eli Georgia **93** C1
Trâblous Lebanon *see* Tripoli
Trabzon Turkey **92** B1
Trafalgar, Cabo *c.* Spain **60** B2
Trail Can. **126** D3
Trakai Lith. **42** B3
Tralee Rep. of Ireland **51** B2
Tramore Rep. of Ireland **51** C2
Trang Thai. **75** A3
Trangan *i.* Indon. **71** C3
Transantarctic Mountains Antarctica **119** H2
Transylvanian Alps *mts* Romania **44** B2
Trapani Italy **62** B3
Traralgon Austr. **117** D3
Trat Thai. **75** B2
Traunstein Ger. **56** C3
Traverse City U.S.A. **136** C2
Třebíč Czech Rep. **57** D3
Trebinje Bos.-Herz. **63** C2
Trebišov Slovakia **57** E3
Trebnje Slovenia **62** C1
Treinta y Tres Uru. **153** C4
Trelew Arg. **153** B5
Trelleborg Sweden **47** C4
Tremblant, Mont *h.* Can. **128** C2
Tremiti, Isole *is* Italy **62** C2
Tremonton U.S.A. **132** D2
Třemošná Czech Rep. **55** F3
Tremp Spain **61** D1
Trenčín Slovakia **57** D3
Trenque Lauquén Arg. **153** B4
Trent *r.* U.K. **52** C3
Trento Italy **62** B1
Trenton Can. **137** E2
Trenton *MO* U.S.A. **135** E2
Trenton *NJ* U.S.A. **137** F2
Trepassey Can. **129** E2
Tres Arroyos Arg. **153** B4
Três Corações Brazil **155** C2
Três Lagoas Brazil **154** B2
Tres Lagos Arg. **153** A5
Três Marias, Represa *resr* Brazil **155** C1
Três Pontas Brazil **155** C2
Tres Puntas, Cabo *c.* Arg. **153** B5
Três Rios Brazil **155** D2
Treuenbrietzen Ger. **55** F1
Treviglio Italy **62** A1
Treviso Italy **62** B1
Trevose Head U.K. **53** A4
Tricase Italy **63** C3
Trichur India **85** B3
Trida Austr. **117** D2
Trier Ger. **54** C3
Trieste Italy **62** B1
Triglav *mt.* Slovenia **62** B1
Trikora, Puncak *mt.* Indon. **71** D3
Trim Rep. of Ireland **51** C2
Trincomalee Sri Lanka **85** C4
Trindade Brazil **154** C1
Trinidad Bol. **152** B2
Trinidad *i.* Trin. and Tob. **145** D3
Trinidad U.S.A. **134** C3
Trinidad and Tobago *country* West Indies **145** D3
Trinity Bay Can. **129** E2
Tripoli Greece **65** B3
Tripoli Lebanon **92** B2
Tripoli Libya **101** D1
Tristan da Cunha *i.* S. Atlantic Ocean **160** D8
Trivandrum India **85** B4
Trivento Italy **62** B2
Trnava Slovakia **57** D3
Trogir Croatia **63** C2
Troia Italy **62** C2
Troisdorf Ger. **54** C2

Uberaba Brazil **154** C1
Uberlândia Brazil **154** C1
Ubombo S. Africa **109** D2
Ubon Ratchathani Thai. **75** B2
Ubstadt-Weiher Ger. **55** D3
Ubundu Dem. Rep. Congo **105** C3
Ucayali *r.* Peru **150** B3
Uch Pak. **86** B2
Ucharal Kazakh. **89** F2
Uchiura-wan *b.* Japan **78** D2
Uchur *r.* Rus. Fed. **95** K3
Ucluelet Can. **126** C3
Udaipur India **86** B2
Uday *r.* Ukr. **45** D1
Uddevalla Sweden **47** C4
Uddjaure *l.* Sweden **46** D2
Uden Neth. **54** B2
Udhampur India **86** B1
Udine Italy **62** B1
Udomlya Rus. Fed. **43** E2
Udon Thani Thai. **74** B2
Udupi India **85** B3
Ueda Japan **79** C3
Uekuli Indon. **73** D2
Uele *r.* Dem. Rep. Congo **104** C2
Uelen Rus. Fed. **124** A2
Uelzen Ger. **55** E1
Uere *r.* Dem. Rep. Congo **105** C2
Ufa Rus. Fed. **41** E3
Ugalla *r.* Tanz. **105** D3
Uganda *country* Africa **105** D2
Uglegorsk Rus. Fed. **81** F1
Uglich Rus. Fed. **43** E2
Uglovka Rus. Fed. **43** D2
Ugra Rus. Fed. **43** D3
Uherské Hradiště Czech Rep. **57** D3
Úhlava *r.* Czech Rep. **55** F3
Uichteritz Ger. **55** E2
Uig U.K. **50** A2
Uíge Angola **104** B3
Üijöngbu S. Korea **77** B2
Uinta Mountains U.S.A. **132** D2
Uis Mine Namibia **106** A2
Üisöng S. Korea **77** B2
Uitenhage S. Africa **109** C3
Uithuizen Neth. **54** C1
Uivak, Cape Can. **129** D1
Ujjain India **86** B2
Ukholovo Rus. Fed. **43** F3
Ukhrul India **74** A1
Ukhta Rus. Fed. **40** E2
Ukiah U.S.A. **133** B3
Ukkusissat Greenland **125** I2
Ukmergė Lith. **42** E2
Ukraine *country* Europe **44** D2
Ulaanbaatar Mongolia *see* Ulan Bator
Ulaangom Mongolia **80** C1
Ulan Bator Mongolia **80** D1
Ulanhad China *see* Chifeng
Ulanhot China **81** E1
Ulan-Khol Rus. Fed. **41** D4
Ulan-Ude Rus. Fed. **81** D1
Ulan Ul Hu *l.* China **87** D1
Ulchin S. Korea **77** B2
Ülenurme Estonia **42** C2
Ulhasnagar India **85** B3
Uliastai China **81** D1
Uliastay Mongolia **80** C1
Ulithi *atoll* Micronesia **71** D2
Ulladulla Austr. **117** E3
Ullapool U.K. **50** B2
Ullswater *l.* U.K. **52** B2
Ullŭng-do *i.* S. Korea **77** C2
Ulm Ger. **56** B3
Ulsan S. Korea **77** B2
Ulsta U.K. **50** [inset]
Ulster *reg.* Rep. of Ireland/U.K. **51** C1
Ultima Austr. **116** C3
Ulua *r.* Hond. **143** D3
Ulubey Turkey **65** C3

Uludağ *mt.* Turkey **65** C2
Ulundi S. Africa **109** D2
Ulungur Hu *l.* China **89** F2
Uluru *h.* Austr. **114** C2
Ulverston U.K. **52** B2
Ul'yanovsk Rus. Fed. **41** D3
Ulysses U.S.A. **134** C3
Uman' Ukr. **44** D2
Umba Rus. Fed. **40** C2
Umboi *i.* P.N.G. **71** D3
Umeå Sweden **46** E3
Umeälven *r.* Sweden **46** E3
Umet Rus. Fed. **45** F1
Umingmaktok Can. **124** E2
Umlazi S. Africa **109** D2
Umm Keddada Sudan **103** A3
Umm Lajj Saudi Arabia **90** A2
Umm Ruwaba Sudan **103** B3
Umm Sa'ad Libya **101** E1
Umpqua *r.* U.S.A. **132** B2
Umpulo Angola **106** A1
Umtata S. Africa **109** C3
Umuarama Brazil **154** B2
Una *r.* Bos.-Herz./Croatia **63** C1
Una Brazil **151** F4
Unaí Brazil **154** C1
Unalakleet U.S.A. **124** B2
'Unayzah Saudi Arabia **90** B2
Underwood U.S.A. **134** C1
Unecha Rus. Fed. **43** D3
Ungarie Austr. **117** D2
Ungarra Austr. **116** B2
Ungava, Péninsule d' *pen.* Can.
125 H2
Ungava Bay Can. **129** D1
Unggi N. Korea **77** C1
Ungheni Moldova **44** C2
Unguja *i.* Tanz. *see* Zanzibar Island
União da Vitória Brazil **154** B3
Unini *r.* Brazil **150** C3
Union City U.S.A. **138** C1
Uniondale S. Africa **108** B3
Uniontown U.S.A. **137** E3
United Arab Emirates *country* Asia
91 C2
United Kingdom *country* Europe
48 C2
United States of America *country*
N. America **130** D3
Unity Can. **124** E3
Unst *i.* U.K. **50** [inset]
Unstrut *r.* Ger. **55** E2
Upa *r.* Rus. Fed. **43** E3
Upemba, Lac *l.* Dem. Rep. Congo
105 C3
Upington S. Africa **108** B2
Upolu *i.* Samoa **111**
Upper Alkali Lake U.S.A. **132** B2
Upper Arrow Lake Can. **126** D2
Upper Klamath Lake U.S.A. **132** B2
Upper Liard Can. **126** C1
Upper Lough Erne *l.* U.K. **51** C1
Uppsala Sweden **47** D4
'Uqlat aş Şuqūr Saudi Arabia **90** B2
Ural *r.* Kazakh./Rus. Fed. **88** C2
Uralla Austr. **117** E2
Ural Mountains Rus. Fed. **41** F2
Ural'sk Kazakh. **88** C1
Ural'skiy Khrebet *mts* Rus. Fed. *see*
Ural Mountains
Urambo Tanz. **105** D3
Urana Austr. **117** D3
Uranium City Can. **124** E3
Uray Rus. Fed. **40** F2
Ure *r.* U.K. **52** C2
Uren' Rus. Fed. **40** D3
Urengoy Rus. Fed. **40** G2
Ures Mex. **142** A2
Urganch Uzbek. **88** D2
Urk Neth. **54** B1

Urla Turkey **65** C3
Urmia, Lake *salt l.* Iran **93** C2
Uroševac Serb. and Mont. **64** B2
Uruáchic Mex. **142** B2
Uruaçu Brazil **151** E4
Uruapan Mex. **142** B3
Urubamba *r.* Peru **150** B4
Urucara Brazil **151** D3
Uruçuí Brazil **151** E3
Urucurituba Brazil **151** D3
Uruguai *r.* Brazil **154** B3
Uruguaiana Brazil **152** C3
Uruguay *r.* Arg./Uru. **149**
Uruguay *country* S. America **153** C4
Ürümqi China **89** F2
Urunga Austr. **117** E2
Urup *r.* Rus. Fed. **45** F2
Uryupinsk Rus. Fed. **45** F1
Urziceni Romania **44** C3
Usa Japan **79** B4
Usa *r.* Rus. Fed. **94** F2
Usa *r.* Rus. Fed. **37**
Uşak Turkey **65** C3
Usakos Namibia **108** A1
Ushakova, Ostrov *i.* Rus. Fed. **94** H1
Ushtobe Kazakh. **89** F2
Ushuaia Arg. **153** B6
Usinsk Rus. Fed. **40** E2
Uskhodni Belarus **42** C3
Usman' Rus. Fed. **43** E3
Usogorsk Rus. Fed. **40** D2
Ussel France **58** C2
Ussuriysk Rus. Fed. **78** B2
Ust'-Donetskiy Rus. Fed. **45** F2
Ustica, Isola di *i.* Italy **62** B3
Ust'-Ilimsk Rus. Fed. **95** I3
Ust'-Ilych Rus. Fed. **40** E2
Ustka Pol. **57** D2
Ust'-Kamchatsk Rus. Fed. **95** M3
Ust'-Kamenogorsk Kazakh. **89** F2
Ust'-Kara Rus. Fed. **40** F2
Ust'-Kulom Rus. Fed. **40** E2
Ust'-Kut Rus. Fed. **95** J3
Ust'-Labinsk Rus. Fed. **45** E2
Ust'-Luga Rus. Fed. **42** C2
Ust'-Nem Rus. Fed. **40** E2
Ust'-Nera Rus. Fed. **95** L2
Ust'-Omchug Rus. Fed. **95** L2
Ust'-Ordynskiy Rus. Fed. **95** I3
Ust'-Port Rus. Fed. **40** H2
Ust'-Tsil'ma Rus. Fed. **40** E2
Ust'-Ura Rus. Fed. **40** D2
Ustyurt Plateau Kazakh./Uzbek.
88 C2
Ustyuzhna Rus. Fed. **43** E2
Usvyaty Rus. Fed. **43** D2
Utah *state* U.S.A. **133** D3
Utah Lake U.S.A. **132** D2
Utena Lith. **42** C2
Utica U.S.A. **137** E2
Utiel Spain **61** C2
Utikuma Lake Can. **126** D2
Utrecht Neth. **54** B1
Utrera Spain **60** B2
Utsjoki Fin. **46** F2
Utsunomiya Japan **79** C3
Utta Rus. Fed. **41** D4
Uttaradit Thai. **74** B2
Uummannaq Greenland *see* Dundas
Uummannaq Fjord *inlet* Greenland
125 I2
Uusikaupunki Fin. **47** E3
Uvalde U.S.A. **141** E3
Uvarovo Rus. Fed. **45** F1
Uvinza Tanz. **105** D3
Uvs Nuur *salt l.* Mongolia **80** C1
Uwajima Japan **79** B4
'Uwayriḍ, Ḥarrat al *lava field*
Saudi Arabia **90** A2
Uweinat, Jebel *mt.* Sudan **102** A2

Watson Lake Can. **126** C1
Watsonville U.S.A. **133** B3
Watubela, Kepulauan *is* Indon. **71** C3
Wau P.N.G. **71** D3
Wau Sudan **103** A4
Wauchope Austr. **117** E2
Waukegan U.S.A. **136** C2
Wausau U.S.A. **136** C2
Waveney *r.* U.K. **53** D3
Waverly U.S.A. **135** E2
Waycross U.S.A. **139** D2
Wayne U.S.A. **135** D2
Waynesboro *GA* U.S.A. **139** D2
Waynesboro *VA* U.S.A. **137** E3
Waynesville U.S.A. **139** D1
Wazirabad Pak. **86** B1
Wear *r.* U.K. **52** C2
Weatherford U.S.A. **141** E2
Weaverville U.S.A. **132** B2
Webequie Can. **128** B1
Webi Shabeelle *r.* Somalia **103** C4
Webster U.S.A. **135** D1
Webster City U.S.A. **135** E2
Weert Neth. **54** B2
Wee Waa Austr. **117** D2
Wegberg Ger. **54** C2
Wegorzewo Pol. **57** E2
Weiden in der Oberpfalz Ger. **55** F3
Weifang China **82** B2
Weihai China **82** C2
Weilmoringle Austr. **117** D1
Weimar Ger. **55** E2
Weinan China **82** A2
Weinsberg Ger. **55** D3
Weipa Austr. **115** D1
Weir *r.* Austr. **117** D1
Weirton U.S.A. **137** D2
Weishan China **74** B1
Weißenburg in Bayern Ger. **55** E3
Weißenfels Ger. **55** E2
Weißkugel *mt.* Austria/Italy **56** C3
Wejherowo Pol. **57** D2
Wekweti Can. **126** D1
Welch U.S.A. **136** D3
Weldiya Eth. **103** B3
Welkom S. Africa **109** C2
Welland *r.* U.K. **53** C3
Wellesley Islands Austr. **115** C1
Wellington Austr. **117** D2
Wellington N.Z. **118** B3
Wellington S. Africa **108** A3
Wellington U.S.A. **135** D3
Wellington, Isla *i.* Chile **153** A5
Wellington, Lake Austr. **117** D3
Wells Can. **126** C2
Wells U.K. **53** B4
Wells U.S.A. **132** D2
Wells, Lake *salt flat* Austr. **114** B2
Wellsford N.Z. **118** B2
Wells-next-the-Sea U.K. **52** D3
Wels Austria **56** C3
Welshpool U.K. **53** B3
Wembesi S. Africa **109** C2
Wemindji Can. **128** C1
Wenatchee U.S.A. **132** B1
Wenchang China **83** B4
Wenchi Ghana **100** B4
Wendelstein Ger. **55** E3
Wendeng China **82** C2
Wendisch Evern Ger. **55** E1
Wendo Eth. **103** B4
Wendover U.S.A. **132** D2
Wengyuan China **83** B3
Wenling China **83** C3
Wenshan China **83** A3
Wentworth Austr. **116** C2
Wenzhou China **83** C3
Wepener S. Africa **109** C2
Werda Botswana **108** B2

Werdau Ger. **55** F2
Werder Ger. **55** F1
Wernberg-Köblitz Ger. **55** F3
Wernigerode Ger. **55** E2
Werra *r.* Ger. **55** D2
Werris Creek Austr. **117** E2
Wertheim Ger. **55** D3
Wesel Ger. **54** C2
Wesendorf Ger. **55** E1
Weser *r.* Ger. **55** D1
Weser *sea chan.* Ger. **55** D1
Wessel, Cape Austr. **115** C1
Wessel Islands Austr. **115** C1
Wesselton S. Africa **109** C2
West Antarctica *reg.* Antarctica **119** I2
West Bank *terr.* Asia **92** B2
West Bend U.S.A. **136** C2
West Bromwich U.K. **53** C3
Westburg Ger. **54** C2
Westerholt Ger. **54** C1
Western Australia *state* Austr. **114** B2
Western Cape *prov.* S. Africa **108** B3
Western Desert Egypt **102** A2
Western Ghats *mts* India **85** B3
Western Sahara *terr.* Africa **100** A2
Westerschelde *est.* Neth. **54** A2
Westerstede Ger. **54** C1
Westerwald *hills* Ger. **54** C2
West Falkland *i.* Falkland Is **153** B6
West Frankfort U.S.A. **136** C3
West Frisian Islands Neth. **54** B1
West Indies *is* Caribbean Sea **145** D2
West Loch Roag *b.* U.K. **50** A1
Westlock Can. **126** D2
Westmalle Belgium **54** B2
West Memphis U.S.A. **138** B1
Weston U.S.A. **137** D3
Weston-super-Mare U.K. **53** B4
West Palm Beach U.S.A. **139** D3
West Plains U.S.A. **135** E3
West Point U.S.A. **135** D2
Westport N.Z. **118** B3
Westport Rep. of Ireland **51** B2
Westray Can. **127** E2
Westray *i.* U.K. **50** C1
West Siberian Plain Rus. Fed. *see*
   Zapadno Sibirskaya Ravnina
West-Terschelling Neth. **54** B1
West Town Rep. of Ireland **51** B1
West Virginia *state* U.S.A. **137** D3
West Wyalong Austr. **117** D2
West Yellowstone U.S.A. **132** D2
Wetar *i.* Indon. **71** C3
Wetaskiwin Can. **126** D2
Wetzlar Ger. **55** D2
Wewak P.N.G. **71** D3
Wexford Rep. of Ireland **51** C2
Weyakwin Can. **127** E2
Weyburn Can. **124** F3
Weyhe Ger. **55** D1
Weymouth U.K. **53** B4
Whakatane N.Z. **118** C2
Whale Cove Can. **127** F1
Whalsay *i.* U.K. **50** [inset]
Whangarei N.Z. **118** B2
Wharfe *r.* U.K. **52** C3
Wharton U.S.A. **141** E3
Wha Ti Can. **126** D1
Wheatland U.S.A. **134** B2
Wheeler Peak *NM* U.S.A. **140** C1
Wheeler Peak *NV* U.S.A. **133** D3
Wheeling U.S.A. **137** D2
Whernside *h.* U.K. **52** B2
Whistler Can. **126** C2
Whitby U.K. **52** C2
White *r.* Can./U.S.A. **126** B1
White *r.* U.S.A. **138** B2
White, Lake *salt flat* Austr. **114** B2
White Bay Can. **129** E2
White Butte *mt.* U.S.A. **134** C1

White Cliffs Austr. **116** C2
Whitecourt Can. **126** D2
Whitefish U.S.A. **132** D1
Whitehaven U.K. **52** B2
Whitehead U.K. **51** D1
Whitehorse Can. **126** B1
White Lake U.S.A. **138** B3
White Mountain Peak U.S.A.
   133 C3
White Nile *r.* Sudan/Uganda **103** B3
White Sea Rus. Fed. **40** C2
White Sulphur Springs U.S.A. **132** D
Whiteville U.S.A. **139** E2
White Volta *watercourse* Burkina/Ghan
   100 B3
Whitewater Baldy *mt.* U.S.A. **140** C2
Whitewater Lake Can. **128** B1
Whitewood Can. **127** E2
Whithorn U.K. **50** B3
Whitianga N.Z. **118** C2
Whitney, Mount U.S.A. **133** C3
Whitsunday Island Austr. **115** D2
Whyalla Austr. **116** B2
Wichelen Belgium **54** A2
Wichita U.S.A. **135** D3
Wichita Falls U.S.A. **141** E2
Wick U.K. **50** C1
Wickenburg U.S.A. **140** B2
Wicklow Rep. of Ireland **51** C2
Wicklow Head Rep. of Ireland
   51 D2
Wicklow Mountains Rep. of Ireland
   51 C2
Widnes U.K. **52** B3
Wiehengebirge *hills* Ger. **55** D1
Wiehl Ger. **54** C2
Wieluń Pol. **57** D2
Wien Austria *see* Vienna
Wiener Neustadt Austria **57** D3
Wieringerwerf Neth. **54** B1
Wiesbaden Ger. **54** D2
Wiesloch Ger. **55** D3
Wiesmoor Ger. **54** C1
Wieżyca *h.* Pol. **57** D2
Wight, Isle of *i.* U.K. **53** C4
Wigtown U.K. **50** B3
Wijchen Neth. **54** B2
Wilcannia Austr. **116** C2
Wild Coast S. Africa **109** C3
Wilge *r.* S. Africa **109** C2
Wilhelm, Mount P.N.G. **110**
Wilhelmshaven Ger. **54** D1
Wilkes-Barre U.S.A. **137** E2
Wilkes Land *reg.* Antarctica **119** G2
Wilkie Can. **127** E2
Willcox U.S.A. **140** C2
Willebroek Belgium **54** B2
Willemstad Neth. Antilles **145** D3
William, Mount Austr. **116** C3
William Creek Austr. **116** B1
Williams U.S.A. **140** B1
Williamsburg U.S.A. **137** E3
Williams Lake Can. **126** C2
Williamson U.S.A. **136** D3
Williamsport U.S.A. **137** E2
Williamston U.S.A. **139** E1
Williston S. Africa **108** B3
Williston U.S.A. **134** C1
Williston Lake Can. **126** C2
Willits U.S.A. **133** B3
Willmar U.S.A. **135** D1
Willowmore S. Africa **108** B3
Willowvale S. Africa **109** C3
Wills, Lake *salt flat* Austr. **114** B2
Willunga Austr. **116** B3
Wilmington Austr. **116** B2
Wilmington *DE* U.S.A. **137** E3
Wilmington *NC* U.S.A. **139** E2
Wilnsdorf Ger. **54** D2
Wilson U.S.A. **139** E1

X

Xi Ujimqin Qi China see Bayan Ul Hot
Xiushan China **83** A3
Xiuying China **83** B3
Xixia China **82** B2
Xizang Zizhiqu *aut. reg.* China **74** A1
Xo'jayli Uzbek. **88** C2
Xuancheng China **82** B2
Xuanwei China **83** A3
Xuchang China **82** B2
Xuddur Somalia **103** C4
Xun Jiang *r.* China **83** B3
Xunwu China **83** B3
Xuwen China **83** B3
Xuyong China **83** A3

Y

Ya'an China **83** A2
Yabēlo Eth. **103** B4
Yablonovyy Khrebet *mts* Rus. Fed. **81** D1
Yadkin *r.* U.S.A. **139** D1
Yadong China **87** C2
Yagnitsa Rus. Fed. **43** E2
Yagoua Cameroon **104** B1
Yahk Can. **126** D3
Yahualica Mex. **142** B2
Yahyalı Turkey **92** B2
Yaizu Japan **79** C4
Yakima U.S.A. **132** B1
Yako Burkina **100** B3
Yakumo Japan **78** D2
Yakutat U.S.A. **126** B2
Yakutat Bay U.S.A. **126** A2
Yakutsk Rus. Fed. **95** K2
Yakymivka Ukr. **45** E2
Yala Thai. **75** B3
Yallourn Austr. **117** D3
Yalova Turkey **65** C2
Yalta Ukr. **45** D3
Yalu Jiang *r.* China/N. Korea **77** A1
Yamagata Japan **78** D3
Yamaguchi Japan **79** B4
Yamal, Poluostrov *pen.* Rus. Fed. *see* Yamal Peninsula
Yamal Peninsula Rus. Fed. **40** F1
Yamba Austr. **117** E1
Yambio Sudan **103** A4
Yambol Bulg. **64** C2
Yamburg Rus. Fed. **40** G2
Yamethin Myanmar **74** A1
Yamoussoukro Côte d'Ivoire **100** B4
Yampil' Ukr. **44** C2
Yamuna *r.* India **87** D2
Yamzho Yumco *l.* China **87** D2
Yana *r.* Rus. Fed. **95** L2
Yan'an China **82** A2
Yanaoca Peru **150** B4
Yanbu' al Baḥr Saudi Arabia **90** A2
Yancheng China **82** C2
Yanchep Austr. **114** A3
Yangcheng China **82** B2
Yangchun China **83** B3
Yangdok N. Korea **77** B2
Yangjiang China **83** B3
Yangôn Myanmar *see* Rangoon
Yangquan China **82** B2
Yangshuo China **83** B3
Yangtze *r.* Qinghai China **80** C2
Yangtze *r.* China **83** C2
Yangtze *r.* China **74** B1
Yangtze, Mouth of the China **82** C2
Yangzhou China **82** B2
Yanji China **77** B1
Yankton U.S.A. **135** D2
Yano-Indigirskaya Nizmennost' *lowland* Rus. Fed. **95** L2
Yanskiy Zaliv *g.* Rus. Fed. **95** L2

Yantabulla Austr. **117** D1
Yantai China **82** C2
Yaoundé Cameroon **104** B2
Yap *i.* Micronesia **71** D2
Yapen *i.* Indon. **71** D3
Yapen, Selat *sea chan.* Indon. **71** D3
Yaqui *r.* Mex. **142** A2
Yaraka Austr. **115** D2
Yaransk Rus. Fed. **40** D3
Yaren Nauru **112**
Yarīm Yemen **90** B3
Yarkant He *r.* China **89** E3
Yarlung Zangbo *r.* China **80** C3
Yarmouth Can. **129** F3
Yarongo Rus. Fed. **40** F2
Yaroslavl' Rus. Fed. **43** E2
Yaroslavskiy Rus. Fed. **78** B2
Yarram Austr. **117** D3
Yartsevo Rus. Fed. **43** D2
Yasnogorsk Rus. Fed. **43** E3
Yasothon Thai. **75** B2
Yass Austr. **117** D2
Yatağan Turkey **65** C3
Yathkyed Lake Can. **127** F1
Yatsushiro Japan **79** B4
Yavari *r.* Brazil/Peru **150** C3
Yavatmal India **87** B2
Yavi, Cerro *mt.* Venez. **146**
Yavoriv Ukr. **44** B3
Yawatahama Japan **79** B4
Yazd Iran **93** D2
Yazoo City U.S.A. **138** B2
Ydra *i.* Greece **65** B3
Ye Myanmar **75** A2
Yecheng China **89** E3
Yécora Mex. **142** B2
Yefremov Rus. Fed. **43** E3
Yegorlyk *r.* Rus. Fed. **45** F2
Yegorlykskaya Rus. Fed. **45** F2
Yegor'yevsk Rus. Fed. **43** E2
Yei Sudan **103** B4
Yekaterinburg Rus. Fed. **40** F3
Yelets Rus. Fed. **43** E3
Yélimané Mali **100** A3
Yell *i.* U.K. **50** [inset]
Yellowknife Can. **126** D1
Yellow River *r.* China **82** B2
Yellow Sea N. Pacific Ocean **81** E2
Yellowstone *r.* U.S.A. **132** E1
Yellowstone U.S.A. **134** A2
Yel'sk Belarus **42** C3
Yemen *country* Asia **90** B3
Yemva Rus. Fed. **40** E2
Yenakiyeve Ukr. **45** E2
Yenangyaung Myanmar **74** A1
Yên Bai Vietnam **74** B1
Yendi Ghana **100** B4
Yenice Turkey **65** C3
Yenifoça Turkey **65** C3
Yenisey *r.* Rus. Fed. **80** C1
Yeoval Austr. **117** D2
Yeovil U.K. **53** B4
Yeppoon Austr. **115** E2
Yerbogachen Rus. Fed. **95** J2
Yerevan Armenia **93** C1
Yereymentau Kazakh. **89** E1
Yermish' Rus. Fed. **43** F2
Yershov Rus. Fed. **41** D3
Yesan S. Korea **77** B2
Yeşil' Kazakh. **89** D1
Yeşilova Turkey **65** C3
Yetman Austr. **117** E1
Ye-U Myanmar **74** A1
Yeu, Île d' *i.* France **58** B2
Yevlax Azer. **41** D4
Yevpatoriya Ukr. **45** D2
Yeysk Rus. Fed. **45** E2
Yezyaryshcha Belarus **42** C2
Yibin China **83** A3
Yichang China **82** B2

Yichun *Heilong.* China **81** E1
Yichun *Jiangxi* China **83** B3
Yilan China **78** A1
Yıldız Dağları *mts* Turkey **64** C2
Yıldızeli Turkey **92** B2
Yinchuan China **82** A2
Yingchengzi China **77** B1
Yingde China **83** B3
Yingkou China **82** C1
Yingshan *Hubei* China **82** B2
Yingshan *Sichuan* China **82** A2
Yingtan China **83** B3
Yining China **89** F2
Yirga Alem Eth. **103** B4
Yishui China **82** B2
Yitong China **77** B1
Yiwu China **80** C2
Yixing China **82** B2
Yiyang China **83** B3
Yizhou China **83** A3
Yli-Kitka *l.* Fin. **46** F2
Ylitornio Fin. **46** E2
Ylivieska Fin. **46** E3
Yogyakarta Indon. **73** C2
Yoko Cameroon **104** B2
Yokohama Japan **79** C3
Yola Nigeria **101** D4
Yonezawa Japan **79** D3
Yong'an China **83** B3
Yongchun China **83** B3
Yongdeng China **82** A2
Yŏngdŏk S. Korea **77** B2
Yongkang China **83** C3
Yongsheng China **74** B1
Yongzhou China **83** B3
Yopal Col. **150** B2
York Austr. **114** A3
York U.K. **52** C3
York *NE* U.S.A. **135** D2
York *PA* U.S.A. **137** E3
York, Cape Austr. **71** D3
Yorke Peninsula Austr. **116** B3
Yorketown Austr. **116** B3
Yorkshire Wolds *hills* U.K. **52** C3
Yorkton Can. **124** F3
Yoshkar-Ola Rus. Fed. **41** D3
Youghal Rep. of Ireland **51** C3
Young Austr. **117** D2
Younghusband Peninsula Austr. **116** B3
Youngstown U.S.A. **137** D2
Youvarou Mali **100** B3
Youyi Feng *mt.* China/Rus. Fed. **89** F2
Yozgat Turkey **92** B2
Ypé-Jhú Para. **154** A2
Yreka U.S.A. **132** B2
Yr Wyddfa *mt.* U.K. *see* Snowdon
Yssingeaux France **59** C2
Ystad Sweden **47** C4
Ysyk-Köl *salt l.* Kyrg. **89** E2
Ytri-Rangá *r.* Iceland **46** [inset]
Yuanjiang China **74** B1
Yuan Jiang *r.* China **74** B1
Yuanmou China **74** B1
Yuba City U.S.A. **133** B3
Yūbari Japan **78** D2
Yucatán *pen.* Mex. **143** C3
Yucatan Channel Cuba/Mex. **144** B2
Yuendumu Austr. **114** C2
Yueyang China **83** B3
Yugorsk Rus. Fed. **40** F2
Yukagirskoye Ploskogor'ye *plat.* Rus. Fed. **95** M2
Yukon *r.* Can./U.S.A. **126** B1
Yukon Territory *admin. div.* Can. **124** C2
Yulin *Guangxi* China **83** B3
Yulin *Shaanxi* China **82** A2
Yulong Xueshan *mt.* China **74** B1
Yuma *AZ* U.S.A. **140** B2

All mapping in this atlas is generated from Collins Bartholomew digital databases. Collins Bartholomew, the UK's leading independent geographical information supplier, can provide a digital, custom, and premium mapping service to a variety of markets. For further information:
Tel: +44 (0) 141 306 3752
e-mail: collinsbartholomew@harpercollins.co.uk

We also offer a choice of books, atlases and maps that can be customized to suit a customer's own requirements. For further information:
Tel: +44 (0) 141 306 3209
e-mail: business.gifts@harpercollins.co.uk

or visit our website at: www.collinsbartholomew.com